Modern Conspiracies
in America

Modern Conspiracies in America

Separating Fact from Fiction

Michael D. Gambone

ROWMAN & LITTLEFIELD
Lanham • Boulder • New York • London

Published by Rowman & Littlefield
An imprint of The Rowman & Littlefield Publishing Group, Inc.
4501 Forbes Boulevard, Suite 200, Lanham, Maryland 20706
www.rowman.com

86-90 Paul Street, London EC2A 4NE

British Library Cataloguing in Publication Information Available

Library of Congress Cataloging-in-Publication Data
The hardback edition of this book was previously cataloged as follows:

Names: Gambone, Michael D., 1963- author.
Title: Modern conspiracies in America : separating fact from fiction /
  Michael D. Gambone.
Description: Lanham : Rowman & Littlefield, [2022] | Includes
  bibliographical references and index.
Identifiers: LCCN 2021054681 (print) | LCCN 2021054682 (ebook)
Subjects: LCSH: United States—History—20th century. |
  Conspiracies—United States—History. | Conspiracy theories—United
  States—History. | United States—History—21st century. | Political
  culture—United States—History—20th century. | Political
  culture—United States—History—21st century. | Critical thinking.
Classification: LCC E741 .G35 2022 (print) | LCC E741 (ebook) | DDC
  973.9—dc23/eng/20211122
LC record available at https://lccn.loc.gov/2021054681
LC ebook record available at https://lccn.loc.gov/2021054682

ISBN 979-8-8818-0388-9 (paperback)
ISBN 978-1-5381-6463-1 (cloth)
ISBN 978-1-5381-6464-8 (electronic)

This works is dedicated to my mentor and friend
Dr. Claire Hirshfield

Contents

Contents

Preface

If not for two people, I would probably be mostly happily oblivious about conspiracy theories. Aside from some *Mythbusters* episodes, the odd urban legend in high school, and the ritual of talking about Kennedy assassination conspiracies in class, the idea did not occupy much space in my mind. That changed a few years ago.

An old friend from high school introduced me to a whole new universe of conspiracy theories online. It was a nice distraction from a book that I was finishing while on sabbatical leave from Kutztown University back in 2015. I was frankly stunned by the scope and scale of what is out there. From Morgellons, to "fake" snow, to vaccines causing ADHD, to those long lines in the sky behind airplanes that apparently are part of a cabal by the global power structure to enslave the world, there are almost more evil plans than any one person can name much less understand. Every one of these topics had multiple websites and threads. Some, like Snopes or Metabunk, are solely devoted to debunking conspiracy theories. The total internet bandwidth devoted to both must be staggering.

Lunch with an old mentor pushed my interest in conspiracies further along. Dr. Claire Hirshfield taught me one class on African history at Penn State but left a permanent imprint on my intellectual life. One of her best abilities was provoking curiosity. We talked about an adult education course she was teaching that focused on famous conspiracies like the *Protocols of the Elders of Zion*. It was fascinating. I had never really understood just how deeply fear, suspicion, and scapegoating are woven into history.

All of these conversations made me curious and, being a history teacher at a state college in Pennsylvania for the last twenty-two years, I decided to develop a class that focused on twentieth-century American conspiracies.

During the process, I realized that simply describing conspiracies in American history wouldn't be enough. What I also needed to do was develop a way for my students to explain *why* conspiracies existed and *how* we could understand whether or not they were real. Developing the course became a fascinating exercise in history, politics, culture, media studies, technology, and psychology.

Plus, a little marketing. When I launched the course in 2016, I decided to have some fun. I bought a small drone at Best Buy, placed a big, homemade billboard that simply read "They Are Watching" next to the main student walkway to my class building, and put on my best Men in Black suit. When classes changed, I orbited my new drone around the sign as hundreds of students walked by, briefly tearing them away from their cell phones with that strange sight.

It worked. The course filled and then overfilled. Within a year, the class took up three-quarters of my total teaching load.

The course also evolved over time. What started as an effort to apply logic to internet craziness and conspiracy theories shifted to using the same yardstick to evaluate evidence of real conspiracies. The FBI found a constant stream of Soviet spies after World War II. What separated them from individuals singled out by Joe McCarthy? What was the difference between the first August 1964 clash in the Gulf of Tonkin and the second?

Once I worked out the kinks in my class, I decided to take the next step: publish what I learned to see if more people might be interested. It seems like the moment is just right for a book like this. We live in strange, paranoid, partisan times, where informed, civil public debate is becoming increasingly rare. Cable television and social media accounts for some of this trend, but there is more to it. We also seem to have forgotten how to be patient and listen.

At the end of the day, I think that we need to do more than improve our understanding about the way things happened in the past. We need to rediscover the lost skill of agreeing to disagree.

Michael D. Gambone
Reading, Pennsylvania

Acknowledgments

There are many people who deserve recognition for their help with this book. I want to thank Dr. Claire Hirshfield, who has been one of my most important mentors from the time that I was an undergraduate at Penn State University to the present day. She was and continues to be a constant source of inspiration and encouragement.

I would also like to thank the students who have enrolled in my Conspiracies and Modern American History course at Kutztown University. I started teaching it back in 2016 and have been impressed by our students' curiosity and passion for the topic. I learned that almost all of them have a favorite conspiracy. More importantly, what we all learned was how best to understand conspiracies in a way that involved both evidence and civility. We busted another myth in the process, the one about this generation of college students being hypersensitive "snowflakes" incapable of reasonable discussion. That was not true by a long shot. Classes follow a healthy combination of common sense and collegiality. Being part of that process makes me much more optimistic about the future.

Many thanks to our staff at the Rohrbach Library, particularly Dawn Boody, who kept the pipeline of interlibrary loan material moving and, on more occasions than I probably remember, patiently dealt with overdue books.

As with all academic projects, my wife, Rachel, continues on as my first editor. If an idea combines common sense with evidence and clarity, she lets me know. If I don't quite cut the mustard, she has the loving candor refined over thirty years of marriage.

Lastly, I would like to thank Thalia, who was an undergraduate at the University of Pittsburgh as I started work on the book. Her studies involve both political science and literary criticism, and she has applied that impressively sharp lens on her father's work. I am raising a young person who has all the potential in the world and the work ethic to reach their goals. More than any parent could ask.

Anarchists rally against the European Union, 2007. (Public domain via Wikimedia Commons: https://commons.wikimedia.org/wiki/File:AnarchistAntiEU_Upscaled.png.)

Introduction

The general population doesn't know what's happening, and it doesn't even know that it doesn't know.[1]

—Noam Chomsky

A conspiracy theorist is a person who tacitly admits that they have insufficient data to prove their points. A conspiracy is a battle cry of a person with insufficient data.[2]

—Neil deGrasse Tyson

ENEMIES EVERYWHERE

We are overwhelmed with conspiracies. They seem to be around every corner. We see Russian agents hiding among US government officials, something that makes older people (like me) unhappily reminded about the long-gone Cold War. Many believe our elections are rigged by foreign and domestic plotters. As COVID-19 cut a swath through the country and the world, some people argued that it was all fake and designed to take away our freedom. It seems like today, no one escapes the vortex of skepticism, cynicism, paranoia, and fear that occupies our thoughts almost constantly.

None of these beliefs are on the fringe anymore. They are not for disheveled people wearing sandwich boards and ringing bells on street corners declaring that end of the world is near. After January 6, we don't roll our eyes and almost immediately forget about the "deep state" in America. Conspiracies are in the mainstream today. They are front and center in presidential politics. Donald Trump and the Tea Party before him brought conspiracy beliefs to our living rooms and kitchen tables. Barack Obama joked about conspiracy theories regarding his background at the White House Correspondents' Dinner in 2011. Donald Trump was not joking when he joined in with the chorus of people who demanded to see Barrack Obama's complete birth certificate. Trump was equally serious when he brandished a *Breitbart* article about the "thousands" of Muslims who celebrated after the World Trade Center attacks in 2001. Steve Bannon, the publisher of *Breitbart*, sat on the National Security Council for a few months before he left the Trump administration in August 2017. Conspiracies are serious business today.

WHO ARE "THEY"?

We use the word all the time. We play the pronoun game every time we are either unsure or simply disinterested about the details of a story. When you bottom out your car in a pothole on the way to work, the first thing that comes to mind is: "They should do something about that." Who? The state department of transportation? The local municipality? Who?

We use generalizations all the time. We always refer to "the military" as if it is a giant, monolithic block, when anyone who has been in it knows the kaleidoscope variations inside such a giant organization. College teachers aren't much better when they use the term "students" like it is a catchall for the ridiculously diverse array of human beings who sit in my classes every day. Try stuffing a lacrosse player, a pre-med student, and a member of the Monty Python Club into the same box. It is a bad fit.

The "mainstream media" (another generalization) does not help one bit. Copy editors and newsreaders can be incredibly lazy when it comes to expressing precision in sound bites. "Critics have questioned the _____," is a common trope that you can hear almost every night on the evening news. Who knew critics could always be so consistently, well, critical? My favorite is still "The CIA remains shrouded in secrecy." I would be worried if it wasn't, but we are supposed to assume that the statement means something if it is recited with careful diction and the kind of weighty cadence that they teach in news anchor school.

So we take short cuts when we approach information, which always leads to trouble. None of this is new. Certainly, fears that "They" are up to something is also old news. Humans have always had scapegoats. They are useful shortcuts that connect paranoia and blame. In America, they have been French, British, Irish, Italian, Russian, and, most recently, Latin American and Russian. (Again. More on that later.) All you have to do is Google "Salem witch trials" to get a sense about how the concept gets defined and redefined over time.

What is different about all this today?

BLAME THE INTERNET

Whenever we talk about modern conspiracy belief, the discussion almost always leads us to the internet. It is not a hard step to take. The worldwide web is its own vast universe. The internet has been part of the public domain for a generation now. It is part of our daily lives, almost like the air we breathe. That doesn't make it any easier to comprehend. Writing in 2016, Stephanie Pappas tried to answer the question: "How Big Is the Internet, Really?"

> In 2014, researchers published a study in the journal *Supercomputing Frontiers and Innovations* estimating the storage capacity of the Internet at 10^{24} bytes, or 1 million exabytes. A byte is a data unit comprising 8 bits, and is equal to a single character in one of the words you're reading now. An exabyte is 1 billion billion bytes.[3]

Jargon like this never helps in reality, so Pappas took it a step further, framing the issue by using an old journalist's trick:

> [Martin] Hilbert and his colleagues took their own stab at visualizing the world's information. In their 2011 *Science* paper, they calculated that the information capacity of the world's analog and digital storage was 295 optimally compressed exabytes. To store 295 exabytes on CD-ROMS would require a stack of discs reaching to the moon (238,900 miles, or 384,400 kilometers), and then a quarter of the distance from the Earth to the moon again, the researchers wrote. That's a total distance of 298,625 miles (480,590 km). By 2007, 94 percent of information was digital, meaning that the world's digital information alone would overshoot the moon if stored on CD-ROM. It would stretch 280,707.5 miles (451,755 km).[4]

This helps a little bit, but who can really imagine a stack of CD-ROMs that extends past the moon? For that matter, how many Americans still remember what a CD is today?

In reality, it is impossible to imagine, yet alone comprehend, how much information is contained online today. And that is the point. Having access to this vast potpourri of images, videos, documents, spreadsheets, music, and commentary is not the same as being able to understand even a tiny part of it. We all know about being part of the "information age," but that does not automatically translate into the talent, wisdom, or experience necessary to separate good, accurate information from the junk.

And yet the internet is becoming a dominant platform for news, particularly for younger audiences. A 2016 Pew Research Center study noted that although television was the primary (57 percent) venue where Americans got news, almost four in ten (38 percent) found it online. Among the eighteen to twenty-nine crowd, half get their information online. The same is true for people ages thirty to forty-nine years. According to the Pew report, print newspapers are the clear dinosaur in this story. Only 5 percent of young adults still get their information from this traditional source, compared with 10 percent of people ages thirty to forty-nine, and 23 percent of people fifty to sixty-four.[5]

So, the internet has the potential to help an increasing number of us to be geniuses or idiots. As a professional historian, I love what the worldwide web offers. I can access documents produced by governments, corporations, or private organizations in a matter of seconds. I wrote a book about American veterans during the COVID-19 pandemic and followed this process. Online archives have thousands of artifacts available today, a sharp contrast to a time when this process involved travel to a physical building and tedious hours spent working through finding aids.

And that is a big problem. The internet has the potential to be an endless series of blind alleys, which can frustrate any researcher. But there is more to the problem than frustration. Michael Crichton, of all people, put his finger on it back in 1995, when the internet was young. A passage from *The Lost World* reads:

> This idea that the whole world is wired together is mass death. . . . Mass media swamps diversity. It makes every place the same. Bangkok or Tokyo or London: there's a McDonald's on one corner, a Benetton on another, a Gap across the street. Regional differences vanish. All differences vanish. In a mass-media world, there's less of everything except the top ten books, records, movies, ideas. People worry about losing species diversity in the rain forest. But what about intellectual diversity—our most necessary resource? That's disappearing faster than the trees. But we haven't figured that out, so now we're planning to put five billion people together in cyberspace. And it'll freeze the entire species. Everything will stop dead in its tracks.[6]

What Crichton seems to be describing, at least in intellectual terms, is the death of curiosity. With Google or Wikipedia available in the palm of your hand, answers become easy. In effect, we have rediscovered intermediaries because they make the vastness out there easier to handle. We are increasingly surrendering curiosity for convenience. It is a trend that I have observed over almost three decades of teaching, and it worries me.

THE HARDWIRED PARTS

It may be that conspiracy belief is simply a hard-wired part of our mental makeup that exists in the subconscious and is largely out of our control. Rob Brotherton made this basic argument in *Suspicious Minds: Why We Believe in Conspiracy Theories* (2015). He points out that paranoia exists and it may be part of our survival instinct. Approaching the unknown with caution is simple common sense, or "prudent paranoia" as one psychologist put it.[7]

Beyond the most basic instinct to survive, Brotherton points out other attributes that may also influence the way we think. For example, it appears that people seek order wherever they look. Establishing patterns satisfies the desire to impose some type of control over our environment. A variety of psychological experiments have pointed to the subconscious need to be in charge of things, and that influences both what we see and how we think.[8]

We also have a tendency to follow paths of least resistance when asking questions and seeking answers. The clinical term for the tendency is "confirmation bias," the point at which our beliefs start to guide our search for facts.[9] People affected by confirmation bias tend to accept sources that agree with their beliefs and dismiss ones that challenge their existing bias.

There is a big difference between scientific inquiry that satisfies something resembling objectivity and a gigantic echo chamber constructed out of our prejudices. Most people are somewhere in between those two points. We are not hostages to our subconscious desires. We are also not blank slates—or "sheeple," to use a popular internet term—ready to accept every answer that experts hand us. We have free will, common sense, and more than enough tools to make our own decisions.

WHAT NEXT?

The purpose of this book is fairly straightforward. I plan to present the topic of conspiracies the same way I approach it in class. I begin with definitions so that we can understand the starting points of the discussion. Then I move to methods, basic components in a logical toolbox that can be applied to not only conspiracies but also historical events or contemporary issues that anyone might come across. Lastly, I apply these definitions and tools to a series of case studies. At this point, I test the definitions and the methods, illustrating where they apply and where they fall short. One thing I always point out is the basic fact that absolute truths don't exist. We can look for truth but will never completely find it. That is not an original idea. A few Greeks talked about the concept a few thousand years ago.

The end goal is also fairly simple: I will offer the reader a chance to learn how to separate nonsense from the facts.

Chapter 1 lays out some useful tools to dissect conspiracies. First, I will define what a conspiracy means. This is important because it establishes a baseline for most of what will follow in the book. Very often, we identify something as a conspiracy when it clearly is not. Chapter 1 will also address some basic logic, such as the relationship between a claim and a proof. It will introduce key terms—correlation and causation—that set out very important distinctions in any discussion about conspiracies.

The chapters that follow offer some interesting case studies of famous (and maybe not so famous) conspiracies. Chapter 2 addresses a conspiracy prevalent after World War I that still lingers today: *The Protocols of the Elders of Zion*. Chapter 3 looks at the Communist conspiracies that populated one of the most paranoid periods of the Cold War. Chapter 4 takes on the Kennedy assassination not only for its obvious impact on American history but also for the reasons conspiracy theories resonated with the public in the sixties, and still do. Chapter 5 looks at the theories swirling around the September 11 attacks, some of which are plausible and some that are clearly on the fringe of logic. Chapter 6 devotes attention to school shootings with a specific focus on conspiracies surrounding Sandy Hook Elementary School, a narrative that added an extra layer of tragedy on an already terrible moment in American history. Chapter 7 examines the phenomena known as "chemtrails," which offers the idea that the Earth is being sprayed from the sky for a variety of evil purposes. Chapter 8 addresses the 2016 election and the cascade of conspiracy claims that flowed out of the presidential contest, ones that continued right into the next administration. Chapters 9, 10, and 11 reflect the reality that the tempo of conspiracies and their impact on American history definitely has accelerated in the very recent past. The country was (and is) saturated with the overlapping impacts of a global pandemic, widespread belief in a "deep state" conspiracy against the country, and accusations about a stolen election that show no signs of slowing down.

As we apply parts of a basic methodology to our case studies, it will become clear that some parts of some of these conspiracies are *real*. They are not a matter of perception or personal belief. They are real and supported by objective facts. The United States was subject to a coordinated campaign of Soviet spying throughout the Cold War. These cases are well documented and stretch over decades. What is important to understand for our purposes is where reality parted ways with actual Russian espionage, facts, and real history under the guidance of people like Joe McCarthy. That point of departure is what we are looking for in this book, that separation from what is real toward what can best be described as fantasy. When that happens, the conversation shifts to a discussion of a *conspiracy theory*. We will talk more about this difference in the next chapter.

What is the best way to see this separation? It's pretty simple, actually. Follow the facts. First learn how to find them and interpret them and understand their limits. Then apply the facts. They will help you separate real threats from perceived ones and find out after all if they are watching.

Mathematics class, 2005. (Public domain via Wikimedia Commons: https://commons
.wikimedia.org/wiki/File:Mathematics_lecture_at_the_Helsinki_University_of_Technol
ogy.jpg.)

Chapter One

Building a Toolbox
for the Logical Mind

Do not guess, try to count, and if you cannot count, admit that you are guessing.[1]

—G. Kitson Clark

WHAT IS A CONSPIRACY?

One of the basic rules that I learned many years ago in graduate school was to define my terms. That way, everyone in the discussion can have a starting point. It does not mean that everyone agrees with the definition, but that they at least know where to begin. I have done the same thing in my classes for years.

In *Suspicious Minds*, Rob Brotherton took a simple, effective approach to defining his key terms. He looked them up. The *Oxford English Dictionary* explains a *conspiracy* as: "a secret plan by a group to do something unlawful or harmful."[2] So, here is our starting point. And it is interesting to see that, from the very beginning, we are making assumptions and value judgments. Conspiracies are secrets, plans hatched away from broad daylight where they can be kept safe from prying eyes, eyes that might see a crime in progress or some kind of bad act that will result in harm. According to this standard, not only are conspirators criminals, they also are evil by definition.

The definition of a *conspiracy theory* is separate, distinct, and less clear as far as an outcome is concerned. The *Merriam-Webster's Collegiate Dictionary* describes it as: "A theory that explains an event or set of circumstances as a result of a secret plot by usually powerful conspirators."[3] We still assume

1

secrecy is an important part of a conspiracy, but with the added element that plotters are powerful actors moving behind the scenes. Conspiracy theories are tempting shortcuts that explain why something happened. According to the definition, they also have the quality of feeding paranoia without adding much clarity to the story.

"Conspiracy theory" is also a loaded term. Many believers argue that the CIA invented the term after the Kennedy assassination to discredit skeptics.[4] In other words, the term "conspiracy theory" was produced by a conspiracy! Although this claim has been debunked by a number of sources, it lingers on in the debate as a trigger term.[5] It is one of the reasons why contemporary advocates of conspiracies use the word "truth" to describe what they do. "Architects & Engineers for 9/11 Truth" is one example.[6]

Academics (at least the good ones) tend to be very careful about what they mean when they talk about conspiracy theories. Historian Kathryn Olmsted defines them in terms that are both tentative and neutral. In her book *Real Enemies*, she says: "A *conspiracy theory* is a proposal about a conspiracy that may or may not be true; it has yet to be proven."[7] Olmsted is cautious for good reasons. We can't, as an audience, know what the motives for a conspiracy might be, good or evil, without proof. The same is true of the conspiracy itself. Lacking evidence, we are right to call into question whether or not it exists. I like Olmsted's approach, because identifying a possible conspiracy is only the first step in a process that places the burden of proof on both the theorist to make their point and the reader to test whether or not it is valid.

JUST WHERE ARE THE CONSPIRACIES?

How common are conspiracies? According to Emma James and Chris Flemming: "As far as we are aware, we do not live in a world with one or two powerful conspiracies in operation—but in one in which *millions* of minor ones—and perhaps a few medium ones are grinding away all the time."[8] Some of these millions of conspiracies involve a broad range of criminal activity. According to the FBI, there were nearly eight million crimes committed against property in the United States in 2015, for example.[9] Some conspiracies are fun. Brotherton points out that parents plan surprise birthday and graduation parties for their children.[10] Spouses purchase secret gifts of jewelry or plan travel to celebrate anniversaries and so on. However, we seem to be more attracted to the idea of large, evil schemes to unseat governments or upset the global balance of power for the drama. If there is anything that twenty-six James Bond movies prove, people love a story where good and evil clash on a global scale.

In reality, it is pretty obvious that conspiracies are *normal*, even mundane, if you think about it.

A FORMULA FOR EXAMINING CONSPIRACIES

Definitions aside, we also need a method for breaking down conspiracies and conspiracy theories into components that align with logic or at least common sense. This formula is useful because it can apply to virtually any conspiracy or theory a reader may run across in their internet travels. If you have ever worked on a research paper in school or studied basic philosophy, many of these terms will be familiar. That is because quite a few of them have been around for hundreds if not thousands of years. In that respect, we are re-inventing a <u>very</u> old wheel.

The Claim

Most conspiracies start with a basic claim, a statement that lays out a blueprint describing the actor(s), their goal(s), and their method(s). Just how simple or complex the claim might be depends on the conspiracy or our understanding of it. For example, the CIA organized a military, economic, and political plot to overthrow Guatemalan president Jacobo Arbenz in 1954, claiming he was pro-communist and would open the door for a Soviet invasion of Latin America. The CIA's effort seems pretty straightforward on the surface. The agency followed the logic of the Cold War and a potential threat to US national security. With hindsight, we understand now that it was only one layer to the story. Further investigation by scholars revealed the Guatemalan coup to be much more complicated, both in terms of Arbenz's relationship with communism and US conflicts of interests (CIA director Allen Dulles owned stock in a company threatened by Arbenz's reforms). It is important to understand that it is possible for claims to evolve.

The claims made by conspiracy theories sometimes tend to take on a life of their own, partly because they lack concrete proof. (We'll talk more about evidence later.) The Kennedy assassination offers a good example. Accepting the idea that Lee Harvey Oswald was a patsy for more powerful interests, the list of potential antagonists includes institutions (the CIA, the Defense Department, the Federal Reserve) as well as individuals (Nikita

Khrushchev, Lyndon Johnson, Cuban exiles, Jackie Kennedy). Their alleged goals are equally diverse. Some claims focus on Kennedy's death as retaliation for a past act like the failure of the Bay of Pigs invasion or the president's alleged affair with mobster Sam Giancana's mistress. Other claims make the point that Kennedy died to prevent something from happening such as American withdrawal from Vietnam or signing the Nuclear Test Ban Treaty.

Some conspiracy claims are gigantic. These "superconspiracies" (some authors have also used the term "nesting conspiracies") consist of interlocking levels of actors, motives, and methods.[11] In his 1992 movie, *JFK*, Oliver Stone took the idea of a conspiracy claim to this level by basically implicating everyone—LBJ, the Defense Department, Cuban exiles, the CIA, and so forth—in the president's death. Conspiracy theorist David Icke takes Stone's idea even further, if that is possible. Icke is an advocate of the idea that shape-shifting reptilian aliens from a planet located in the fourth dimension have replaced global leaders.[12] In just one sentence, Icke has transformed a conspiracy into an interplanetary, trans-dimensional event, truly redefining what the term "super" in conspiracies really means.

Historical Context

Conspiracies don't happen in a vacuum. It is important to know as much as possible about the atmosphere surrounding the conspiracy. Are the times defined by a crisis? War is a common man-made disaster that places stress on people and cultivates the search for scapegoats. Traditional armies threaten a country's ability to exist. Other forms of war are much more diverse. The Cold War lasted for decades but spread conflict across a whole range of activities, from espionage and subversion to insurgencies and complex propaganda campaigns.

Economics matter. Hard times like the Great Depression are also a crisis, creating a foundation of broad suffering and discontent. Just like wartime, we have traditionally looked for someone to blame for hard times. In the thirties, the book *Merchants of Death* captured public attention by blaming Wall Street for American entry into World War I.[13] On the flip side are the good times, where growth promotes ever-increasing expectations and also highlights the gap between haves and have-nots. Kennedy assassination theories flourished in the 1960s, a period of time when the post-World War II boom in America was rolling on.

Politics matter. Conspiracy theories are incredibly tempting and useful tools to apply against political opponents. In 1964, Richard Hofstadter wrote the now classic essay "The Paranoid Style of American Politics" to reflect upon the ugliness that roiled the landscape in his times. But Hofstadter also pointed out that the bitter debate and finger pointing characterizing the early 1960s could be traced back into the nineteenth century and beyond.[14] As bad as we think the 2020 election was and partisanship is today, it has a sadly rich history in America.

Lastly, race and ethnicity matters. In his book *A Culture of Conspiracy*, Michael Barkun examines the blending of folklore, urban legend, rumor, and conspiracy belief, particularly among African Americans.[15] This is an important part of context. The legitimate historical record is littered with horrific acts perpetrated by official power against the disenfranchised. In the modern era, historical context is defined by the Tuskegee Experiment, which speaks not only to decades of bad acts but also, more importantly, deliberate efforts to cover up the truth. Consequently, polling indicates that African Americans tend to accept conspiracy claims made against the government at a higher rate than white audiences. A 2013 survey by Public Policy Polling found that African Americans believed (54 percent) that the Bush administration deceived the country regarding Iraqi weapons of mass destruction as opposed to the 41 percent of white respondents. The same separation appeared regarding the belief that the CIA spread crack cocaine in American inner cities. The survey found that 22 percent of African Americans believed this to be true versus 13 percent of whites.[16]

All of these factors affect any conspiracy theory. They determine how much plausibility a claim might have. They decide their credibility. It was easy to believe that Communists were within the United States in the late 1940s after headlines shouting "Atomic Spy Ring Smashed by FBI" became commonplace. The historical context of a claim affects its credibility, public acceptance, and durability where the basic elements of the time continue and remain relevant.

EVIDENCE

This is the real meat of any conspiracy. When you look into any claim, your first question should be: What supports it? To be plausible and follow a basic logical flow, proof should always follow the claim. The strongest claims will also have multiple sources of evidence that corroborate and verify what is being offered by the speaker or writer. Journalists (at least good ones) usually cite a series of sources that do this. We will talk about different types of evidence below.

ANALYSIS

Ideally, you should be analyzing conspiracy theories from the first claim, to its historical context, and all of its proposed evidence. Language matters. For example, when I look at any claims, official or otherwise, *pronouns* are always a big red flag. As I mentioned earlier, ordinary people and media figures get lazy when it comes to generalizations. "They" pops up constantly in conversations and news broadcasts. The same is true with vague protagonists like "some," as in "some believe," or the inevitable "critics," who always seem to appear when a writer needs to express opposition to an action, a policy, or a person. On the other end of the scale are scientific terms, which are invoked to make a claim sound like it has authority. Dane Wigington, an advocate of climate control conspiracies, is often guilty of using and misusing science to make his point. He peppers terms like "anthropomorphic" (man-made) or "nucleated" (to form around a central body) throughout his website to lend it credibility.[17]

You should apply the same scrutiny to historical context. What makes a conspiracy theory plausible at any particular time may evolve. Many Americans believed that Japanese immigrants were a danger to national security in the hysterical aftermath of Pearl Harbor. Dial the Wayback Machine to 1919 and people thought the same thing about Eastern European immigrants. Reset it to 1840, and the same fear applied to the Irish, and so on. The passage of time can sometimes give us a little more objectivity. Sometimes a lot.

When it comes to analyzing evidence, precision is even more important. It may sound obvious, but it is important to remember that not all evidence is created equal. A lab report that records the amount of lead in water is a good example of science at work, although it is important to understand what type of science was used to produce it. This type of evidence is dramatically different than the 9/11 Commission Report, which is a classic primary source but one with considerable complexity and political baggage. Both the lab report and the 9/11 Commission are on a different planet than the classic YouTube video, which may include an ominous soundtrack and many quick-cut edits, but very little substance.

As you analyze a conspiracy, or any claim in general, it is good to understand that finding the "objective truth" is a great goal, but basically an impossible one. Seeking out ironclad, absolute proof is a holy grail, one that will be subject to debate, parsing, deflection, and a lot of frustration. That is normal.

In class, I borrow a legal term and use the "beyond a reasonable doubt" standard. Truth is not an absolute. Neither is the lack of truth. It is a matter of degree. The *Washington Post*'s "Pinocchio Test" is a good example of how this works. The *Post* started publishing fact-checking back in 2007 and made it a regular feature of the paper in 2011. It adopted the Pinocchio Test to measure degrees of deception:

- *One Pinocchio.* "Some shading of the facts. Selective telling of truth."
- *Two Pinocchios.* "Significant omissions and/or exaggerations."
- *Three Pinocchios.* "Significant factual error and/or obvious contradictions."
- *Four Pinocchios.* "Whoppers."[18]

So, as you move forward, remember that you will never find a definite end point to your story. What you can look for is an answer that reaches a certain threshold of proof that may satisfy both your curiosity and basic logic. It is possible.

MORE TOOLS TO CONSIDER

Beyond our basic formula—claim, historical context, evidence, analysis—there are a few more tools to think about and use as you analyze conspiracy theories.

PRIMARY SOURCES

A primary source is one with direct access to an event. Eyewitnesses are pretty common primary sources. The same is true for an agency or a person directly involved in an event or responsible for it. Historians use diaries or memoirs to get a window to the past in order to understand what went on at a certain point in time. The same is true for official documents. Policy papers and official reports often contain key actors involved in an event. They provide the "smoking gun" proof that links individuals and institutions to historical events. The Watergate tapes or the *Pentagon Papers* are famous examples of official documents that have exposed activity hidden from public scrutiny. Generations of reporters and researchers have searched for primary sources like these to expose conspiracies.

SECONDARY SOURCES

A secondary source is one that has indirect access to an event. We see these every day on editorial pages or in bookstores. Journalists may write about issues, but they do it as bystanders or observers. Bob Woodward broke the Watergate story and later wrote John Belushi's biography, but that did not mean he was actually there to see conspiracies to obstruct justice or smuggle drugs onto the set of *Saturday Night Live*. The same is true about historians. In graduate school, my main area was Cold War policy in Central America during the 1950s. All of this happened before I was born. I am a bystander to this part of history, but it did not stop me from working my way through mountains of official documents at the National Archives in College Park, Maryland.

CORRELATION

Correlations describe a connection between two or more things. We use the idea in a variety of ways. Medical studies examine the correlation between types of nutrition and severity of illness in patients. Marketing companies use correlations to determine consumer purchases in grocery stores according to shelf height. Correlations are part of popular culture. A group of students at Albright College invented a game called Six Degrees of Kevin Bacon in 1994 to demonstrate how easy it was to draw a line (or "connect the dots") between the actor and anyone else in Hollywood.[19]

The game also points out a serious pitfall with using correlations; just about anything can be linked with something else. The website tylervigen. com offers "Spurious Correlations," flow charts like the "per capita cheese consumption correlates with number of people who died by becoming tangled in their bedsheets" that are frankly hilarious.[20]

There is a good point inside that joke. Medical science and marketing demonstrate just how useful correlations can be. They establish simple links. They also have obvious limits. Relying too much on this one device is tempting and can lead the amateur researcher down a rabbit hole that can be hard to escape.

CAUSATION

This is an important term. The formal definition of causation is "the act or process of causing something to happen or exist."[21] You might have heard the phrase "cause and effect" at some point. This is what causation is talking about. When you look for causation, you are looking for a direct link between an event and the reason it happened. There is not much of a gray area when it comes to causation. Like G. Kitson Clarke said at the start of this chapter, "Do not guess, try to count, and if you cannot count, admit that you are guessing." When you hang your argument on causation, you are deliberately avoiding the guessing game.

CONFIRMATION BIAS

This term defines both the research and the researcher. According to RationalWiki, confirmation bias is "the tendency for people to (consciously or *un*consciously) seek out information that conforms to their preexisting viewpoints."[22] We tend to listen to our friends more than strangers or rivals, especially when they agree with us. That tendency has been true for as long as there have been humans on earth, but it has taken on new additions in the recent past. If you have a Facebook account, you get to "friend" people with whom you communicate. Basically, you can control your audience if you want. Trolls need not apply. If they do, they can quickly be banned.

The same is true with your news feeds. You can subscribe or bookmark sources of information that conform to your interests and, back to the original point, your biases. Algorithms built into the system pick up where you leave off, feeding you news and advertisements that mirror your search history. The end result resembles a sort of mental echo chamber, where our bias gets magnified until it is so loud that it drowns out everything else.

NORMALCY BIAS

Conspiracy theorists sometimes use this term to describe the mass of people (or "sheeple") who look for normalcy despite obvious evidence to the contrary. Some individuals are natural optimists and tend to see life as a glass half full. Normalcy bias speaks more to what happens when people are facing a disaster. If you live on a flood plain or below sea level in New Orleans, ignoring the possibility that a storm might destroy your home, you might suffer from normalcy bias.[23] Conspiracy believers use the term to describe a condition when threats exist in plain sight without provoking any public reaction.

ANALOGY

The term describes a similarity between like features of two things and compares them. The English language is filled with analogies. We try to use "layman's terms" to make complicated things clearer. A doctor can compare the human heart to a pump. An economist will illustrate the impact of federal interest rate changes by comparing them to tuning an old carburetor. An analogy is a good shortcut because it appeals to images rather than facts. It requires imagination instead of an intricate knowledge of the topic.

FALSE ANALOGY

To paraphrase the old saying, the devil is in the lack of details. A false analogy takes the comparison of two things and starts warping it out of shape, badly, depending on how far you stretch the comparison. A false analogy can take the points of comparison beyond common sense to absurd, crazy levels. A common example that appears on the internet is: "Employees are like nails. Just as nails must be hit in the head in order to make them work, so must employees."[24] Some false analogies are a little subtler. "Government is like business, so just as business must be sensitive primarily to the bottom line, so also must government."[25] This is true to a point, but if you think about it, the analogy does not hold. Governments are not profit driven. They have the greater public good in mind (or should).

TIME TO GET STARTED

So, we have the basic components of our toolbox. We have the four parts of a formula—the claim(s), historical context, evidence, and analysis—that we will apply to a series of case studies in the next chapters. We also have a few key terms to apply to the discussion. You have the option to use all, some, or none of them. If you want to expand your personal toolbox further, take a look at a more comprehensive glossary of terms featured at the back of the book.

Be patient. All the tools in the world won't matter if you aren't willing to use them to do more than what you can do right now. I always offer my students an option when we start class. Opinions and informed judgments are two very different things. Your opinions matter to you. An informed judgment needs to be supported by facts and logic. Keep your opinions. Develop your judgment.

That might be the best way to approach our toolbox.

1930

EL GOBIERNO
MUNDIAL INVISIBLE

o

**EL PROGRAMA JUDIO
PARA SUBYUGAR AL
MUNDO**

Spanish edition of the *Protocols of the Elders of Zion*, 1930. (Public domain via Wikimedia Commons: https://commons.wikimedia.org/wiki/Category:Protocols_of_the_El ders_of_Zion#/media/File:Protocols_Spain_1930.jpg.)

Chapter Two

The Protocols of the Elders of Zion

There is no need to exaggerate the part played in the creation of Bolshevism and the bringing about of the Russian revolution by these international and for the most part atheistical Jews. It is certainly a very great one; it probably outweighs all others.[1]

—Winston Churchill, 1920

THE INTERNATIONAL JEWISH CONSPIRACY

After World War I, a story about an international Jewish conspiracy to take over the world swept through Europe, crossed the Atlantic, and settled in the United States. The motives, methods, and overall plan were in a book that appeared under different titles: *The Protocols of the Elders of Zion*, *The Protocols of the Learned Elders of Zion*, and *The Protocols of the Wise Men of Zion*, among others. Whatever it was called, the work was a bombshell that reached into almost every corner of the world.

As you read the *Protocols*, a few quirks start to stand out. The book manages to be both tantalizingly detailed and surprisingly vague. For example, a good part of the *Protocols* is a great study of the dark side of human nature, particularly on how to manipulate the worst tendencies in people:

PROTOCOL No. 1
The Basic Doctrine

3. It must be noted that men with bad instincts are more in number than the good, and therefore the best results in governing them are attained by violence and terrorization [*sic*], and not by academic discussions. Every man aims at

13

power, everyone would like to become a dictator if only he could, and rare indeed are the men who would not be willing to sacrifice the welfare of all for the sake of securing their own welfare.[2]

The *Protocols* also talks about some of the institutions that would support a global takeover, especially those responsible for religion, media and public education:

PROTOCOL No. 16
Brainwashing

1. In order to effect the destruction of all collective forces except ours we shall emasculate the first stage of collectivism—the UNIVERSITIES, by re-educating them in a new direction. THEIR OFFICIALS AND PROFESSORS WILL BE PREPARED FOR THEIR BUSINESS BY DETAILED SECRET PROGRAMS OF ACTION FROM WHICH THEY WILL NOT WITH IMMUNITY DIVERGE, NOT BY ONE IOTA. THEY WILL BE APPOINTED WITH ESPECIAL PRECAUTION, AND WILL BE SO PLACED AS TO BE WHOLLY DEPENDENT UPON THE GOVERNMENT.

PROTOCOL No. 14
Assault on Religion

5. IN COUNTRIES KNOWN AS PROGRESSIVE AND ENLIGHTENED WE HAVE CREATED A SENSELESS, FILTHY, ABOMINABLE LITERATURE.[3]

There are twenty-four *Protocols* in all and they set out an extensive list of actions. But the document never gets into details. The Protocols do not reveal the names of specific people or agencies that might be involved or responsible for the conspiracy. The reader does not learn anything tangible like a timeline or a specific date when the unnamed conspirators might finally launch their plan. In short, the *Protocols* are a great example of how a vague group of conspirators, "they," loom over world events ready to take over from within. Yet in 1919, it seemed that "they" had a perfect opportunity, as the world staggered out of the "War to End All Wars" and into an uncertain future.

HISTORICAL CONTEXT:
LIVING IN THE AFTERMATH OF WORLD WAR I

World War I was a bona fide, man-made disaster. The scope and scale of the war were almost impossible to comprehend at the time. Political, social, and economic collapse followed in its wake and traveled around the world for decades. Approximately ten million soldiers died as a result of the conflict. The cheering men who marched off to war died in the trenches and barbed wire along the Western Front in France and Belgium, in Russia, the mountains of Italy, and other places. A generation lost to war rippled through the lives of wives, children, and families left behind in its wake.

World War I led to the final collapse of monarchy in a broad swath of Europe. Instability and revolution saw the end of the Hohenzollerns (Germany), Romanovs (Russia), Habsburgs (Austria-Hungary), and Ottomans (Turkey). The war not only ushered in the end of monarchy but ultimately discredited the system that had governed Europe for centuries. The secret diplomacy conducted by elites had resulted in disaster, leaving millions of disillusioned survivors with the unavoidable sense that, as Stephen Bronner explains: "history operates behind our backs."[4] When Woodrow Wilson spoke of "Open covenants of peace, openly arrived at," his message expressed the widespread desire for transparency in government that might avoid another disaster like World War I.[5]

Economic suffering also followed the war. This was especially true in Germany, exhausted by years of wartime industrial mobilization, crippled by more than two million combat deaths, and made responsible for tens of billions of reparations by the victorious Allies. In response, the new government in Berlin began printing money to cover its debts and sent the country into an even deeper downward spiral. When the war broke out in 1914, 4.2 German marks equaled one US dollar. By November 1, 1923, that ratio had skyrocketed to 130 billion marks to a dollar. By the end of the same month, it took an impossible 4.2 trillion marks to reach the same threshold.[6]

Germany's deep economic decline affected most of the rest of the industrialized world. Prior to WWI, Germany shouldered England aside as the largest economy in Europe. In 1919, by virtue of the Treaty of Versailles, the Allies took the step of gutting the German economy to punish the country and eliminate it as a threat to their security. The decision made a certain amount of sense, but it also effectively crippled the main engine of the continent's economic future. As a result, Europe never completely recovered from the Great War. Strikes, labor unrest, and declining standards of living became the new norm in England, France, and other Allied countries. Although the United States avoided most of these problems, millions of dollars in bad loans to German businesses after World War I were one of the causes of the Great Depression.

As these problems unfolded, disease ravaged Europe and the rest of the world after the war. Influenza, or the "Spanish Flu" as it was known in the

United States, killed between twenty and one hundred million people world-wide in the year after World War I. Approximately 675,000 victims were Americans, more than five times the number who died in the trenches.[7] A doctor stationed at Camp Devens, Massachusetts, wrote in September 1918: "It is horrible. One can stand to see one, two, or twenty men die, but to see these poor devils dropping like flies get on your nerves. We have been averaging about 100 deaths a day, still keeping it up."[8] When influenza reached American cities, the impact was much worse. In October 1918, the first month the disease took hold of Philadelphia, approximately eleven thousand people reportedly died, although the number is probably low given just how overwhelmed local authorities were at the time.[9]

There is one last detail to think about that ties these other parts of the story together. World War I produced something like a crisis of faith in Western civilization. The war took almost every scientific advancement of the industrial age and put it to the purpose of taking human life. Modern weapons like the machine gun and poison gas were brutally efficient at killing and incapacitating. More mundane inventions such as the telephone and barbed wire contributed to the carnage in their own ways. Barbed wire entanglements tormented soldiers throughout the war. The British historian J. F. C. Fuller described the battlefield in the following terms:

> Their carefully planned war was . . . smashed to pieces by firepower . . . so devastating that . . . there was no choice but to go under the surface . . . like foxes. Then . . . to secure these trenches from surprise . . . each side . . . spun hundreds of thousands of miles of steel web around its entrenchments. . . . Armies, through their own lack of foresight, were reduced to the position of human cattle. They browsed behind their fences and occasionally snorted and bellowed at each other.[10]

For many people, even the concept of progress seemed to be the enemy. It was not only faith in industry or technology that was called into question but also any sense of optimism that the future might be better, safer, or more prosperous. The war had taken that faith along with its millions of deaths.

The postwar was a much more cynical time, something Ernest Hemingway captured in his 1925 poem "The Age Demanded":

> The age demanded that we sing
> and cut away our tongue
> The age demanded that we flow
> and hammered in the bung.
> The age demanded that we dance

and jammed us into iron pants.
And in the end the age was handed
the sort of shit that it demanded.[11]

Author David Aaronovitch put it a different way, noting: "Everywhere peoples stared out of the abyss."[12] Much of the postwar life existed in a free-falling political, social, and economic vacuum. People openly contemplated the value of both fascism and communism to replace the old, failed political order. The twenties "roared" as many more sought out an escape from the horrible realities of the war. What made a hero had changed. Charles Lindbergh followed the traditional mold of the explorer when he made his solo flight across the Atlantic Ocean in 1927. Other celebrities had different qualities. Charlie Chaplin became a global icon because he made people laugh in comedies produced by the new silent film industry. Babe Ruth made his mark in baseball during its golden age. When asked what he thought about making more money than the president, Ruth reportedly replied: "Why not, I had a better year than he did."[13]

THE SEARCH FOR SCAPEGOATS

Entertainment aside, there was a much darker side to the postwar that appeared right after the guns stopped firing. The 1920s started with more than a few people looking for and finding scapegoats to blame for the horrors of World War I and the suffering that was engulfing the world. Selective memory was at work from the beginning of this process. The same people who sought out and found scapegoats in the 1920s conveniently forgot that when news of war broke in 1914 it was met by cheering crowds in most world capitals.

So, who was to blame? In his memoirs, German general Erich von Ludendorff pointed to "secret agitation" at home, which tainted incoming conscripts and undercut the effort of loyal veterans on the Western Front.[14] On the opposite end of the political scale, David Aaronovitch notes that leftists blamed capitalism in general.[15]

Unfortunately, perceptions of Jews fit both categories. Jews were "agents of radical change" throughout modern history.[16] They were members of the educated, merchant class that were prominent in European nationalist revolutions of 1848, the Paris Commune in 1871, and the 1905 Russian Revolution. During the Russian Revolution, Jewish members of the Communist Party prompted official concerns regarding their activities. A British Foreign Office report published in 1919 argued that the Russian revolutionary movement: "originated in German propaganda and was, and is being carried out by international Jews."[17] The mainstream media of the day picked up on this theme after the war. An editorial in the British newspaper *The Times* on May 8, 1920 noted:

> When come this uncanny note of prophecy, prophecy in part fulfilled, in parts far gone in the way of fulfillment? Have we been struggling these tragic years to . . . extirpate the secret organization of German world domination only to find underneath it, another, more dangerous because more secret? Have we escaped a *Pax Germanica* only to fall into a *Pax Judeaica*?[18]

The bigger question in the minds of many Western leaders and citizens was just how far this activism went. The conventional wisdom of 1919 extended Jewish revolutionary activity into other suspected subversive groups, real or otherwise, a list that included anarchists, communists, the Illuminati, and the Freemasons.[19] Sadly, these perceptions and suspicions dovetailed with widespread and deeply entrenched anti-Semitism in Europe and the United States.

Fear of secret, internal enemies exploiting unrest appeared in America during the Red Scare. Labor troubles and racial tensions peppered the United States in the year after the war. Seattle workers called a general strike at the start of 1919. In September, 340,000 steelworkers attempting to unionize went on the picket line. Two months later, 400,000 members of the United Mine Workers under John L. Lewis struck in November. Editorial pages were filled with concerns that radicals and anarchists might take advantage of the situation. One writer noted: "It is only a middling step from Petrograd to Seattle."[20] In the meantime, race riots erupted in Texas, Illinois, and Washington, DC, during the summer of 1919, resulting in dozens of deaths and hundreds of injuries.

These events provided very loud background noise to what amounted to a coordinated terrorist attack. As strikes and riots spread, the US Post Office intercepted thirty-four bombs mailed to a number of local, state, and federal officials, a list that included Attorney General A. Mitchell Palmer, Supreme Court Associate Justice Oliver Wendell Holmes, Postmaster General Albert S. Burleson, and businessmen like John D. Rockefeller.[21] The discovery triggered a massive search for culprits.

Terror and paranoia reached hysterical levels as civic leaders demanded justice. Spurred on by wartime mobilization, conservative interests— nativists and nationalists alike—blamed recent immigrants for disloyalty. Law enforcement focused in particular on recent immigrants with ties to radical political and labor organizations. Palmer, aided by the newly created General Intelligence Division led by a youthful J. Edgar Hoover, initiated more than four thousand arrests in thirty-three cities. Approximately five hundred were eventually deported, many without basic due process.[22]

The Red Scare in America came because the war and a long history of suspicion and hatred of immigrants stoked it. The public applauded the Palmer Raids because they provided shortcuts: a clear enemy and a simple solution to a national problem. The actual truth was a casualty of this desire. The Red Scare effectively prepared the country for the *Protocols*. The next step involved focusing the "problem" on Jews and giving it a push from one of the most famous Americans of the time.

THE IMPORTANCE OF HENRY FORD

Americans have always had a love affair with entrepreneurs. Self-made men like Andrew Carnegie and J. P. Morgan fascinated the public because they symbolized all the best qualities of hard work, individualism, and economic success in the great industrial age. For a person living at the 1920s United States, it is hard to imagine a more iconic figure than Henry Ford.

Ford was a self-made man who defined success in modern America. He had embraced the internal combustion engine and developed an assembly line process that could turn out millions of his famous Model T sedans each year. More importantly, the head of the Ford Motor Company could afford to pay his assembly line workers an unprecedented $5 a day.

Henry Ford also hated Jews. At the start of World War I, Ford was against the conflict, claiming in public meetings that global conflict had been caused by "German-Jewish bankers."[23] The same prejudice continued into the postwar. According to historian Vincent Curcio: "Ford had an abiding nostalgia for an idealized, healthier rural past. He saw modern culture, with its jazz, flappers, bootleg liquor, and liberal urban press as the enemy of his social dreams; he thought Jews, in large measure, were behind these social depredations."[24] Ford saw a Jewish hand in the history of American tragedy. He believed, for example, that Jewish bankers were behind Lincoln's assassination because of his support for the Greenback Party.[25]

Consequently, when the *Protocols of the Elders of Zion* arrived in America, Henry Ford became one of its most vocal and influential supporters. Ford's celebrity as a great American captain of industry lent credibility to the conspiracy. More importantly, Ford had a gigantic loudspeaker that came in the form of his company newspaper, the *Dearborn Independent*, which premiered at the beginning of 1919. The paper mainly focused on local issues, but eventually reporters for the *Independent* and Ford himself began to run articles on larger stories, particularly immigration, the Russian Revolution, and the causes of World War I. As Aaronvitch notes: "Like a Ford car, the components were being assembled by different people. Soon they would be put together, and the thing would begin to move."[26] The May 22, 1920 edition of the paper was dedicated to "The International Jew: The World's Foremost Problem." It did not waste any time getting to the point:

> The Jew is the world's enigma. Poor in his masses, he yet controls the world's finances. Scattered abroad without country or government, he yet presents a unity of race continuity which no other people has achieved. Living under legal disabilities in almost every land, he has become the power behind many a throne.[27]

The following month, the *Dearborn Independent* began publishing sections of the *Protocols* as part of its "International Jew" series. Ford eventually published both the series' editorials and the *Protocols* under the title: *The International Jew*. The book went on to sell more than a half million copies in the US market.

Ford's well-funded media campaign gave the *Protocols* story enormous momentum in the United States that carried back across the Atlantic. His stance inspired the young Nazi leader Adolph Hitler to pursue his own conspiracy. Ford is the only American mentioned by name in *Mein Kampf. The International Jew* was translated into German and published throughout the country.[28] Hitler kept a portrait of Ford and when asked why in 1931, he told the *Detroit News*: "I regard Ford as my inspiration."[29] Years after the conspiracy was soundly debunked in the United States and most nations, German propaganda would keep the story alive in millions of minds for years.

THE *PROTOCOLS* AS EVIDENCE

The actual evidence in this case study is easy to find. Unlike the Kennedy assassination or the September 11 attack, you do not have to wade through witness statements, agency reports, videos, or complex debates about metallurgy and the melting point of steel. The evidence for the great global Jewish conspiracy is the actual *Protocols of the Elders of Zion*. When the document surfaced in 1919, it became a primary source for both believers and debunkers, a place it basically still occupies today. As I noted earlier, the publication contains twenty-four sections that describe a conspiracy whose main goal is destroying the existing power structure and replacing it with a world empire ruled by a supreme Jewish leader.

But where did it come from? One researcher traced it back to an 1897 meeting of the First Zionist Congress in the Swiss city of Basel. Russian academic Sergei Nilus claimed in a 1911 edition of the published *Protocols* that they were part of "Zionist executive archives" located somewhere in France. Nilus spoke of a "Jewish-Freemason conspiracy that will surely lead to the end of our vile world."[30]

It looked like the original source of the *Protocols* was a moving target. As it turned out, finding the origins of the conspiracy became the key to understanding whether or not it was actually real. What is interesting is just how quickly research into the origins of the document led scholars and journalists to the conclusion that it was both a fake from the start and evidence of an actual conspiracy.

ANALYSIS OF THE *PROTOCOLS*: UNPEELING THE LAYERS

Ironically, just as the *Protocols* story was beginning to peak around the world, its foundation began to crumble. Careful research into its origins began in 1920. It uncovered important and disturbing similarities between the *Protocols* and older works of fiction. In 1921, the London *Times* revealed additional details that linked the *Protocols* with an 1864 work of fiction by French author Maurice Joly in 1864, titled *Dialogues in Hell between Machiavelli and Montesquieu*. Joly wanted to criticize the policies of the French leader Louis Napoleon (otherwise known as Napoleon III) through an imagined discussion between two historical figures.

A basic, side-by-side look at the two books reveals that *Protocols* 1 through 19 are almost exactly the same as the first seventeen dialogues in Joly's work.

Seventeenth Dialogue	*Protocols*, No. 17
Montesquieu: . . . Now I understand the apologue the god Vishnu; you have a hundred arms like the Hindu idol and each one	Our kingdom will be an apologia of the divinity Vishnu, in whom is found its personification—in our hundred hands will be, one in

of your fingers touches a spring. In the same way that you touch everything, are you also able to see everything?

Machiavelli: Yes, for I shall make of the police and institution so vast that in the heart of my kingdom half the people shall see the other half.

If, as I scarcely doubt, I succeed in attaining this result, here are some of the forms by which my police would manifest themselves abroad: men of pleasure and good company in the foreign courts, to keep an eye on the intrigues of the princes and of the exiled pretenders . . . the establishment of political newspapers in the great capitals, printers and book stores placed in the same conditions and secretly subsidized.

each, the springs of machinery of social life. We shall see everything without the aid of official police . . . In our programs, one-third of our subjects will keep the rest under observation.

Our agents will be taken from the higher as well as the lower ranks of society, from among the administrative class who spend their time in amusements, editors, printers, and publishers, booksellers, clerks, and salesmens, workmen, coachmen, lackeys, et cetera.

Source: Will Eisner, *The Plot: The Secret Story of the Protocols of the Elders of Zion* (New York: W.W. Norton & Company, 2005), 82.

American media also took up the cause of investigating the *Protocols* as well. The *New York Herald* assigned reporter Hermann Bernstein to examine the origins of the *Protocols*, which he published in February 1921 in the book *The History of a Lie*. The book was a bombshell. During his research, Bernstein received documents from a Dr. Harris Houghton that pointed him to Piotr Ivanovitch Rachkovsky, a secret policeman who worked for the Russian tsar. In 1892, Rachkovsky published the book *Anarchism and Nihilism*, which describes Jews "governing by discrete means both monarchies and republics."[31]

One of Rachkovsky's particular talents was forgery. He applied this skill to building the *Protocols* around the 1892 book and the other works of fiction mentioned above. Rachkovsky basically crafted a fantasy, but one he calculated would resonate with the prejudices of his day. His purpose was simple: the work was intended to discredit reformers who were challenging the Russian monarchy. The 1903 version of the *Protocols* was part of a Russian pogrom against Jews and a crackdown on political dissidents. When he received a 1905 copy of Nilus's book in 1905, Tsar Nicholas embraced it and contributed $12 million for publication and distribution of anti-Semitic literature in Russia.[32]

THE UNKILLABLE *PROTOCOLS*

Henry Ford finally admitted his mistake in 1927 regarding the *Protocols*, years after it had been debunked, and issued a reluctant apology. And yet, the book would not die. Direct references to the *Protocols* appear in *Mein Kampf* (1925):

> The extent to which the whole evidence of the people is based on a continual lie is shown in an incomparable manner in *The Protocols of the Elders of Zion*, which the Jews hate so tremendously. The *Frankfurter Zeitung* [a German newspaper] is forever moaning to the people that they are supposed to be a forgery; which is the surest proof that they are genuine. What many Jews do perhaps unconsciously is here consciously exposed.[33]

Belief in the *Protocols* became an ingrained part of the Nazi Party platform. The book served as one of the pillars of the Nazi movement and later provided a justification for a race war against the Jews and the Final Solution. As a German academic noted in 1942:

> Not only is each people morally justified in exterminating hereditary criminals—but any people that still keeps and protects the Jews is just as guilty of an offense against public safety as someone who cultivates cholera germs. [34]

A reasonable person might think that the final defeat of Hitler and the discovery of the horror of extermination camps throughout the Nazi empire would put a stake through the heart of the *Protocols*. And yet that did not happen. David Aaronovitch notes that twelve editions of the *Protocols* were published in Argentina after 1945, helping rumors that a "Chief Rabbi Gordon" was attempting to create a Jewish state in Patagonia as late as the nineteen seventies.[35] References to the book also appear in Article 17 of the 1988 Hamas *Covenant*:

> Zionist organizations which take all sorts of names and shapes such as the Free Masons, Rotary Clubs . . . and the like. . . . Those Zionist organizations control vast material resources, which enable them to fulfill their mission amidst societies, with a view of implementing Zionist goals.[36]

In 2004, the Iranian documentary *Al-Sameri wa al-Saher* examined Jewish control of Hollywood, claiming that the activity was "in total compliance with the *Protocols of the Elders of Zion*.[37] The *Protocols* were even bound up in the September 11 terrorist attacks. A recurrent myth that emerged in the aftermath of the World Trade Center disaster was that no Jews died when the towers collapsed because they were warned by the Israeli Mossad.[38]

So, what accounts for the *Protocols*, long, irrational half-life? How could a work of fiction continue to be accepted as a fact? One possible answer lies in the fact that scapegoats are too convenient to ignore. Blaming Jews for the man-made catastrophe that was World War I was as easy as doing the same while lower Manhattan burned in 2001.

You can find another, more important factor in history. In chapter 1, we talked about the term "confirmation bias" and just how much it influences conspiracy theories. Anti-Semitism has a long and powerful history. It set the framework for the conventional wisdom in Europe and the United States for centuries. Many towns blamed Jews for the onset of the Black Death (1347–1351). "Blood libel," the belief that Jews routinely murdered Christians to drain them of their blood for the Passover meal, appears as early as the twelfth century.[39] The ongoing undercurrent of anti-Semitism made it easy to transition from routine prejudice to more elaborate theories about a Jewish conspiracy.

In this respect, belief and perception are more important than intellect. Henry Ford was not a stupid man, but he was someone who allowed his prejudices to overcome his intelligence. The same was true for the professionals, intellectuals, artisans, and workers—a broad range of economic and social interests—to buy into the Nazi mythology surrounding the *Protocols*. Training, education, experience, and a whole range of things that make up a normal human being are not foolproof protection from fear or prejudice.

Conspiracies are also useful tools and timeless ones. Writing about the *Protocols* in her 1951 book *The Origins of Totalitarianism*, Hannah Arendt's commented that "The chief political and historical fact of the matter is that the forgery is being believed. That fact is more important than the (historically speaking, secondary) circumstance that it is a forgery."[40] Blaming the outsider to rally a majority is a very old device, something we will talk about in more detail throughout the rest of the book.

Army-McCarthy hearings, 1954. (Public domain via Wikimedia Commons: https://com mons.wikimedia.org/wiki/File:Welch-McCarthy-Hearings.jpg.)

Chapter Three

The Russians Are Coming!

A man steeped in falsehood . . . part of a conspiracy so immense and an infamy so black as to dwarf any previous venture in the history of man.[1]

—Joseph McCarthy, referring to Secretary of State
George C. Marshall, June 1951

Have you no sense of decency sir, at long last?[2]

—Joseph N. Welch during Army-McCarthy Hearings, June 9, 1954

BAD NOSTALGIA: THE OLD COLD WAR

Some conspiracies are real. Sometimes we worry about enemies among us because there really are enemies living among us in America. The Cold War is rich with examples of spies, subversion, and traitors, but it also presents a problem for educators: more and more people don't remember it. When I started teaching in 1994, the average student generally understood what the Cold War meant. Milestones like the Berlin Wall, the Cuban Missile Crisis, or Richard Nixon's summit in China weren't hard examples to mention whenever the subject came up.

Today, it is a different story for my average freshman, born in 2004. To this group of youngsters, America's conflict with the former Soviet Union is as remote as the Civil War, the American Revolution, or the Middle Ages, for that matter. Ironically, more than thirty years after the official death of the Soviet Union, the best reminder of the bad old days of the Cold War is our own recent presidential elections and the endless refrains about Russian interference.[3]

During the Cold War, both the United States and the USSR fought a covert conflict of espionage, assassination, and sabotage for decades, mostly outside of each other's borders, but not always. Spies from both the Central Intelligence Agency and its Soviet counterpart, the Komitet Gosudarstvennoy Bezopasnosti (otherwise known as the KGB), operated in Cold War hotspots like Vietnam, Cuba, Chile, Angola, and right here at home. For many Americans, the spy was normal fixture of life, a pop culture hero to be found in the fiction of Ian Fleming and brought to life by Sean Connery as James Bond.

The point when the Cold War really reached into the United States can be traced back to the Red Scare of the late 1940s and early 1950s. During that time, a general sense of unease rooted in the postwar US-Soviet rivalry was transformed into a moment when fear turned Americans against each other and paranoia about Russian meddling in the government reached hysterical proportions that ruined lives and careers.

Anti-Communism became a driving force in American diplomacy and an important credential for politicians. Administrations from Harry Truman to Richard Nixon built their foreign policy decisions around either confronting or "containing" the perceived threat of global Communism. Two generations of Americans paid the price for these decisions in Korea and Vietnam. Similarly, politicians built their reputations around the vague idea that being "hard" on Communism was a critical part of their party platforms and personal beliefs, something that lasted well into Ronald Reagan's presidency.[4]

This chapter will explore the actual nature of the communist threat and, perhaps more importantly, its limits. Soviet spies lived and worked within the United States for years. Many if not most of these people were Americans who betrayed both security agreements while government employees as well as the basic tenants of citizenship. These spies were real. However, there are bigger questions that are also important. Not every person accused of treason was a traitor. When it came to the covert Cold War, where did tangible reality end and fear mongering and opportunism begin? At what point did political gain matter more than the truth? What impact did it have on the country and its faith in basic institutions? These are some of the questions that we will talk about in the next few pages.

CLAIM: THE WHEELING, WEST VIRGINIA, SPEECH

Probably the most famous claim about the communist menace was articulated by Wisconsin Republican Senator Joseph McCarthy during a speech in Wheeling, West Virginia, on February 20, 1950:

The reason why we find ourselves in a position of impotency is not because our only powerful potential enemy has sent men to invade our shores . . . but rather because of the traitorous actions of those who have been treated so well by this Nation. It has not been the less fortunate, or members of minority groups who have been traitorous to this Nation, but rather those who have had all the benefits that the wealthiest Nation on earth has had to offer . . . the finest homes, the finest college education and the finest jobs in government we can give.

This is glaringly true in the State Department. There the bright young men who are born with silver spoons in their mouths are the ones who have been most traitorous.

I have here in my hand a list of 205 . . . a list of names that were made known to the Secretary of State as being members of the Communist Party and who nevertheless are still working and shaping policy in the State Department.

As you know, very recently the Secretary of State proclaimed his loyalty to a man guilty of what has always been considered as the most abominable of all crimes—being a traitor to the people who gave him a position of great trust—high treason.[5]

McCarthy's claims were a bombshell made when Cold War fears were running rampant. Stories of spies and traitors peppered American newspapers after World War II. The arrests of atomic scientists Alan Nunn May and Klaus Fuchs prepared the ground for public paranoia. Current events stoke public fear even more. Headlines screamed about the collapse of China to communist revolution in 1949 and the first successful Soviet atomic test that same year. The North Korean invasion of South Korea in 1950 and Chinese intervention edged the world toward World War III.

McCarthy not only rode the wave of fear then starting to engulf the country, he also gave it focus and structure. In his "conspiracy so immense," he made it clear that people understood the US government was the source of the problem. Fuchs and May were individual traitors. Accusing the entire State Department ramped up the story to a whole new level.

McCarthy's claim also appealed to economic and social resentments. When he spoke about "the bright young men who are born with silver spoons in their mouths," McCarthy was referring to a special kind of betrayal from Ivy League–educated elites who represented America's best and brightest. During the Great Depression, Franklin Roosevelt referred to them as his "brain trust," a group of academics and policy makers who built popular New Deal programs and later applied their talents to mobilization for World War II. However, their position could cut both ways. Ivy League experts also received much of the blame for the economic dislocations that followed victory in 1945 as well as the series of Cold War reverses ending the decade.

Lastly, McCarthy made sure that he made his claims in full view of the American media. After the Wheeling speech, major news dailies around the country featured headline stories of McCarthy's claims and official efforts to investigate them. The *New York Times* featured his statement that eighty-one individuals, including one who served as "one of our foreign ministers," were implicated, although he refused to provide names or specific details, a habit that constantly frustrated McCarthy's critics but did not interrupt his rise in the Senate.[6]

HISTORICAL CONTEXT:
THE NATURE OF THE COMMUNIST THREAT

As I mentioned at the start of the chapter, many people don't remember the basic ideas that separated the United States and the Soviet Union during the heyday of the Cold War. What motivated the hostility between these two countries for most of the twentieth century? Literally thousands of books have been written on the topic. At its core, the Cold War was a conflict over basic concepts. Historian Nicholas Riasanovsky provides one of the clearest explanations of Communism and the discussion requires a little bit of patience.

Communism centers on the idea of "dialectical materialism," in which material wealth is the sole measure of a person to the exclusion of everything else. Intellect, spirituality, creativity, and all the features that make up a human being take second place. Materialism divides individuals and society as a whole between haves and have nots. According to Karl Marx, the gap between rich and poor—each living in a separate economic class—is the source of conflict (the "dialectic") that will be resolved only after revolution destroys the elites who control the capitalism and the class system.[7]

As it played out, the Cold War was also a struggle over strategic resources (like oil) and key points on the map (like the Suez Canal) that granted access to them. The Cold War was about power (or hegemony, to use the academic term) and the ability to influence the course of world events. The Cold War was a moral contest as well. It was a contest between one system that believed in the existence of God pitted against one that did not. Even so, there were times when the so-called Free World led by the United States regularly tolerated horrible violations of basic human rights in the name of freedom. Anyone who grew up after 1945 remembers bits and pieces of these basic elements as they played out in Korea, Berlin, Laos, Vietnam, Nicaragua, Afghanistan, and a hundred other places.

The United States fought Communism long before the Cold War began. As the Russian Revolution raged in 1919, the United States joined a coalition of European countries intent on destroying Communism before it could gain a foothold and spread. An American infantry regiment joined one hundred thousand troops from fourteen other nations that intervened in the Russian Revolution to accomplish just that. They failed. Americans are still buried in the permafrost near Archangel to mark that failure.

When the USSR emerged out of the Russian Revolution, Soviet communists made their own plans. They formed the Communist International (also known as the Comintern) to fight: "by all available means, including armed force, for the overthrow of the international bourgeoisie and for the creation of an international Soviet republic as a transition stage to the complete abolition of the State."[8] "All available means" meant providing economic, military, and political aid to like-minded revolutionaries in China, Cuba, North Korea, and dozens of other countries. It also meant an ongoing campaign of espionage, sabotage, and assassination against the West and Western Allies. Soviet efforts did not automatically translate into a disciplined or effective global campaign against capitalism. But they did succeed in keeping tensions high as revolutions rose and fell in concert with a series of breaking scandals that brought the Cold War into America's own backyard.

AMERICAN TRAITORS

There is evidence of Soviet espionage against Western industrial nations and the United States as early as the 1920s. Moscow recognized American economic power as well as its talent for research and development and wanted to "glean industrial secrets from US businesses."[9] Soviet leaders also looked for political intelligence that they could use to gauge official US policy. To accomplish this, communist operatives actively recruited Americans within the US government. These individuals included Whittaker Chambers, who took charge of a cell of communist agents during the early part of FDR's New Deal. Chamber's cell included Alger Hiss in Department of Agriculture and Harry Dexter White at the Department of the Treasury.[10] All three men would become central to McCarthy's investigations of the US government years later.

Despite the wartime alliance between the United States and the USSR, Soviet espionage actually increased during World War II. The Manhattan Project and the US atomic bomb program generated intense Russian interest. During the war, covert operatives successfully recruited Klaus Fuchs, a German refugee physicist; Theodore Hall, an American scientist; and David Greenglass, who worked as a machinist at the Los Alamos test facility.[11] During and after the war, additional spy rings continued to operate in San Francisco, New York City, and Washington, DC.

Spy scandals rippled through America in the late 1940s. When Elizabeth Bentley turned herself into the FBI's New York field office at the end of 1945, it caused a sensation. Bentley started her career as a Soviet agent in the late 1930s. During World War II, she controlled political and military assets who had access to some of the upper tiers of the US government. When Bentley confessed her activities to American authorities, it exposed a massive security failure and triggered a scramble in official Washington to avoid blame.[12]

The FBI was particularly vulnerable since one of its primary responsibilities was ferreting out spies. In the wake of Bentley's confession, Director J. Edgar Hoover buried the Truman administration in memos warning the president of real and suspected Soviet espionage. Truman ignored most of his specific concerns but issued an executive order in March 1947 "prescribing procedures for the administration of an employees' loyalty program in the executive branch of government." Between 1947 and 1956, five million federal workers underwent additional security screening, resulting in 2,700 dismissals and 12,000 resignations.[13]

In the meantime, a miffed Hoover began leaking his files to sympathetic lawmakers in the Republican-controlled Congress as well as Thomas Dewey when he ran against Truman in 1948. That same year, the *New York World-Telegram* published the Elizabeth Bentley story, catapulting the private, official debate into a public firestorm.[14] Sensing an opportunity, the House Un-American Affairs Committee (HUAC) convened hearings that summer to investigate just how far communists had penetrated the upper echelons of the US government. The committee called both Alger Hiss and Harry Dexter White to testify. Both men denied all charges against them.

Investigations from both the press and official Washington received a boost from multiple directions in 1950. In January, Hiss was convicted of perjury for lying to Congress about his relationship with Whittaker Chambers. Not two weeks later, Klaus Fuchs, a British physicist who had worked on the Manhattan Project, was arrested and confessed to selling secrets to the Russians. Fuchs led the FBI to David Greenglass, Julius Rosenberg, and his wife Ethel.[15] The spy ring story ignited by Elizabeth Bentley almost two years earlier gained a new lease on life. J. Edgar Hoover prodded the story along in Senate testimony, claiming that "54,000 known Reds and nearly 500,000 sympathizers," were active in the United States.[16]

ENTER "TAILGUNNER JOE"

It was very clear to most people that there were real threats to American national security. At the same time, this made the issue incredibly tempting for young politicians interested in promoting their own careers. They did so regardless of party. When Richard Nixon and John Kennedy entered Congress in 1946, they represented the Republican and Democrat parties in a bitter fight over social welfare programs and the legacy of the New Deal. In terms of foreign policy, both men were dyed-in-the wool Cold Warriors, however.

The real virtuoso when it came to politicizing national security issues was a little-known senator from the state of Wisconsin, Joseph McCarthy. Although technically exempt from military service as a circuit court judge, McCarthy volunteered for the Marine Corps and was commissioned as a lieutenant in 1942. He served as an intelligence officer for a bomber squadron in the Solomon Islands during World War II. McCarthy adopted the nickname "Tailgunner Joe" to exaggerate his combat service. He volunteered to be an observer on twelve combat missions but falsely claimed another twenty in order to qualify for a Distinguished Flying Cross and multiple awards of the Air Medal that the Marine Corps did not officially approve until 1952.[17]

McCarthy turned out to be a pretty mediocre senator. As his first term was coming to an end, his legislative record of accomplishments was fairly thin. The freshman senator also lacked compelling, "hot button" issues to rally his constituents back in Wisconsin. According to historian David Oshinsky, McCarthy had his political epiphany during lunch with two friends and advisors—Edmund Walsh, dean of the Georgetown University School of Foreign Relations, and political science professor of the school, Charles Kraus—in January 1950. As they ate, McCarthy considered old age pensions or possibly a St. Lawrence Seaway construction project to restart his political career. However, he noted that neither really had "some real sex appeal" to capture national attention.[18] Walsh shrewdly suggested "Communism in government," an idea that could exploit widespread concerns about spies in particular and the Cold War in general.

He did just that in Wheeling. McCarthy took real evidence of plotting, combined it with suspicion, and unleashed the story on a ready-made audience. Armed with what appeared to be a hard count of 205 traitors in the US government, the Wisconsin senator jumped into the Cold War fray with both feet. The problem, as it turned out, was that McCarthy would not provide the list he enjoyed waving in front of the cameras. His list shrank to fifty-seven names and later grew to eighty-one "loyalty risks."[19] Initially, it looked like McCarthy's political gambit was beginning to come apart over its own lack of detail. But, as it sometimes happens, he discovered that it was better to be lucky than good.

HISTORY SAVES MCCARTHY

As McCarthy bumbled his way forward into the waiting arms of the American media, defenders of the Truman administration began to mobilize. Chaired by Senator Millard Tydings (Democrat, Maryland), Congress convened a committee to investigate McCarthy's claims. The 313-page majority report, published in July 1950, noted that his charges were "perhaps the most nefarious campaign of half-truths and untruth in the history of this Republic."[20]

At that moment, history intervened. North Korea crossed the Thirty-Eighth Parallel into South Korea in June, a month before the Tydings Committee report became public. The war shifted the entire political dynamic in America. Stunned by the unexpected attack on the other side of the world and escalating US casualties, the public wanted answers and McCarthy seemed to have them. Political retribution for being perceived as "soft" on Communism followed right on the heels of the North Korean invasion. Tydings, who had held his seat since 1926, would be forced out of the Senate in the 1950 Congressional midterm elections.

McCarthy's star rose as the Cold War heated up. He was awarded the chairmanship of the Senate Internal Security Subcommittee and later the Committee on Government Operations. These bodies existed to oversee US security concerns. For the most part, however, they gave McCarthy a platform to browbeat opponents and ruin careers. No one was safe. Witnesses were called to testify about past acquaintances, social contacts, and political affiliations, some as far back as the 1930s. When McCarthy could not find direct evidence, he skillfully wove together series of correlations that were a master class in "guilt by association." During the 1952 presidential campaign, the senator turned his sights on George C. Marshall, accusing the former five-star general and secretary of state of a "baffling pattern of decisions" that seemed to be serving the "world policy of the Kremlin."[21] In a testament to McCarthy's power at the time, Republican candidate Eisenhower refused to contradict him and omitted a reference to Marshall from a speech he gave in Wisconsin during the lead-up to the election.

THE RIPPLE EFFECT

The paranoid wave urged on by McCarthy and fellow red baiters like California Congressman Richard Nixon carried into nearly every corner of America. Hollywood appeared to be a clearinghouse for communists. As early as 1947, the president of the Screen Actors Guild, Ronald Reagan, began naming names of producers, directors, and actors he believed followed the Communist Party line.[22] Similar accusations landed on writers and playwrights like Arthur Miller, who was accused of subverting American ideals through works such as *Death of a Salesman* (1949). As time passed, the ripple effect of suspicion carried across the country, touching celebrities and normal folks alike. Linus Pauling, a quantum chemist and molecular biologist, won the Nobel Prize for chemistry in 1954, but ran afoul of the US government because he opposed nuclear weapons. Pauling was denied a visa to attend a 1952 meeting of scientists in London. Scenes like this played out across the country in businesses, school boards, unions, and professional organizations. People risked their continued employment for a perceived lack of loyalty to the country. Friendships and family relations shattered for the same reason, many never to recover. In its search for enemies, it seemed like many of the fundamental institutions binding America together were coming apart.

EVIDENCE: INVESTIGATING THE INVESTIGATOR

As we noted earlier, in 1950, there was serious, tangible evidence of Soviet plotting against the United States that traveled back for decades. This basic fact was both McCarthy's greatest asset and his greatest weakness. During his Wheeling speech, McCarthy did not draw a clear line between threats identified in the past, in some cases, years in the past, and a "clear and present danger" to the United States.

However, his critics did. As Oshinsky notes, Democratic lawmakers and newspapers investigated McCarthy's Wheeling claims and found them in the public record going back to the mid-1940s. The original claim that 205 communists worked in the State Department reflected a 1946 report by then Secretary of State James Byrnes to the Congress on potential security risks, not actual communists. The fifty-seven names that McCarthy later offered were derived from a 1948 House Appropriations Committee finding regarding State Department employee "security problems."[23]

CBS journalist Edward R. Murrow took the same yardstick to McCarthy's claims during committee hearings in the early 1950s. Murrow applied basic investigative journalism and logic to the senator by simply comparing McCarthy's claims against the existing public record. Appearing on the CBS television program *See It Now*, and using publicly available documents, Murrow repeatedly exposed McCarthy's exaggerations, distortions, and outright lies. For example, one of McCarthy's favorite false tropes was that the FBI had named the American Civil Liberties Union as a communist front organization. This claim was caught on film during McCarthy's investigation of State Department employee Reed Harris and rebroadcasted by Murrow on his program. By illustrating these moments again and again, Murrow basically disassembled McCarthy before a national television audience.

The back and forth between Murrow and McCarthy reached a high point when the senator predictably condemned Murrow as a communist, "the leader and the cleverest of the jackal pack which is always found at the throat of anyone who dares to expose individual Communists and traitors."[24] However, given the choice between canceling *See It Now* and continuing a TV program that was riveting a national audience, CBS kept Murrow on the air.

As it turned out, McCarthy turned out to be his own worst enemy. In 1954, he decided to investigate the United States Army, attempting to make a case that communist agents had penetrated the Army Signal Corps. Because McCarthy was actually one of the subjects of the investigation, he ceded his chairmanship to Senator Karl Mundt, a South Dakota Republican. This did not prevent him from sitting on the committee and sparring with the Army legal team over the next thirty-six days, all in full view of the television cameras.

McCarthy's bullying and grandstanding backfired badly. The moment came on the thirtieth day of hearings when he was abruptly taken to task by Joseph N. Welch, a counsel for the Army, who perfectly framed the moment:

> Senator, may we not drop this? We know he belonged to the Lawyers Guild. . . . Let us not assassinate this lad further, senator. You've done enough. Have you no sense of decency, sir? At long last, have you left no sense of decency?[25]

At the end of the exchange, the audience broke into applause.

It was clear that McCarthy's ugly style overwhelmed his shaky evidence. Most Americans, including the millions of veterans who served in World War II and Korea, rejected his absurd claims about the Army. His Gallup Poll approval dropped significantly in the wake of the hearings, from 50 percent to just 32 percent.[26] The Army-McCarthy hearings also struck a raw nerve in the new president, Dwight Eisenhower, who left the Army as a five-star general and deeply resented McCarthy's attacks on an institution that had defined his adult life. Behind the scenes, Eisenhower began working with the Senate to undercut McCarthy. Publicly, the president invoked executive privilege to starve McCarthy's investigation of official documents.[27]

Caught between declining popularity and a growing backlash orchestrated by the White House and Senate rivals in both parties, McCarthy's political career spiraled downward. He was officially censured by his Senate colleagues in December 1954 for "obstructing constitutional processes" and lost control of key committee assignments. A little more than two years later, he was dead, from what his death certificate described as "Hepatitis, acute, cause unknown," although many authors have speculated that the cause was McCarthy's alcoholism.[28]

ANALYSIS: WHAT DID THE SECOND RED SCARE MEAN?

There is little question that the opposition between communism and capitalism developed into open conflict for most of the twentieth century. The United States and an alliance of Western nations tried to kill communism during the 1917 Russian Revolution and failed, kicking off a geopolitical feud that lasted for decades. Although the two sides paused their open battling to defeat Hitler, war in the dark corners of the world moved forward.

When fears of communist conspiracy reappeared in the late 1940s, they were built upon ongoing Soviet intrigue, but other more subjective factors might have mattered even more to the story. American conspiracists understood the value of suspicion, fear, and resentment, especially as it applied to domestic politics, even more specifically to Democrats in office. As popular as Franklin Roosevelt and the New Deal had been, he and the party had enemies who disliked the idea of growing federal power and the elitism that came with it.

When Roosevelt died in 1945, administration opponents in the Republican Party saw a chance to roll back not only the power of the state but also the control eastern liberal policy makers had over the country. What they saw was as much political rebellion as it was social rebellion. But they could not close the deal. Republicans surged back into Congress in 1947, but Harry Truman shocked the country by winning the presidency in his own right the following year. During the campaign, Truman gave as good as he got, railing against the "do nothing Congress" before cheering crowds.[29] By the time McCarthy had his 1950 "epiphany," American political partisanship was increasingly entrenched and bitter.

Republican opposition morphed into a bitter stew of claims regarding treason, class war, and more than a few pointed references to social deviancy. As McCarthy mentioned in his 1950 speech: "those who have had all the benefits that the wealthiest Nation on earth has had to offer . . . the finest homes, the finest college education, and the finest jobs in government we can give."[30] In contrast to these Ivy League elites were the common, hardworking folk. McCarthy placed himself on this side of the country and its beliefs, a place he described as "Americanism with its sleeves rolled."[31]

Accompanying this anger was a deep streak of homophobia. Code words for homosexuality appeared frequently in McCarthy's speeches as well as those of other Cold Warriors like Richard Nixon.[32] McCarthy described

Secretary of State Dean Acheson as "the Red Dean of Fashion," who sported "a lace handkerchief, a silk glove, and . . . a Harvard accent."[33] At points, the media picked up this thread. During the 1952 presidential campaign, the *New York Daily News* referred to Democrat candidate Adlai Stevenson as "Adelaide" and derided his "fruity voice" during speeches.[34] To minds like these, traitors challenged not only American national security and democracy but also our fundamental moral values.

But hatred had its limits. It was this kind of ugliness that broke McCarthy and discredited him. When he attacked the US Army in 1954, McCarthy tried to draw the military into the steamy narrative saturating American institutions in power. However, the public recoiled from this idea, refusing to believe that the military was that corrupted by outside influences. In fact, it is not hard to understand their conclusion, given the tens of millions of citizens who could claim veteran's status by 1954. McCarthy's charges on the military were not just an abstract argument. They were an attack on Americans who proudly served and wanted to enjoy the rewards of that service.[35]

THE LEGACY OF MCCARTHYISM

To be sure, there were clear and consistent communist efforts to infiltrate US institutions and sabotage American policy during the Cold War, efforts that extended far beyond McCarthy's death. One of the stories pushed off the front page by the September 11 attacks was the arrest of a Cuban spy, Ana Belén Montes, who had infiltrated the senior ranks of the Defense Intelligence Agency by 2001.[36] Concerns regarding an ongoing communist conspiracy were definitely real.

When politics entered the story, the line between real and fake began to blur, unfortunately. McCarthy and a whole generation of Democrat and Republican American politicians understood the potent value of fear and repeatedly invoked the Red Menace to generate traction with voters.

So, the hunt for communists continued. J. Edgar Hoover was convinced that Martin Luther King was a communist agent and ordered FBI surveillance of the civil rights leader. The FBI began an official counterintelligence program (COINTELPRO) in 1956 with the express purpose of quashing threats to American security. As the country entered the 1960s, the Bureau's focus shifted from an increasingly irrelevant American Communist Party toward other known and suspected dissident groups. Based upon its suspicions about their loyalty and possible links with Moscow, tentative or fictitious as they were, the FBI conducted ongoing investigations of the Black Panthers, the Students for a Democratic Society, the Vietnam Veterans Against the War, and many other organizations. Throughout, the Bureau freely discarded the law in order to protect its vision of America. It conducted wiretaps, searched mail, and conducted surveillance without probable cause or warrants. It was also common practice for the FBI to plant false stories in the media, harass activists, and attempt to provoke targeted groups to violence. Many of these abuses spilled into the press in 1976 when the Senate Select Committee to Study Governmental Operations, chaired by Frank Church (Democrat, Idaho), published its findings. The Church Committee offered a damning judgment of the FBI, saying, "Many of the techniques used would be intolerable even if all of the targets had been involved in violent activity, but COINTELPRO went beyond even that."[37] In the end, the FBI, like McCarthy, became a problem bigger than communism when it flaunted its own power at the expense of the law and common sense.

The twentieth-century endpoint for McCarthyism appeared during Ronald Reagan's presidency. When he denounced the nuclear freeze movement in 1982 for containing communist sympathizers and "foreign agents," Reagan's strong words fell on deaf ears.[38] The "Great Communicator" couldn't rally a cynical and distrustful public around a time-honored concept. In the wake of Vietnam, the *Pentagon Papers*, Watergate, the Church Committee's revelations, and, frankly, McCarthy's own crusade, playing the communist card simply didn't have the same power as it did a generation earlier.

That last point deserves a few more moments of attention. We usually blame the collapse of public faith in government on the 1960s. The New Left, student radicals, spoiled Baby Boomers, and advocates from a kaleidoscope of causes are the usual culprits. However, a strong case can be made that McCarthy fired the starting gun that launched a series of very public attacks on official authority and the trustworthiness of our elected leaders. In his tirades against the president, his staff, cabinet officials, senior military officers, and a whole host of people who represented the pillars of postwar American stability, McCarthy undercut some our most important foundations.

Polaroid photograph of the assassination of President John F. Kennedy, taken an estimated one-sixth of a second after the fatal shot. (Public domain via Wikimedia Commons: https://commons.wikimedia.org/wiki/File:Moorman_photo_of_JFK_assassination.jpg.)

Chapter Four

The Assassination of John F. Kennedy

The shots which killed President Kennedy and wounded Governor Connally were fired by Lee Harvey Oswald.[1]

—Warren Commission Report, 1964

What really happened?[2]

—Nikita Khrushchev, 1964

THE DEATH OF A PRESIDENT

Being president can be dangerous business. John F. Kennedy was not the first chief executive to be murdered while in office. Lincoln's death is probably the most famous, but assassin's bullets also cut down James Garfield (1881) and William McKinley (1901). The list of actual assassination attempts is disturbingly long and includes Andrew Jackson, Teddy Roosevelt, William Howard Taft, Herbert Hoover, Franklin Roosevelt, Harry Truman, Gerald Ford, Ronald Reagan, George W. Bush, and Barrack Obama. The most common method has been pistols (Jackson, Roosevelt, Taft, FDR, Ford, Reagan), although bombs (Hoover, Truman), a hand grenade (Bush), and ricin in an envelope (Obama) have all been used in failed assassination attempts.

What made Kennedy's death unique was that it was the first to be captured by the age of television. Dozens of still pictures and the Zapruder film recorded Kennedy's death. Kennedy's funeral, which featured the heartbreaking image of his son John saluting his father, was nationally televised and is now deeply embedded in our memories.

41

Kennedy's death also occurred at the height of the Cold War, a little more than a year after the Cuban Missile Crisis, the Berlin Crisis, and the Laos Crisis, a time when world tensions were ratcheted up to an extreme level. My parents recalled people buying canned goods to prepare for a war, something that I found chilling and a little depressing at the same time. Regardless, for most Americans at the time, the prospect of having the leader of the so-called Free World die was not tolerable. It was a clear and definite tripwire that people knew would lead to global conflict.

Most people today tend to focus on the images of Kennedy's death rather than the historical context. Context is important, not only when it comes to understanding the general atmosphere of the country at the time but also just how much of a role Cold War tensions had on official decision making. We will come back to this point later.

ASSASSINATION CLAIMS: SIMPLE AND COMPLEX

The first part of the basic claim is very simple: the president of the United States died on November 22, 1963, in Dallas, Texas. However, one step beyond that point, the debate begins over who was responsible. The official story, provided by the 1964 Warren Commission Report, maintains that Lee Harvey Oswald was the "lone gunman."

Skeptics have questioned the credibility of this statement ever since. Alternate conspiracy claims challenging the official version of the Kennedy assassination are the opposite of simple. In the years after his death in Dallas, they have become part Americana, part classical Greek Hydra. Conspiracy theories grow, are debunked, and surge back again even stronger than ever, challenging everything in their path. While sorting through all the various branches of Kennedy assassination theories, a few basic trends do stand out.

First, most of these theories agree that John F. Kennedy was assassinated by a conspiracy of actors rather than a lone gunman. Second, some argue that Kennedy likely died as retaliation for one of his policies, such as the failed 1961 Bay of Pigs invasion and the "purge" of CIA leadership following it. A third school of thought maintains that Kennedy died to prevent him from enacting a policy, such as the withdrawal of US forces from Vietnam, or shifting power from the Federal Reserve to the US Treasury. This last theory is interesting because it has a bit of the *Protocols of the Elders of Zion* buried within it.

There are a series of related, smaller sub-claims that exist beneath this basic architecture explaining both the actors involved in the conspiracy and their motives. For many, Kennedy's death was a clear sign of the rise of what

Dwight Eisenhower labeled the "military industrial complex" on January 17, 1961:

> This conjunction of an immense military establishment and a large arms industry is new in the American experience. The total influence—economic, political, even spiritual—is felt in every city, every State house, every office of the Federal government. We recognize the imperative need for this development. Yet we must not fail to comprehend its grave implications. Our toil, resources and livelihood are all involved; so is the very structure of our society.
>
> In the councils of government, we must guard against the acquisition of unwarranted influence, whether sought or unsought, by the military-industrial complex. The potential for the disastrous rise of misplaced power exists and will persist.
>
> We must never let the weight of this combination endanger our liberties or democratic processes. We should take nothing for granted. Only an alert and knowledgeable citizenry can compel the proper meshing of the huge industrial and military machinery of defense with our peaceful methods and goals so that security and liberty may prosper together.[3]

This school of thought pursues the idea that presidents are basically figureheads for the modern power structure. This power structure, or the "establishment," as it was commonly known fifty years ago, was made up of private corporate interests (Standard Oil, IBM, Ford, etc.) along with their government counterparts in the Defense Department, the CIA, the National Security Council, the Treasury Department, and a host of other federal agencies.[4] At best, the ongoing interaction between the two sets of actors living in each other's pockets was a conflict of interest over public policy. At worst, their relationship represented an ongoing bastardization of democracy. Regardless, there is an element of truth in this history that gave credence to later conspiracy belief

Ironically, Eisenhower was just as guilty as any other president of encouraging the relationship. When he organized his cabinet in 1953, people jokingly (or mockingly) referred to it as containing "nine millionaires and a plumber," for the wealthy men present.[5] Eisenhower's man in charge of the Defense Department, Charles "Engine Charlie" Wilson, once famously said during his confirmation hearing: "for years I thought that what was good for our country was good for General Motors and vice versa," failing to acknowledge the conflict of interest between his new job and the fifty thousand shares of GM he held in his stock portfolio.[6] By the time Kennedy arrived to the White House in 1961, his new secretary of defense, Robert S. McNamara, freshly arrived from running the Ford Motor Company, served as a living example of the "military-industrial complex."

THE KENNEDYS:
AMERICAN ROYALTY IN HISTORICAL CONTEXT

For better and worse, the Kennedys are the closest thing to royalty that we have in America. They have been heroes to millions of admirers, embodying the best and most idealistic qualities of public service and sacrifice that we can know. In contrast, the Kennedys have also been media fodder for all their faults, a traveling road show of all the worst attributes of power, corruption, misconduct, and tragedy.

Truth be told, the Kennedy family was part of this power structure long before Joseph P. Kennedy's son became president. They were part of American royalty by design, a path deliberately planned and executed over the course of years. World War II proved to be a costly opportunity for the family. The older boys went to war, seeking recognition in highly dangerous combat assignments. According to well-known family lore, the oldest son and heir apparent, Joseph P. Kennedy Jr., died during a bombing mission over Normandy. Like his older brother, John F. Kennedy joined the Navy and assumed command of a PT boat in the South Pacific. When he ran for Congress in 1946, he was a badly injured, legitimate war hero. The extent of his injuries would not become public until after his death.

As a lawmaker, Kennedy was charming, witty, and cultured in a way that kept him in the public eye. This was especially true after his marriage to Jacqueline Bouvier in 1953, which bolstered his status even further. In many respects, Jackie Kennedy overshadowed her husband in the Senate and, later, the White House.

Once he became president, the Kennedy mystique expanded to include those around the young president. David Halberstam beautifully captured the atmosphere surrounding the new president's arrival to the White House:

> the new men were tough—"hard-nosed realists" was a phrase often used to define them, a description they themselves had selected. They had good war records; they were fond of pointing out that they were the generation which had fought the war, that they had been the company commanders, had borne the brunt of the war and lost their comrades. This gave them special preparation for the job ahead, it was the company commanders replacing the generals, and even here was seen virtue."[7]

The carefully crafted product that was John Kennedy often clashed with reality during his rise, and people at the time knew it. While the young congressman and senator struck a heroic pose, his legislative record did not. Many contemporary critics saw him as a product of his father Joseph Kennedy's political ambition, as a man who lacked his own person convictions and direction. When Kennedy won the 1957 Pulitzer Prize for *Profiles in Courage*, many saw his father's hand in the prestigious award, manipulating the process to pave the way toward the 1960 election. Allegations that Kennedy employed a ghostwriter for the book turned out to be true. Commentators characterized Kennedy as a lightweight, a leader who should have shown "less profile and more courage" against McCarthy in the 1950s.[8] Eleanor Roosevelt, FDR's widow and a major figure in the Democratic Party, refused to endorse him in 1960 and offered a scathing assessment of the candidate: "I feel that I would hesitate to place the difficult decisions that the next President will make with someone who understands what courage is and admires it, but has not quite the independence to have it."[9]

The struggle over the Kennedy myth affected both his time in office and his long-term legacy. The scope and scale of the myth affected his rhetoric and approach to the Cold War. Kennedy's acceptance speech at the Democratic convention in July 1960 was a window to his worldview:

> We stand today on the edge of a New Frontier—the frontier of the 1960s—a frontier of unknown opportunities and perils—a frontier of unfulfilled hopes and threats. Woodrow Wilson's New Freedom promised our nation a new political and economic framework. Franklin Roosevelt's New Deal promised security and succor to those in need. But the New Frontier of which I speak is not a set of promises—it is a set of challenges. It sums up, not what I intend to offer the American people, but what I intend to ask them. It appeals to their pride, not their pocket-book—it holds out the promise of more sacrifice instead of more security.[10]

Pursuing his vision of a "New Frontier" is one of the reasons that Kennedy staffed his administration with "hard-nosed realists" who would challenge communists at every turn.

Yet, this approach had real limits that were obvious even while Kennedy was alive. Most Cold Warriors who were part of Kennedy's leadership—his "whiz kids," as the contemporary media knew them—saw no combat during World War II. There were exceptions. One Kennedy aide, Roger Hilsman, served in Burma as part of the Office of Strategic Services (OSS) and was wounded in combat. Kennedy's secretary of labor, Arthur Goldberg, was also with the predecessor of the CIA, organizing transportation workers in occupied Europe. The rest were enthusiastic, determined, and largely out of their depth. American history in the 1960s is littered with near disasters (Cuba) and complete failures (Vietnam) that resulted from inexperience made worse by a lack of wisdom. Democrat Party veteran and Kennedy's ambassador to the United Nations, Adlai Stevenson, privately put it another way: "They've got the damnedest bunch of boy commandoes running around . . . you ever saw."[11]

Grabbing hold of the Cold War to burnish the White House's public image was a double-edged blade. As much as the Kennedy team wanted to make sure the world knew about its toughness and willingness to fight the Soviets on any front, the approach had definite risks. Cuba is the best and most direct example. Confronting Khrushchev over missiles involved an international audience with ringside seats to a classic superpower conflict. However, the ongoing series of covert operations to kill Castro and sabotage his regime were something American leaders deliberately hid from the public for a variety of reasons, particularly after Kennedy's death. This secret war and the ongoing cover-up would factor heavily into the Warren Commission Report, the "official story," and shape the conspiracy debate for years afterward.

DALLAS

Although we know that Kennedy died in Dallas, Texas in 1963, generally, we skip over the reasons that he was there in the first place. The main answer is politics. When 1963 started, the Gallup Poll recorded Kennedy's approval rating at 74 percent. By October, that number had slipped to 58 percent, high by modern standards but an alarming trend only a year before the 1964 general election.[12] What was the cause? Foreign affairs probably played a part. The unraveling situation in South Vietnam, punctuated by a Buddhist monk burning himself to death in June 1963, undoubtedly alarmed many Americans. But it was Kennedy's domestic record that probably weighed more heavily on the president. Kennedy failed to get tax cuts through Congress. His civil rights record created controversy. Northern liberals and civil rights leaders grew increasingly impatient over the White House's tentative approach. Southern segregationists denounced federal intervention when it came under the leadership of Attorney General Robert F. Kennedy.

Kennedy could legitimately blame circumstances on his political woes. Southern Democrats held his administration in contempt and Lyndon Johnson's presence did not do much to change that fact. The Old South allied with Republicans to very effectively block Kennedy's policy initiatives. A good part of the blame rests with Kennedy as well. The repeated failures of his domestic platform resulted from an absence of leadership. Simply put, Kennedy set his own priorities. He once remarked to Richard Nixon: "Foreign affairs is the only important issue for a President to handle, isn't it? . . . I mean, who gives a shit if the minimum wage is $1.15 or $1.25, compared to something like Cuba."[13]

So, Kennedy was in Dallas to recover political momentum going into his re-election campaign. He arrived to plant his flag in a state that he won by just 2 percent of the vote in 1960.[14] He wanted the crowds to see him as the presidential motorcade moved through the city. That is one of the reasons Kennedy refused to use a plastic (not bulletproof) bubble top that would have partially blocked him from onlookers.[15]

And he died. The nation reeled in shock. After the shock had died down, people looked for answers. It was a natural sequence of events, but, ironically, in the attempt to provide answers, the US government made a tragedy that much worse.

THE PURPOSE OF THE WARREN COMMISSION

The official commission to investigate the assassination of John F. Kennedy was created by executive order a week after his death. Its express purpose was "to ascertain, evaluate, and report upon the facts relating to the assassination of the late President John F. Kennedy and the subsequent violent death of the man charged with the assassination."[16] The commission was chaired by Earl Warren, chief justice of the Supreme Court, and made up mainly of legislators: Senators Richard Russell (Democrat, Georgia) and John Sherman Cooper (Republican-Kentucky); and Representatives Hale Boggs (Democrat, Louisiana) and Gerald Ford (Republican, Michigan). John J. McCloy, former president of the World Bank, and Allen Dulles, former director of the CIA, rounded out the membership. Most of these names are lost to time, but in 1964, the commission's membership was to project balance, stability, and prestige onto a catastrophe.

At the time, the American policy establishment might have been more in need of reassurances than the public. US policy makers were terrified that Kennedy's shocking death might escalate Cold War tensions to the breaking point. Many administration officials suspected a conspiracy behind Kennedy's death, specifically blaming the Soviets or the Cubans. Richard Helms, the deputy director of Central Intelligence for Plans, held Moscow responsible. Robert Kennedy believed it was Cuban exiles seeking revenge for the Bay of Pigs.[17] All agreed that the Warren Commission should avoid any finding that might escalate the Cold War.

From the start, the agenda was clear, at least to the upper tier of US leaders. Oswald was the key. As the Warren Commission went to work, it deliberately underplayed key parts of Oswald's background, his defection to the Soviet Union in 1959 and his membership in the New Orleans branch of the Fair Play for Cuba Committee, prior to the assassination. At the same time, the commission also spent a great deal of time focused on making it clear that Oswald was the lone gunman. This particular blinder built serious flaws into the final Warren Commission report, as we will see later in the chapter.

The Warren Commission also set off a scramble among federal officials desperate to avoid being cast in a bad light after Kennedy's death. J. Edgar Hoover latched onto the single gunman theory partially because he believed that communists were at fault, but also because the focus on Oswald could deflect attention from just how badly the FBI had mishandled the threat to the president. Agents in New Orleans and Dallas had interviewed Oswald three times in 1962 and 1963. The Bureau knew that Oswald was a potential threat to the government and worked at a location along the motorcade route but did not place him on its Security Index. Weeks prior to Kennedy's visit, the CIA notified the Bureau that Oswald had visited the Soviet and Cuban embassies in Mexico City. Privately, Hoover characterized the Bureau's handling of the whole situation as "gross incompetence."[18]

For its own part, the CIA desperately wanted to avoid any links the commission might find between itself and Cuba. Still smarting from the abortive Bay of Pigs Operation, the last thing Langley wanted were additional questions that might shed light on ongoing operations to kill Fidel Castro and overthrow his government. Their target had no intention of making their lives easy. Just two months before Kennedy's death, Castro told the Associated Press that "United States leaders should think that if they are aiding in terrorist plans to eliminate Cuban leaders, they themselves will not be safe."[19]

The Secret Service lacked the same options as its brother agencies. Kennedy's death represented the first chief executive assassinated since William McKinley. As such, the agency could not escape the scrutiny of the Warren Commission. The commission recognized that the Secret Service "treated direct threats against the president adequately." However, the report acknowledged its responsibility for the president's death by noting, "it failed to recognize the necessity of identifying other potential sources of danger to his [Kennedy's] security." The report took the Secret Service to task regarding the security of the motorcade route. The commission also addressed the lack of proper coordination with local law enforcement and other federal agencies.[20]

Regardless, the Warren Commission attempted to be even handed about Dallas. Its report noted concluded that "The complexities of the Presidency have increased so rapidly in recent years that the Secret Service has not been able to develop or to secure adequate resources of personnel and facilities to fulfill its important assignment. This situation should be promptly remedied."[21]

Overall, both the Warren Commission and the federal agencies on the ground when Kennedy died in Dallas skewed the report's scrutiny and, ultimately, their own accountability. The Secret Service took a few well-earned, but softened, hits. Otherwise, the FBI and CIA essentially conspired to reduce or eliminate their exposure. In effect, the Warren Commission report suffered from a problem we apply to many modern conspiracy theories. It took short-cuts and cherry-picked its evidence. Ironically, this built-in flaw would fuel skepticism and speculation for the next sixty years and beyond.

ASSASSINATION EVIDENCE: TOO MUCH AND TOO LITTLE

The primary agenda of the Warren Commission was not to root out every last bit of the truth regarding the Kennedy assassination. In fact, its stated purpose according to Executive Order 11130 was: "to ascertain, evaluate, and report upon the facts relating to the assassination of the late President John F. Kennedy and the subsequent violent death of the man charged with the assassination."[22] In other words, the commission existed to assign blame for Kennedy's death to Lee Harvey Oswald. The evidence simply followed a conclusion prepared before the Warren Commission met. To any reasonable person, this seems like a serious, basic logical flaw. Yet, it became official US policy only days after Kennedy died.

This is unfortunate because there was no shortage of evidence. The FBI field investigation following Kennedy's assassination generated 25,000 interviews and 2,300 investigative reports. The Secret Service conducted an additional 1,500 interviews. Gerald Posner noted in his 1996 book, *Case Closed*, that 75 people took 510 photos of the assassination.[23] A review of the Warren Commission report includes hundreds of pages devoted to individual testimony, ballistics reports on Oswald's rifle, fingerprint and fiber tests, and the pistol used to kill Officer J. D. Tippit after the assassination.

When the Warren Commission followed the mandate to fix blame on Oswald, it built a very specific pipeline for all the data that came next. Or what did not. In reality, the Kennedy assassination was a complex event, made up of dozens of separate, interlocking components. Two particular examples of just how badly the commission treated the evidence stand out.

The first is with respect to the so-called Magic Bullet that struck Kennedy and Texas governor John Connolly. The commission's primary interest was justifying where the bullets came from—Oswald in the book depository—rather than how the bullets struck their targets. The commission report endorsed the idea that the first bullet hit both Kennedy and John Connolly, and the second comprised the fatal headshot that killed the president. It definitively agreed that both came from the Texas Book Depository.

The lack of attention to the first bullet's path once it hit Kennedy invited a series of controversies. The first bullet penetrated Kennedy's back and exited his throat before striking Connolly in the back, chest, right wrist, and thigh. The Warren Commission report never clearly explained just how it managed to accomplish this before being deposited on a hospital stretcher outside Parkland Memorial Hospital in Dallas.

The second controversy involved the span of time it took to make the shots. According to the Warren Commission, the fastest that Oswald could have fired all three shots—including a missed first shot—was 4.5 seconds.[24] Given the time constraints cited by the commission, the clunky quality of Oswald's surplus Mannlicher-Carcano rifle, and the fact that he was shooting at a moving target, many observers concluded that it was impossible for only one shooter to hit both Kennedy and Connolly.

Medical authorities added no clarity to the muddled evidence. In the chaos that reigned inside the Parkland Memorial Hospital emergency room, doctors mistakenly identified damage to Kennedy's throat as an entrance wound. The military doctors assigned to perform Kennedy's autopsy at Bethesda Naval Hospital lacked experience with bullet wounds. Dr. Pierre Finck, an Army physician assigned to the autopsy team, was its only ballistics expert, although he had never examined an actual gunshot wound.[25] Consequently, doctors missed basic steps during the examination and misread much of the physical evidence.

Constant interference from the Kennedy family did not help. The autopsy was rushed in part because Kennedy's inner circle wanted to conceal evidence of Addison's disease as well as the president's repeated bouts of venereal disease. The Warren Commission did not include autopsy x-rays or photos out of respect for the family's privacy.[26]

The end result was an official story handicapped by evidence withheld, mishandled, missed, or suppressed by the Warren Commission. Historian Kathyrn Olmsted describes the US government's examination of the evidence as "rushed, incompetent, and unconvincing."[27] Many studies of the Kennedy assassination have recorded skepticism at the highest levels of American government. Richard Russell, a member of the Warren Commission, stated flatly in private conversations with Lyndon Johnson, that he did not believe in the Magic Bullet.[28] The American public obviously shared Russell's behind-the-scenes skepticism. Gallup polls over the next fifty years note widely and consistently held doubts about the Warren Commission's basic conclusions.[29] In effect, the commission failed in its mission. The people simply didn't buy the official story.

ANALYZING THE ASSASSINATION (I):
EARLY DOUBTS, TESTS, AND SKEPTICISM

Blaming the Warren Commission for all the doubts and skepticism that followed its report is only part of the story. It is ironic that the gigantic, almost

nine-hundred-page document effectively became a treasure trove for generations of conspiracy theorists searching for evidence of a secret cabal against
John F. Kennedy. But other factors contributed to the spreading sense that the
government was lying about what happened to the president.

Context matters. According to Kathryn Olmsted, many early skeptics about
Kennedy's assassination were victims of McCarthy's political purges in the
1950s.[30] Having suffered at the hands of a conspiracy-minded senator, they
were perfectly willing to believe that their government was capable of terrible
things. They were not alone. A broad spectrum of American political interests also seemed primed to believe in the worst. Only a year after Kennedy's
death, Richard Hofstadter published what became a famous commentary
titled "The Paranoid Style of American Politics."[31] Hofstadter constructed
a convincing narrative that linked together a deep history of American conspiracy belief. His examples stretched back to the founding of the country and
included Masons, Jesuits (and Catholics in general), the Illuminati, and Irish
immigrants, among many others. Hofstadter never mentions the *Protocols*,
but he makes clear the powerful impact of religion on American conspiracy
belief, something not lost on those reflecting on the death of America's only
Catholic president at that time.

Importantly, Hofstadter doesn't stop with anti-immigrant nativists or angry
American liberals in his study. He includes the modern American Right, particularly groups like the John Birch Society who believed that the country had
already been taken over by dangerous foreign interests:

> The old American virtues have already been eaten away by cosmopolitans and
> intellectuals; the old competitive capitalism has been gradually undermined by
> socialist and communist schemers; the old national security and independence
> have been destroyed by treasonous plots, having as their most powerful agents
> not merely outsiders and foreigners as of old but major statesmen who are at the
> very centers of American power. Their predecessors had discovered conspira-
> cies; the modern radical right finds conspiracy to be *betrayal from on high.*[32]

Hofstadter built the foundation for understanding why Americans were ready
to invest in their own paranoid theories about evil. The rest of American history in the 1960s relentlessly added to that foundation. When the *Pentagon
Papers* were published in 1971, the multi-volume collection of official documents was a bombshell illustrating decades of official lies and deceit. The so-
called credibility gap, popularized by Senator J. William Fulbright, became a
regular part of national politics. Revelations about the Watergate conspiracy
hardened public attitudes further, as did documents released about the FBI's
Counterintelligence Program (COINTELPRO) and the Church Committee's
report on abuses committed by a host of federal agencies that includes the

IRS and the CIA.[33] In the cascade of revelations, that struck one body blow after another against American institutions, it seemed like Hofstadter's American conservatives were right. The country *had* been betrayed "from on high."

Conspiracy theories about the Kennedy assassination flowed from and into this fractured public trust. A good part of this discussion came from mass market publications that appeared almost immediately after Kennedy's death. *Esquire* magazine offered thirty-five theories regarding the assassination in its December 1966 edition.[34] Edward Jay Epstein published *Inquest: The Warren Commission and the Establishment of Truth* in 1966, a book that included interviews with every member of the Warren Commission. That same year Mark Lane published *Rush to Judgment*. Both books were enormously popular, with Lane's spending twenty-nine weeks on the *New York Times* best sellers list.[35]

Mark Lane's main target was the Warren Commission report. *Rush to Judgment* tested the official story by highlighting the logical inconsistencies that appeared in it. For example, the commission was not sure if Oswald fired three or four shots. The commission recognized that at least one shot likely missed the motorcade, the so-called Tague shot witnessed by James T. Tague, who was struck by bullet fragments. When Warren Commission investigators interviewed John Connolly and his wife, Nellie, both testified that separate bullets had wounded Kennedy and the Texas governor, something Connolly repeated in an October 1966 *Life* magazine interview. Lane also dissected the length of time for the shooting proposed by the Warren Commission. The report agreed that approximately five seconds elapsed between the first and last shots. Lane compared that conclusion against FBI tests in 1964, which indicated that it took 2.25 to 2.3 seconds between shots to operate Oswald's Mannlicher-Carcano rifle. He came to the conclusion, again, using the Warren Commission's own data, that it was impossible for Oswald to be the lone gunman.[36]

Rush to Judgment highlighted one of the central points of the debate that raged around the Kennedy assassination. People could debate political agendas or point to murky conspiracies about the "military-industrial complex," but ballistics and basic physics had more weight. Time and distance gave doubters something tangible to get their hands around. Conspiracy theorists argued that the 1.4 seconds between the first impact on Kennedy and Connolly's reaction were too slow for the "Magic Bullet" and too fast for Oswald to reload. The conclusion: there must have been a second gunman.[37]

Other parts of the forensics debate circled around the same principle. The bullet path through Kennedy and Connolly seemed ridiculous with its strange twists and turns. The "pristine" status of the Magic Bullet also raised eyebrows. The lack of damage to the bullet discovered on a hospital gurney contradicted the damage done to the two men it hit.[38]

THE ZAPRUDER FILM

In many ways, the 8mm film taken by Abraham Zapruder from a vantage point only feet away from the presidential motorcade is a unique piece of physical evidence. It is very short at only 26.6 seconds, exposing 486 frames of 8mm Kodachrome II safety film.[39] To modern eyes accustomed to high-definition television and Imax, it is terrible quality video, grainy, jumpy, and incomplete. Approximately five critical seconds are blocked as Kennedy's limousine passes behind a road sign on Elm Street. The film is incomplete, offering only a partial glimpse of a tragic historic moment. It leaves the viewer wanting to know more without a clear way to know how.

The Warren Commission featured individual black-and-white screen shots from the Zapruder film in its final report. However, it took more than a decade before an unedited version of the film became public. The complete Zapruder film did not air until March 1975, when it appeared on ABC's *Good Morning America*.[40]

The Zapruder film captured our attention and has never really let go for a number of reasons. Probably the first and most obvious is that it is vicious, shocking, and even painful to watch. As much as we think modern eyes are accustomed or indifferent to violence, watching the side of the president's head explode is still difficult to see. Also, to follow a trope that has been around forever, the Zapruder film matters to modern audiences because many tend to value the image over the written word. A great deal of ink has been spent commenting on America's fascination with television, but it is worth thinking about how much truth is in the cliché. Baby Boomers started with television and Millennials kept their grandparents' fascination with screen time. Even if it doesn't seem able to answer complex questions, the Zapruder film makes it hard to tear your eyes away from the Kennedy assassination. It is a permanent part of our historical landscape.

Conspiracy theorists latched on to the Zapruder film because it focuses where the Warren Commission did not: the impact of the bullets that killed Kennedy, not their origin in the book depository. What happened in the presidential limousine in the span of 26.6 seconds has since become a universe unto itself. Skeptics picked over Kennedy and Connolly's reactions to the first shot in order to divine when and if the targets had been struck separately. The part of the film that drew the most attention was the sequence recording the shot that killed Kennedy, specifically the point at which his head snaps to the left and back. For critics of the Warren Commission report, this moment is proof positive that a second gunman, shooting from Kennedy's right, fired the kill shot.

Advocates of the single gunman theory gravitated to the Zapruder film for obviously the opposite reasons. For these individuals—doppelgangers of the academics, journalists, and amateur investigators in the conspiracy crowd—the film was a starting point rather than a final word on Kennedy. As we will see, Zapruder's images invite a whole new series of complicated correlations based upon old evidence and new technology. These have improved our understanding of what happened in Dallas even as they have prolonged the debate.

ANALYSIS OF THE ASSASSINATION (II): THE TEST OF TIME

Although public doubts about the official story have been fairly consistent over the years, analysis of the Kennedy assassination has evolved over time. Advances in medicine, forensics, metallurgy, computer simulations, and other areas have allowed a better understanding of evidence. In 1972, for example, Dr. John Lattimer argued that when Kennedy reached for his throat after being struck by the first bullet, he was assuming the "Thorburn position," a neurological response to damage done to the C-6 vertebra. Kennedy assumed this position at frame 226 of the Zapruder film but was likely first hit by the bullet between frames 223 and 224. Gerald Posner correlated this reaction with eyewitness statements and the Zapruder film to determine that 3.5 seconds passed between the first and second shots, more than enough time for Oswald to work the rifle bolt, aim, and fire.[41]

Under closer scrutiny, the actual path of the Magic Bullet also seemed more plausible. The position of seats in presidential limousine factored into this interpretation. Connolly was sitting in the middle "jump seat" that is offset to Kennedy's left. The president sat on the right side of the rear seat with his arm resting on the car body. Neither of the men shot that day were sitting in the modified Lincoln like store mannequins. As Kennedy leaned to his right and rested his arm on the car, Connolly was leaning back slightly and turned to his right.

Just how well people understood the physical properties of the Magic Bullet also evolved over time. The bullet did not drill a straight hole through Kennedy. It tumbled, as many projectiles do after striking tissue and bone. After exiting Kennedy, the entry wound in Connolly was elongated, indicating the bullet was moving sideways when it hit.[42]

The bullet left traces that marked a definite path between the two men. Forensic tests done in 1974 by Dr. Cyril Wecht concluded that the lead fragments found in Connally's wrist matched the Magic Bullet. A few years later, the House Select Committee on Assassinations (HSCA) contracted Dr.

Vincent Guinn to use the same neutron activation techniques employed by Wecht.[43] Guinn examined fragments recovered from Connolly's wrist, Kennedy's brain, the presidential limousine, and the Magic Bullet. He found that fragments found on floor of limo matched those found in Kennedy's head.[44] The HSCA report, published in 1979, concluded that the fragments came from two Western Cartridge Co. bullets fired from Oswald's Mannlicher-Carcano rifle. Contrary to a great deal of popular belief, the bullet did not finish its destruction unscathed. A simple examination of the Magic Bullet reveals that it was flattened after ricocheting off bone and flesh.

Although new information offered a clearer picture of what happened in Dallas, it did not address the many layers of conspiracy theory that still cocoons the Kennedy assassination. The HSCA questioned Louie Steven Witt, reported for years to be the infamous "Umbrella Man," who many argued had either signaled an assassination team or killed Kennedy himself with a weaponized umbrella. Witt explained his presence in Dallas as an odd protest against the Kennedy family. His explanation seemed to put one part of the assassination to rest.

Other evidence the HSCA considered did not. Audio tapes gathered from the Dallas Police Department and dismissed by the Warren Commission were re-examined with new technology. One specific item at hand was an old dictabelt recording of a police radio left on before and during Kennedy's death. Expert analysis of the recording and a careful recreation of gunshots in Dallas noted a series of sound "impulse patterns" around Dealey Plaza, one of which the committee concluded came from the grassy knoll.

As a result, when the committee issued its final report, its first three findings were a strange composite of the official story, a debunked theory, and newly interpreted evidence:

I.A. Lee Harvey Oswald fired three shots at President John F. Kennedy. The second and third shots he fired struck the President. The third shot he fired killed the President.

I.B. Scientific acoustical evidence establishes a high probability that two gunmen fired at President John F. Kennedy. Other scientific evidence does not preclude the possibility of two gunmen firing at the President. Scientific evidence negates some specific conspiracy allegations.

I.C. The committee believes, on the basis of the evidence available to it, that President John F. Kennedy was probably assassinated as a result of a conspiracy. The committee was unable to identify the other gunmen or the extent of the conspiracy.[45]

None of these conclusions went unchallenged, particularly the last two. Over the next twenty-five years, the National Academy of Sciences (NAS), the FBI, and a number of academics contested the HSCA's methods and its findings. H. B. McLain, the Dallas police officer whose motorcycle allegedly was the source of the recording, disputed the committee's conclusion from the start, arguing that the engine sound originated from a three-wheeled vehicle and not his own two-wheeled motorcycle.[46] The NAS panel criticized the House Select Committee's experts, noting, "desirable control tests were omitted, and analyses depended on subjective selection of data." The NAS also pointed out flawed statistical analysis and argued that the committee had misread the timeline covered by the original recording.[47]

WILL WE EVER GET TO THE BOTTOM OF THIS STORY?

As far as the Kennedy assassination is concerned, probably not. In part, we can blame the Warren Commission, which enjoys a weird status among its critics. The commission report is an interesting root source of a few problems. It has become the deserved target of conspiracy theorists because of its deliberate omissions and errors. Yet, paradoxically, the contents of report provide a great deal of evidence underpinning conspiracy theories.

Investigations that followed the Warren Commission have tried to fix its errors with mixed success. The House Select Committee made breakthroughs with the benefits of new technology and analysis but foundered on new assumptions. More recent science studies of Kennedy's assassination analysis have created less certainty rather than more. In a 2007 paper by *The Annals of Applied Statistics*, scholars from Texas A&M University contested the conclusions about ballistics made thirty years earlier. Academic specialists in chemistry, engineering, and statistics pointed out that updated forensic technology could identify more elements in the bullets. The authors cast doubt on the conclusion that the bullets fired at Kennedy and Connolly were as unique as previously believed.[48]

In the end, it has been almost impossible for science to keep pace with skepticism. The Warren Commission proved to too many people, for good reasons, that experts cannot be trusted. Kathryn Olmsted makes the observation that experts could "no longer claim undisputed privileged status among the myriad forms of human discourse. Indeed experts, by any measure, have become an endangered species."[49]

As we have noted, past history helped this trend. The events following Kennedy's death constantly reinforced this assumption. The abuses committed during the Vietnam War and Watergate encouraged doubts about authority planted by Joe McCarthy. Revelations about CIA and FBI practices in the 1970s fed the downward spiral.

For a moment it time, it appeared that the doubts fueled by Kennedy's death and a generation worth of mistakes might finally lose its grip on America. When the Soviet Union collapsed in 1991 and the Cold War ended, it seemed like this cycle might be broken. Authors wrote about the possibility of a fresh start for the world.[50] A new generation of leaders who had come of age in the 1960s—Bill Clinton and Tony Blair among them—pledged to reinvent government and rebuild the public trust. The nineties were a hopeful decade that came to an abrupt stop when two planes crashed into the World Trade Center.

(Public domain via Wikimedia Commons: https://commons.wikimedia.org/wiki/
File:National_Park_Service_9-11_Statue_of_Liberty_and_WTC_fire.jpg.)

Chapter Five

9/11

We have come together with a unity of purpose because our nation demands it. September 11, 2001, was a day of unprecedented shock and suffering in the history of the United States. The nation was unprepared. How did this happen, and how can we avoid such a tragedy again?[1]

—9/11 Commission Report, 2004

9/11 was a false-flag operation orchestrated by the Bush administration for primarily imperial reasons.[2]

—David Ray Griffin, 2007

OUR NEW PEARL HARBOR

On the morning of September 11, 2001, Americans witnessed a coordinated terrorist attack on their country. Two civilian jet liners struck the World Trade Center and another hit the Pentagon. A fourth aircraft crashed into rural western Pennsylvania before it could reach its target. The nation watched stunned as the television news broadcast lower Manhattan burning, and panicked crowds fled the carnage as police and fire units scrambled to rescue survivors.

News commentators, struggling at the time for some kind of perspective, looked to history for answers. The September 11 attacks were a defining moment for a country wrenched from a period of peace, just as it had been two generations earlier. But as Americans unpacked the day, people began to ask just how such a catastrophe could have happened in the first place. As they searched for answers, history led them back to Pearl Harbor. NBC newscaster Tom Brokaw wrote, in December 2001:

> Just a week before the Japanese attack the Army commander in Hawaii had received a telegram from Washington describing the breakdown of negotiations with Japan and warning "hostile action possible at any moment."
>
> Six decades later national security experts sounded the alarm about the vulnerability of the United States to terrorist attacks in congressional testimony, newspaper columns, television appearances, and seminars.[3]

The September 11 attacks eventually served as a pretext for the invasion of Afghanistan and Iraq, a "global war on terror," and a dramatic expansion of the domestic security state under the umbrella of the Department of Homeland Security and the Patriot Act. Reeling under the weight of a catastrophe, Americans briefly rallied against real threats to not only an abstract idea like our "national security" but also fear that individual, personal safety was at stake in this new world order.

But questions about how it all started would not go away. The events of September 11 were outrageous, complicated, confusing, and part of a much longer history of terrorism that few Americans understood at the time. More importantly, the tragedy was not an endpoint to an ugly story but, instead, began a policy debate that led Americans into their longest and most divisive modern war. What exactly September 11 *was* became a moving goalpost that invited controversy and suspicion.

The debate over the September 11 attacks sound familiar, and that is the point. True to form, much of the "official story" took the events of September 11 and manipulated them for other purposes. The Bush administration quickly constructed a chain of events linking New York and the Pentagon to Baghdad. However, the audience for this narrative was made up of generations of Americans raised on mistrust of official sources and their motives. Baby Boomers joined the remnants of the McCarthy era and younger Millennials in a chorus of doubts and accusations, all of it amplified by the emerging internet. Bystanders trying to parse truth from speculation had their work cut out for them.

CLAIM: LIHOP OR MIHOP?

The events of September 11 fit under what Michael Barkun characterizes as both "systemic conspiracies" and "superconspiracies." Systemic because the conspiracy had "broad goals, usually conceived as securing control over a country, region, or the entire world."[4] There is a mirror image quality to the term. The label fits either the Osama bin Laden terrorist network intent on attacking American empire or the actual empire, guided by neoconservative hawks in the Bush administration who began a "global war on terror" in Afghanistan, Iraq, and dozens of other places around the world.

Lumping all the evidence into usable bundles produced a variety of results. The official story promoted by the Bush administration and the 9/11 Commission was that the attacks were the result of a coordinated terrorist conspiracy against the United States. Following this line of reasoning, the nineteen hijackers who took control of four civilian airliners were part of the Osama bin Laden terrorist network. What eventually accompanied the official story was a momentous additional claim: that the Iraqi government was directly involved in the 9/11 attacks and posed an ongoing threat to US national security.

A variation on this theory was a scenario where the US government knew an attack would occur on September 11 and let it happen on purpose (LIHOP). According to this school of thought, American officials were directly implicated in the attacks when they deliberately quashed intelligence reports on terrorist preparations, obstructed federal agencies like the FBI from arresting the hijackers, and withheld countermeasures—such as fighters to intercept to planes—that might have prevented the disaster. The LIHOP school is a callback to older historical studies, such as Franklin Roosevelt's alleged knowledge of Japanese plans to attack Pearl Harbor, placing responsibility for events on official inaction.[5]

A variety of individuals and groups see a much darker story surrounding the September 11 attacks. They believe that the United States government and a wide variety of organizations made it happen on purpose (MIHOP) as the direct result of a conspiracy. The MIHOP school of thought portrays the nineteen hijackers as patsies of powerful interests, a cabal that includes the US government, the Mossad (Israel's national intelligence agency), investors who wanted to manipulate the stock market, the CIA, wealthy real estate developers, the Bush family, neoconservative warmongers in the Bush cabinet, and a whole host of actors working separately or as part of a super conspiracy. The methods behind the attacks are just as varied, according to MIHOP. They include drone strikes, remotely piloted planes made to look like civilian airliners, cruise missiles, and controlled demolition, among many others.

There is an interesting anti-Semitic streak in some MIHOP theories. Narratives that assign blame for the September 11 attacks on the Mossad recall earlier accusations promoted by the *Protocols of the Elders of Zion* after World War I. This story gained addition notoriety after the false accusation that no Jews showed up for work in the World Trade Center on September 11 began to make the rounds among conspiracy circles.

THE HISTORICAL CONTEXT OF MODERN TERRORISM

Terrorism was a constant part of the old Cold War. Communist insurgents targeted both civilian and military officials throughout the Vietnam War, for example. The United States responded by creating the Phoenix Program, which conducted an active campaign of assassination and sabotage against the Viet Cong.[6] These small, vicious actions were mostly lost in the nuclear standoff and large-scale wars that plagued the world at the time.

By the 1970s, international terrorism accelerated even beyond existing Cold War standards. The attack on Israeli athletes during the 1972 Munich Summer Olympics captivated and horrified a global audience. Terrorist incidents escalated rapidly from that point, from fifty in 1968 to more than four hundred by 1982.[7] A 1979 CIA report noted a potential change in terrorist tactics, predicting that one future method might be "standoff weapons," such as heat-seeking missiles, to avoid "direct confrontations with authorities."[8]

The 1980s saw a significant increase in terrorism against Americans. One of the most infamous was the truck bombing of Marine peacekeepers in Lebanon in October 1983, an attack that killed 241 Americans. US military personnel in West Germany were the victims of multiple car bombs and armed attacks in 1983 and 1985. Civilians also suffered grievous losses. The time between June 1985 and December 1988 witnessed the hijacking of TWA Flight 847 to Beirut, terrorist assaults on airports in Rome and Vienna, the capture of the *Achille Lauro* cruise ship, and a bomb that destroyed Pan Am Flight 103 over Lockerbie, Scotland. In the meantime, kidnappings of American citizens in Lebanon became sadly routine events.[9]

As these attacks grew in frequency and sophistication, US officials began to realize that the nature of terrorism and war was changing. Terrorists were no longer playing by Cold War rules. They refused to act as superpower proxies and were instead following motives—faith, ethnicity, and cultural identity—that were becoming harder to predict.[10] Looking at the future of terrorism, 1985 RAND study noted:

> Warfare in the future may be less destructive than that in the first half of the twentieth century, but also less coherent. Warfare will cease to be finite. The distinction between war and peace will dissolve. Armed conflict will not be confined by national frontiers.[11]

ESCALATING ATTACKS

The RAND prediction was disturbingly on the mark. The time between the final death of the Soviet Union and the first major attack on US soil was incredibly short. On February 26, 1993, a truck bomb was detonated below the North Tower of the World Trade Center in New York City. It contained more than a half-ton of improvised explosives (IEDs) intended to destroy the North Tower's foundation and send it into the South Tower. The bombing failed although it did kill six people and injured more than a thousand.[12]

The attack provoked one of the largest criminal investigations in FBI history that eventually led to the arrests and convictions of terrorists from Egypt, Palestine, Iraq, Pakistan, and Kuwait. The fact that the US government treated terrorism as crime subject to law enforcement measures is interesting. Home grown, domestic terrorism—like the Oklahoma City attack in 1995—was on the uptick at the time and did fit federal law enforcement better than local and state police agencies. However, the FBI lacked the jurisdiction and reach when it came to investigating terrorist cells, in some cases directly sponsored by foreign countries thousands of miles from US soil.

As the 1990s came to a close, it was very clear that the law enforcement approach was not working. By 1997, American citizens and facilities worldwide made up 40 percent of terrorist targets, up from 25 percent the previous year.[13] Danger abroad was matched by increasing threats at home. The 1996 Khobar Towers attack in Saudi Arabia was preceded a year earlier by the massive truck bombing of the Alfred P. Murrah Federal Building in Oklahoma City. For a moment, Timothy McVeigh became more infamous than a new generation of foreign terrorists.

The threat worsened with the approaching new millennium. Coordinated attacks on American embassies in Nairobi, Kenya and Dar es Salaam, Tanzania, on August 7, 1998, killed 252 people (twelve US citizens) and wounded more than five thousand. Once again, the FBI launched a massive investigation of the two attacks. More than nine hundred special agents deployed overseas, the largest operation of that type in bureau history. In the meantime, millions went toward fortifying US embassies and consulate offices. By 1999, the State Department security budget was $1.7 billion, more than six times larger than the previous year.[14]

The attack on the guided missile destroyer USS *Cole* at the port of Aden on October 12, marked both a change in tactics and an escalation against the United States. A small boat piloted by two al-Qaeda suicide bombers and a load of C-4 military explosives struck the port side approximately midship. The explosion tore open a forty-by-sixty-foot hole through the ship's hull, killed seventeen sailors, and injured thirty-nine. It was the costliest attack on the US Navy since the 1987 Iraqi missile strike against the USS *Stark*.[15]

A few months before the attack on the *Cole*, in June 2000, the National Commission on Terrorism issued a report that was a very critical, bipartisan look at the American war on terror. The commission assessed goals, leadership, methods, and the resources dedicated to combating the growing threat to American security and found the country falling short. In testimony before the Senate, the commission's chairperson, L. Paul Bremer, noted the dynamic, rapidly evolving nature of terrorism itself.[16] The report's authors believed that US policy was generally too passive and overly focused upon defeating the bin Laden network.[17] It suggested that the United States was drifting away from combating state-supported terrorism. The report was a call to action.

After September 11, the National Commission on Terrorism report would be cited as another example of, at best, missed signals or simple incompetence on the part of the US government. In the worst case, it was clear evidence of complicity (LIHOP or MIHOP) in the terrorist attacks on New York and the Pentagon. This criticism has some merit, but it misses a few points.

Hindsight is a great tool. It is easy to see the missed opportunities of 2000 and 2001 as part of a larger conspiracy or a series of coincidental mistakes. But sometimes it is easy to forget two important points about that particular moment in American history. The first involves the evolving nature of the terrorist threat. The US intelligence community and political leaders clearly understood that it was growing worse and becoming more and more unpredictable. However, there is a big difference between knowing something is dangerous and pinpointing where, when, and how it might strike next. By 2000, terrorist organizations had moved from "soft" targets (office buildings) to civilian transportation (both airports and the planes themselves), embassies, and military bases. The types and delivery systems for bombs were also increasingly sophisticated. Improvised explosives in rental trucks had given way to military-grade ordinance carried by boat. Predicting the next evolution of attack prior to September 11 would have taken either incredible powers of research and deduction or a tremendous amount of luck.

Secondly, it is important ask the question: Were people paying attention? In the summer of 2000, Americans focused on a familiar list of distractions: shark attacks, a political scandal in Washington (Gary Condit), and the ongoing stock market boom. The really dominant issue of late 2000 was not terrorism or trivia. It was a bitterly fought presidential election where the key issues were things like Social Security reform and limiting America's role abroad. The end result, or lack of it, widened a chasm in American politics that we still struggle with today. The last thing on most peoples' minds was the plotting of a handful of (mostly) Saudi terrorists who wanted to highjack four civilian passenger jets.

REACTIONS TO 9/11 (I):
CONSTRUCTING FORTRESS AMERICA

In the aftermath of the September 11 crisis, US law and policy underwent significant changes that targeted terrorism. One landmark piece of legislation was the USA Patriot Act, signed by George W. Bush on October 26, 2001.[18] It included attention to the September 11 victims and their families, increased information sharing among intelligence agencies and law enforcement, and the many challenges posed by new communications technology to lawful surveillance.

Much of the Patriot Act became understandably controversial. "Removing obstacles to investigating terrorism," as stated in Title V of the law, meant loosening due process requirements controlling probable cause and police searches. Federal law enforcement argued that they were necessary to combat hard-to-trace disposable cell phones and the sometime impenetrable nature of the worldwide web. Civil libertarians worried about official abuse of this newfound flexibility and its impact on constitutional rights, a concern born out in multiple lawsuits successfully filed against the federal government in the years following September 11.

A less well-known device that followed the September 11 attacks was the national security letter (NSL). A NSL is an "administrative subpoena" that was used by the FBI, CIA, and other government agencies to obtain data without probable cause or a judge's order. National security letters also contained gag orders that prevented individuals or organizations under investigation from discussing them. Between 2003 and 2006, the Justice Department inspector general reported that the FBI alone had issued two hundred thousand NSLs.[19]

The American Civil Liberties Union (ACLU) challenged national security letters in a number of lawsuits. The ACLU argued that the US government-mandated gag order violated the First Amendment. The gag order provision also violated the Fourth Amendment because it subjected recipients to "unreasonable searches and seizures." In 2007, US District Court Judge Victor Marrero agreed and struck down that part of the Patriot Act.[20]

Another result of September 11 was the Department of Homeland Security (DHS). Created only a few weeks after the attacks and led by former Pennsylvania governor Tom Ridge, it laid out its purpose in an official announcement:

> The mission of the Office will be to develop and coordinate the implementation of a comprehensive national strategy to secure the United States from terrorist threats or attacks. The Office will coordinate the executive branch's efforts to detect, prepare for, prevent, protect against, respond to, and recover from terrorist attacks within the United States.[21]

It was the largest government reorganization in American history. In the beginning, DHS contained twenty-two separate federal agencies consolidated under one cabinet post. It included the US Customs Service, the Coast Guard, the Secret Service, the Federal Emergency Management Agency, and the newly created Transportation Security Administration. By 2009, Homeland comprised more than 225,000 employees.[22]

REACTIONS TO 9/11 (II): BUSH DOCTRINE

America's foreign policy also dramatically changed one year after the September 11 attacks. The White House released *The National Security Strategy of the United States of America*, or Bush Doctrine. It represented a sea change in US military strategy:

> It has taken almost a decade for us to comprehend the true nature of this threat. Given the goals of rogue states and terrorists, the United States can no longer solely rely on a reactive posture as we have in the past. The inability to deter a potential attacker, the immediacy of today's threats, and the magnitude of potential harm that could be caused by our adversaries' choice of weapons, do not permit that option. We cannot let our enemies strike first.[23]

Vice President Dick Cheney put the new approach in even more blunt terms in 2003:

> The strategy of deterrence, which served us so well during the decades of the Cold War, will no longer do. Our terrorist enemy has no country to defend, no assets to destroy in order to discourage an attack. Strategies of containment will not assure our security either. There is no containing terrorists who will commit suicide for the purposes of mass slaughter.[24]

Basically, the Bush Doctrine reversed decades of US policy that primarily followed a strategy of self-defense and essentially justified pre-emptive war. Starting in 2002, the United States announced to the world that we would not wait for war to come to us. We had to act first, as we did when the United States deployed a small contingent of special forces and CIA paramilitary operatives to Afghanistan in 2001. A much bigger invasion of Iraq followed in 2003.

A number of writers pointed out that the Bush Doctrine was not so much the starting point for a new era but the endpoint of an old one. As much as the Bush administration portrayed the situation in 2001 as a clear departure, it was, in reality, part of a generational American war with terrorism. In this sense, the attacks on New York and the Pentagon were part of the inheritance of Munich, the *Achille Lauro*, the embassy bombings in Africa, and the USS *Cole*.[25] Regardless of where it was coming from, the global war on terror became the lens through which we saw our new normal.

Paranoia at home added another layer to that lens. The Patriot Act, the Department of Homeland Security, and all the new federal muscle for the war on terror left the impression that the government was everywhere. That was because the government *was* everywhere. In our airports, where long lines and body patdowns of old women and small children reminded travelers just how far things had gone, and not in a good way. We also knew the authorities were online, trolling through data on our emails, our reading choices, and purchase histories. Americans learned to filter their daily reality through this new normal in much the same way that we lived at the peak of the Red Scare, the Korean War, and McCarthy's bursting upon the scene in 1950. It was background noise, but it also rubbed our nerves raw. We learned to live our lives in the twenty-first century with a strange combination of fear about our safety, hope that danger would not reach us, resentment about new obstacles to freedom, and skepticism that security would be guided by wisdom and common sense.

EVIDENCE ABOUT SEPTEMBER 11

There is an enormous amount of evidence related to the September 11 attacks. Much of it initially came from official government efforts to forge a link between al-Qaeda and Iraq. The Bush administration publicly disclosed intelligence intercepts to demonstrate an ongoing relationship between Baghdad and terrorists. Vice President Cheney actively promoted the idea, citing meetings between Iraqi intelligence officials and Mohamed Atta (one of the hijackers) in Prague in April 2001.[26]

Cheney's efforts were part of a larger narrative linking terrorism with Iraqi possession of weapons of mass destruction (WMDs). President Bush, Cheney, and National Security Advisor Condoleezza Rice all repeated this claim in early 2003. Bush used his 2003 State of the Union Address to drive the point home, claiming the United States had evidence that Iraq was attempting to purchase "significant quantities" of uranium from Africa.[27] Probably the best-known example of the administration's campaign was Colin Powell's February 5, 2003, speech at the United Nations, where he spoke about Iraq's massive stockpiling of WMDs, particularly anthrax, and brandished what appeared to be a sealed vial of the substance to drive his point home.

The American media responded with glowing reviews of Powell's performance. The *New York Times* noted that the secretary of state "was all the more convincing because he dispensed with apocalyptic invocations of a struggle of good and evil and focused on shaping a sober, factual case against Mr. Hussein's regime." The *Washington Post* offered an even more aggressive endorsement, headlining its editorial "Irrefutable" and declaring that after Powell's UN presentation "it is hard to imagine how anyone could doubt that Iraq possesses weapons of mass destruction."[28]

The Bush administration's campaign turned out to be highly effective. Kathryn Olmsted points that on September 11, 2001, 3 percent of Americans blamed Iraq for the attacks. By August 2002, that number had risen to 53 percent. In September 2003, 70 percent of the public believed the administration narrative.[29]

That is not to say the administration got a free pass. As time went on, a growing chorus of doubt began to surround the official story. In July 2003, UN weapons inspectors announced that they had found no "evidence or plausible indication of the revival of a nuclear weapons program in Iraq."[30] Media investigations also followed in the wake of the Bush administration and began taking pieces out of it. In May 2002, *Time* magazine and the *New York Times* reported that the FBI in Phoenix and Minneapolis had warned about suspected terrorists taking flight training.[31] At the same time, CBS News ran a story about CIA warnings regarding a plot to hijack airplanes prior to September 11.

Official Washington soon joined in. Senator Bob Graham (Democrat, Florida) formed a committee in the summer of 2002 to investigate the September 11 attacks and soon unearthed evidence of Saudi support for the hijackers. The Bush administration refused to cooperate with the committee, calculating their delay around the approaching 2002 Congressional elections and gains by Republican candidates.[32]

A number of whistleblowers added their voices to the chorus. Joseph Wilson, a former ambassador sent to Africa to look for evidence of Iraqi uranium purchases, found none and went public in a July 2003 *New York Times* editorial titled "What I Didn't Find in Africa,"

> Did the Bush administration manipulate intelligence about Saddam Hussein's weapons programs to justify an invasion of Iraq?
>
> Based on my experience with the administration in the months leading up to the war, I have little choice but to conclude that some of the intelligence related to Iraq's nuclear weapons program was twisted to exaggerate the Iraqi threat.[33]

Almost a year later, Richard Clarke, former national coordinator for Security, Infrastructure Protection and Counter-Terrorism testified before the 9/11 Commission. In his testimony, Clarke claimed that the administration had "cherry-picked" intelligence regarding Iraq and its links to terrorism.[34] He then took his criticism on the road, appearing in dozens of media outlets to take apart the official story. Based on Clarke's testimony and other evidence it collected, in June 2004, the 9/11 Commission determined that there had been no "collaborative relationship" between Iraq and al-Qaeda.[35] Almost a year later, in May 2005, the United Kingdom officially joined the fray. The "Downing Street Memos," British intelligence documents leaked to the press, indicated that head of their secret service had advised Prime Minister Tony Blair "the intelligence and facts were being fixed around the policy."[36]

The relentless cascade of skepticism and new revelations seriously eroded public faith in the official story. This was especially true as a series of policy experts and government agencies openly contested linkages between Iraq and September 11. Basically, the same type of actors who had built the White House's case regarding Iraq and 9/11 were now tearing that scenario down. By June 2004, public belief that Iraq was behind the 9/11 attacks had dropped from 69 percent to 22 percent.[37]

As the dust began to settle around the Bush administration's collapsing credibility, conspiracy theories began to flourish. In the summer of 2006, the Scripps Howard/Ohio University poll found that 36 percent of Americans believed that the Bush administration either helped the attack or deliberately took no actions to stop them. Sixteen percent believed that explosives brought down the towers. Twelve percent believed the Pentagon was hit by a cruise missile. Party affiliation influenced peoples' perspectives as well. More than half of Democrat respondents thought the administration was involved in the attack. Age also mattered. Most eighteen- to twenty-nine-year-olds believed that the government either let the attacks happen (LIHOP) or directly participated in it (MIHOP).[38]

Early conspiracy theories tended to focus on the LIHOP scenario. Georgia House Democrat Cynthia McKinney was a primary advocate of this school as early as 2002 when she asked: "What did this administration know and when did it know it about the events of September 11? Who else knew and why did they not warn the innocent people of New York who were needlessly murdered?"[39] Proponents of LIHOP stressed the case that the FBI deliberately ignored evidence about terrorist preparations in the United States before 9/11. They pointed to Defense Department collusion in the tragedy by calling attention to the absence of fighters scrambled to intercept the inbound jetliners.

Olmsted observes that the LIHOP answer was not satisfying enough for conspiracy theorists. It was too passive an explanation that still left the responsibility for 9/11 in the hands of al-Qaeda. It also presented a logical dilemma for believers who confronted a negative proof, a search for evidence of something that did *not* happen when the government failed to act.

Consequently, the MIHOP school of thought emerged as the next best alternative. In the years that followed, the search for culprits took on a life of its own and, in the process, embraced ideas that were bizarre, staggeringly complex, and sometimes both. One early candidate was the Israeli Mossad. According to a number of theories, the Israeli spy agency either acted on its own accord or as a go-between for neoconservatives in the Bush administration to arrange the September 11 attacks. This scenario accounted for the early myth that no Jews died in the World Trade Center, having received early warning from the Mossad to avoid work that day. Professor Alexander K. Dewdney, a Canadian mathematician and computer scientist, took a far more elaborate take on the New York terrorist attack, naming "Operation Pearl" as a Mossad action involving landing the four civilian jetliners at remote locations and substituting a combination of remotely controlled aircraft and cruise missiles to attack the World Trade Center and the Pentagon.[40]

Theories about the Mossad were only a starting point. As time passed, a variety of MIHOP arguments about very specific and very vague culprits emerged. On the one hand, conspiracy believers pointed to shadowy organizations like the Illuminati and the New World Order as responsible for September 11. Others were much more specific. One theory portrayed the terrorist attacks as a gigantic insurance scam perpetrated by American businessman Larry Silverstein and designed to gather a $4.6 billion payday.[41] Another involved the oil industry. Many 9/11 skeptics pointed to a 1999 speech by Vice President Dick Cheney to the Institute of Petroleum as the "smoking gun" for this conspiracy.

> By some estimates there will be an average of 2 percent annual growth in global oil demand over the years ahead along with conservatively a 3 percent natural decline in production from existing reserves. That means by 2010 we will need on the order of an additional fifty million barrels a day. *So where is the oil going to come from?*
>
> *Governments and the national oil companies are obviously controlling about 90 percent of the assets. Oil remains fundamentally a government business.* While many regions of the world offer great oil opportunities, *the Middle East with two thirds of the world's oil and the lowest cost, is still where the prize ultimately lies,* even though companies are anxious for greater access there, progress continues to be slow.[42]

According to this particular MIHOP scenario, the September 11 attacks were simply an excuse to take over what remained of the world's oil reserves.

To pursue these various threads and many others, the 9/11 Truth Alliance formed in September 2002. The choice of the word "truth" was interesting because many skeptics about September 11 resented the label "conspiracy theorist," believing it was a derogatory term invented by the power structure to discredit them. In the great debate, even individual terms smacked of plotting in high places.

As the various theories about September 11 multiplied, a pattern emerged. Where the official Bush administration at least tried to tie Iraqi links to the terrorist attacks with something resembling a chain of evidence, many LIHOP and MIHOP alternative theories held what might be generously described as a very tentative relationship with the facts. Conspiracy claims about insurance fraud were at least anchored to dollar amounts, if not a detailed understanding of how the insurance industry actually worked in reality. The whole idea about the Mossad conspiracy to alert Jews working in the WTC before the attacks was pure speculation seasoned with a very large dash of anti-Semitism. Gigantic leaps of logic, confusing correlation for causation, and a variety of logical errors guided an enormous number of conspiracy theories in the years after 9/11.

I focus on two of these in my class: the alleged missile attack on the Pentagon and the supposed controlled demolition of World Trade Center Building 7 (WTC 7). The Pentagon attack was prominently featured in the 2005 online documentary *Loose Change*. Among the many pieces of evidence mentioned in the film was the fact that the hole in the side of the Pentagon was too small to have been made by a large passenger aircraft. Impact damage also contained no impression of aircraft wings. According to conspiracy advocate David Ray Griffin: "whatever did hit the Pentagon simply did not cause nearly enough destruction for the official story to be true."[43] Skeptics cited retired Major General Albert Stubblebine as their own argument from authority:

Well there was something wrong. And, so I analyzed it not just photographically, I did measurements . . . I checked the plane, the length of the nose, where the wings were. . . . I took measurements of the Pentagon—the depth of the destruction in the Pentagon.

Conclusion: airplane did not make that hole.[44]

Similar reasoning guides the conspiracy theories about World Trade Center 7. Observers specifically focus on the physical attributes of the WTC 7 collapse. They point to the apparent fact that the building's penthouse began to fall before the walls and main structure. The rate of the collapse has also provoked a significant debate. As WTC 7 fell, conspiracy believers like Architects & Engineers for 9/11 Truth, argue that it did so at "near free fall speed," indicating the lower levels were intentionally blown up.[45] These same skeptics point to a series of flashes that appeared in the windows of WTC 7 as direct evidence of a controlled demolition.

ANALYSIS: BREAKING DOWN SEPTEMBER 11 EVIDENCE

Whenever I cover the various theories flowing around 9/11, I am very careful to make it clear that the official story, LIHOP, and MIHOP parts of the September 11 attacks are what I call "parallel conspiracies" that coexist and reinforce each other. The Bush administration's coordinated effort to build a pretext for the Iraq war fit the textbook definition of a conspiracy. It was "a secret plan by a group to do something unlawful or harmful."[46] As the official story fell apart, it fueled the next waves of conspiracy theories.

The official story was the sum of deliberate exaggeration and manipulation of the facts in order to support a military invasion of Iraq. A quick look at the history of US policy regarding Iraq reveals a bipartisan mistake. Republican neoconservatives, specifically Donald Rumsfeld, Dick Cheney, and Paul Wolfowitz, concocted the invasion plan for Iraq years before the September 11 attacks and promoted the idea through a think tank called the Project for a New American Century (PNAC). Rumsfeld called for Hussein's removal as early as 1998.[47]

Democrats are also responsible for pre-9/11 calculations. When Bill Clinton's secretary of defense, Les Aspin, ordered the Bottom-Up Review of US defense policy in 1993, the intent was to bridge the gap between the just finished Cold War and "An Era of New Dangers."[48] The document argued that the U.S. military should be prepared for two major regional conflicts, specifically against Iraq and North Korea. Readiness was the key: "History suggests that we most often deter the conflicts that we plan for and actually fight the ones we do not anticipate."[49]

All that said, there was a kernel of truth within the official story. Both the US intelligence community and the United Nations knew that Iraq had not complied with the peace terms following the 1991 Gulf War. Powell was especially blunt about this point in his February 2003 UN speech:

> Last November 8, this council passed resolution 1441 by a unanimous vote. The purpose of that resolution was to disarm Iraq of its weapons of mass destruction. Iraq had already been found guilty of material breach of its obligations, stretching back over 16 previous resolutions and 12 years.

> Resolution 1441 was not dealing with an innocent party, but a regime this council has repeatedly convicted over the years. Resolution 1441 gave Iraq one last chance, one last chance to come into compliance or to face serious consequences. No council member present in voting on that day had any illusions about the nature and intent of the resolution or what serious consequences meant if Iraq did not comply.[50]

Powell turned out to be right, but with some important qualifications. Iraq had the components of a nuclear weapons program, but, according to weapons inspector David Kay, the actual program was "dormant" and did not pose an immediate threat to American security in 2003.[51] Once the invasion of Iraq commenced, US forces did discover Iraqi chemical weapons, nerve agents in 2006 and mustard gas in 2008. All told, Operation Iraqi Freedom found more than five thousand chemical warheads, many of them old artillery shells hidden for years from weapons inspectors. Between 2004 and 2011, chemical weapons modified into IEDs wounded US and coalition forces on at least six separate occasions.[52]

For years, the Department of Defense refused to acknowledge the existence of these older WMDs because they did not fit the official narrative in 2003, even if Iraq was actually in violation of UN mandates. The antiwar movement ignored the possibility that they might exist, even after the *New York Times* broke the story in 2014. This strange consensus was a small consolation for individuals actually deployed to Iraq.

The official story about Iraqi links with 9/11 terrorists was entirely debunked by, of all things, officials in the intelligence community. For example, the 9/11 Commission identified Salman Pak as an Iraqi terrorist training camp in 2003.[53] However, in the aftermath of the invasion, multiple sources reported that no such camp existed in Iraq. In September 2006, the Senate Select Committee on Intelligence noted that

> "no credible reports that non-Iraqis were trained to conduct or support transnational terrorist operations at Salman Pak after 1991." DIA (Defense Intelligence Agency) assessed that the foreigners were likely volunteers who traveled to Iraq in the months before Operation Iraqi Freedom began to fight overtly alongside Iraqi military forces . . . DIA said it has "no information from Salman Pak that links al-Qa'ida with the former regime."[54]

In June 2006, the officials from Central Intelligence Agency told the Committee that

> There was information developed after OIF (Operation Iraqi Freedom) that indicated terrorists were trained at Salman Pak; there was an apparent surge of such reporting. As with past information, however, the reporting is vague and difficult to substantiate. As was the case with the prewar reporting, the postwar sources provided few details, and it is difficult to conclude from their second-hand accounts whether Iraq was training al-Qa'ida members, as opposed to other foreign nationals. Postwar exploitation of Salman Pak has yielded no indications that training of al-Qa'ida linked individuals took place there, and we have no information from detainees on this issue.[55]

A November 2003 Defense Intelligence Agency assessment included in the committee report noted that postwar examination of the Salman Pak facility found it "devoid of valuable intelligence."[56]

Next, what makes the "let it happen on purpose" (LIHOP) argument attractive is also its most basic flaw. Hindsight is always the easiest and shortest path for anyone who reaches an event after it happens. Monday morning quarterbacks can pick and choose from the mistakes that they find. As they accumulate, individual errors or coincidences begin to take the form of a pattern that can be then be formed into a conspiracy. In a story that echoed the failures surrounding Lee Harvey Oswald, federal law enforcement overseeing thousands of potential security risks missed a tiny group of would-be terrorists as they took flight training. The intelligence community, sifting through thousands of data points in an increasingly dangerous global environment, warned of the possibility of a terrorist attack without pinpointing a time or location. Once the attack commenced, a military command structure slowly responded to a civilian air traffic control network not designed for weaponized jet liners. Multiple failures across an array of systems illustrated a systemic failure, but not a deliberate conspiracy.

Lastly, there are a number of basic and profound problems with "made it happen on purpose" (MIHOP) conspiracies. Some are clearly based upon fantasy. Conspiracies that include aliens or holographic images of jetliners colliding with the Twin Towers are pretty easy to jettison. The same is true about David Icke's belief that reptilian lizard humanoids were responsible for the September 11 attacks.[57]

Whenever I talk about 9/11 conspiracies in class, I bring out the same idea featured in this book's introduction with an important addition: Does the claim match the proof and, more importantly, is there proportion between the two? In other words, many believers in 9/11 MIHOP conspiracies have assembled large, intricate, complicated narratives that allegedly involve dozens of agencies, thousands of individuals, and a broad array of interlinked actions. All that is well and good, but they also have, as a result, an enormous burden of proof. As I say in class: "Big claims equal big proof." What needs to characterize any MIHOP conspiracy is logic as well as proportion.

Let's look at the evidence related to two important parts of 9/11 mentioned earlier in this chapter: the Pentagon and World Trade Center 7. Any close examination of the Pentagon attack quickly reveals that the actual physical evidence regularly contradicts conspiracy claims. While the producers of *Loose Change* argued that the hole in the side of the Pentagon was only eighteen feet in diameter, a 2003 report submitted by the American Society of Civil Engineers noted that it was actually ninety feet.[58] The plane also did not leave a Wylie Coyote–shaped hole in the Pentagon, a result caused by the wings sheering off once they struck exterior walls that were two feet thick and made of reinforced concrete, brick, and limestone.[59] Pieces of American Airlines Flight 77 were scattered in and around the Pentagon grounds. Investigators found portions of the landing gear, engines, and fuselage throughout the impact area. Many of these fragments still had serial number information on them that was traced back to the plane that took off from Dulles International Airport on September 11. Forensic teams picking through the Pentagon wreckage were also able to identify the remains of 184 of 189 passengers and crew on board Flight 77.[60] Lastly, there were dozens of eyewitness accounts of the strike: one of them, Steve Riskus, noted, "I was close enough (about a hundred feet or so) that I could see the American Airlines logo on the tail as it headed toward the building . . . I clearly saw the AA logo with the eagle in the middle."[61]

The same problems affect conspiracy theories about the controlled demolition of World Trade 7. Architects & Engineers for 9/11 Truth (AE911Truth) have published multiple articles on the collapse of WTC7. They emphasize the fact that the building was not struck by either of the two planes and that "normal office fires" could not have melted structural steel and caused the failure of a "fire-protected" structure.[62] They attribute molten metal found after the collapse to thermite charges placed in WTC 7.[63]

Perhaps the most important part of the AE911Truth case is their belief that the speed of the WTC 7 collapse was too fast to come from structural failure and must have been assisted by demolition charges placed throughout the building. AE911Truth cites video evidence taken from news media and eyewitnesses to emphasize this claim. They also take note that the roof of the WTC 7 began to drop before the building fell and that the entire structure uniformly collapsed, closely resembling a standard controlled demolition.

There are a number of basic problems with the AE911Truth case, some of them more obvious than others. The first has to do with the fact the WTC 7 was struck by burning debris all across its south side, the side facing the two towers hit by aircraft. Most of the images taken during 9/11 are from the building's north side because rubble, smoke, and dust prevented access. However, a photo taken by the New York City Police Department clearly illustrates significant damage to the southwest corner of the building. It is obvious that debris projected from the WTC North Tower hit its neighbor only one hundred yards away.

Just what "normal office fires" did to WTC 7 are open to some additional discussion. The idea that jet fuel and burning office equipment could not melt structural steel is likely correct but probably irrelevant. A study done by *Popular Mechanics* after September 11 argues that the fire in the World

Trade Center buildings was sufficient to weaken the steel, causing a cascading structural failure.[64]

AE911Truth's fixation on controlled demolition also contains an interesting flaw. As much as the organization believes in the idea, they never explain just how dozens or, more likely, hundreds of individual demolition charges were placed in WTC 7, who did the placing, or when it might have happened. MIHOP advocate Kevin Ryan has speculated that some tenants in WTC 1 and 2 may have been responsible for these buildings' destruction, although he has offered no proof.[65] Explaining the "how" part of the conspiracy invites an incredibly detailed and complicated scenario, something involving a finely tuned act of terrorism by a large group of actors. Most accounts offered by 9/11 conspiracy theorists simply gloss over this detail. When they do so, they are ducking the "big claim/big proof" dilemma and cherry-picking their own data. Doing that does not help their case at all.

WHY DO 9/11 CONSPIRACY THEORIES CONTINUE?

Despite their many defects, some obvious, some not, 9/11 conspiracy theories live on more than twenty years after the September 11 attack. There may be a number of reasons for the long shelf life of some of these ideas. The most obvious is the war, which, as of this writing, has moved past its twentieth year. As fighting continues, audiences are periodically reminded about the costs of that one day back in 2001.

Any number of 9/11 conspiracy theories also continue to benefit from a variation on the "argument from authority." Organizations like Architects & Engineers for 9/11 Truth or Scholars for 9/11 Truth provide the conspiracy community with an important gloss of legitimacy, some of it rooted in the substance of their cases, other parts of it in the style that experts and academics lend their arguments. Listening or reading the back and forth over "nanothermite" or the composition of "iron microspheres" pretty quickly exhausts any layperson's understanding of chemistry, structural engineering, physics, or a whole array of highly specialized topics and academic disciplines. But, as we will see with terminology about geoengineering in chapter 7, if it sounds complicated, it must be true.

Optics also matter. David Ray Griffin is one of the better-known practitioners of September 11 conspiracy theories because he lends the "easy authority of a teacher" to his arguments, as David Aaronovitch put it.[66] Griffin is a retired professor of theology, not an engineer or a scientist. That fact was irrelevant when he wrote *The New Pearl Harbor: Disturbing Questions About the Bush Administration and 9/11* in 2004. In the book, Griffin wrote that he only wanted to raise "disturbing questions," bypassing the need for matching claims with proof. In fact, to Griffin, the very nature of his questions seemed to be proof enough of a conspiracy. Regarding MIHOP believers, Griffin writes:

> It is for this reason that I claim only that these revisionists have presented a strong *prima facie* case for official complicity, strong enough to merit investigations by those who do have the necessary resources to carry them out—the press and the US Congress. If a significant portion of the evidence summarized here holds up, the conclusion that the attacks of 9/11 succeeded because of official complicity would become virtually inescapable.[67]

Griffin's perspective speaks to a lot of the current problems within 9/11 conspiracies and the conspiracy culture in general. Apparently, skepticism is a perfectly good substitute for facts, especially if they agree with your own, personal theories about an event or a particular actor. Griffin is basically breathing life back into the old McCarthy trope from the Red Scare that assigns guilt by association. If a bad act is somehow placed anywhere near the US government or any member of the "power structure," it must have happened. As much as 9/11 "Truthers" promise to connect the dots, facts don't matter as much as preexisting beliefs. Academic credentials become a device to repackage bias in what seems to be objectivity and legitimacy.

Finally, one of the most obvious reasons for the persistence of 9/11 conspiracy belief is the internet. It is important to understand that the September 11 attacks occurred just at the point that desktop computers were beginning to become the new normal, along with access to a seemingly bottomless reservoir of information. At the time, media outlets constantly touted the dawn of the new information age in homes, schools, and businesses across the country.

As a researcher, I love the worldwide web. It allows me to organize material and focus my work through online finding aids before I travel out to places like the National Archives in College Park, Maryland, locations that contain millions of linear feet of paper documents. The internet is also its own archive. Millions of documents are available through the miracle of the portable document file (PDF), something my students take for granted today.

The internet is also a great resource for the amateur researcher. Individual US federal agencies have their own online archives. The Central Intelligence Agency, for example, has its own "Freedom of Information Act Electronic Reading Room."[68] George Washington University built its own digital national security archive from declassified official documents that stretch back over decades and covers some of the most controversial aspects of American foreign policy.[69] Real and planned covert operations—from the Bay of Pigs invasion to Operation Northwoods—are now at the fingertips of anyone with a computer or smart phone.

This is both good news and bad. The facts, collected and distributed, can now reach an enormous audience. A new "citizen media" can now hold mainstream media corporations and the government accountable for their actions.[70] With off-the-shelf software and hardware, people can collectively demand transparency from institutions responsible for our lives. This is all good news.

Unfortunately, the worst part of the internet is us. Computers cannot give us wisdom or save us from our own flaws. We can build a website with free software and distribute our thoughts to the world without any filters whatsoever. The web allows great freedoms without any responsibilities. In practice, the worldwide web gives people the chance to verify facts or cherry-pick them. David Aaronovitch puts it very well: "the democratic quality of the Net has permitted the release of a mass of undifferentiated information, some of it authoritative, some speculative, some absurd."[71]

CONCLUSIONS: THE "WHO" AND NOT THE "HOW"

The official government story on September 11 as well as the LIHOP and MIHOP schools all share a common feature, focusing most on "who" perpetrated acts of terrorism more than "how" they were actually accomplished.[72] This is important whether talking about Saddam Hussein, CIA officials in cahoots with neoconservative plotters, or a larger, shadowy globalist conspiracy. Emphasis on the "who" allows us to indulge in suspicions rather than facts. We can connect the dots by emoting instead of logically applying evidence to a claim. Hussein was a believable source of the 9/11 attacks because he had committed crimes against humanity. People see suspicion of the CIA as legitimate because the agency had actively plotted against entire countries. The past record defined what seemed plausible. Kathryn Olmsted put it very well when she said: "*Loose Change* [the movie] demonstrated that you did not need to be an empire to create your own reality."[73]

The internet helps us on our way to this point. It does so by allowing us unprecedented access to bits and pieces of information without any filters from "official" sources or interference by so-called experts. It allows the September 11 audience to be skeptical and make its own conclusions without any concurrent obligations to the many complicated features of a very complicated event. In fact, the internet contributed to premature conclusions because it reinforced our impatience. With a world of information at our fingertips, we looked for more and quickly found it, shared the bounty with like-minded conspiracy theorists, and quickly disappeared down our own custom-built rabbit holes.

But, as I said in the introduction, you can't blame everything on the internet or impatient, amateur researchers. Watching the Bush administration's official story slowly implode helps me understand why people hold experts in such disdain. They deserve it. They concocted information and deflected efforts to hold them accountable.

What we had in the aftermath of September 11 was a very bad dynamic: ahorrifying act of terrorism subsequently manipulated by our own elected officials in an environment filled with distrust and paranoia. Could it get worse? As it turned out, it did.

(Public domain via Wikimedia Commons: https://commons.wikimedia.org/wiki/
File:Police_at_Sandy_Hook.PNG.)

Chapter Six

Sandy Hook

This needs to be investigated. They are clearly using this to go after our guns. . . . Something though, really, is starting to get suspicious here. . . . But the fact that this whole thing could be staged, it's just mind blowing.[1]

—Alex Jones, January 2013

As you begin this school year, remember Ana Grace. Walk with courage, with faith, and with love.[2]

—From a letter by Nelba Marquez-Greene, mother of student slain at Sandy Hook, published in *Education Week*, September 2013

MASS SHOOTINGS IN AMERICA

Adam Lanza attacked the Sandy Hook Elementary School in Newtown, Connecticut, on the morning of December 12, 2012, and murdered twenty-six people, including twenty children. It was not America's first mass shooting, and it wasn't the first time that students were massacred in what was supposed to be a place of safety and learning. But despite the fact that many Americans were growing increasingly numb to an ever-expanding list of gun deaths, no one could ignore the reality of six- and seven-year-olds ripped apart by multiple gunshot wounds.

We do not have a common definition of what a school shooting means. Official sources in government and law enforcement tend to combine mass shootings and school shootings under a single label. According to the Congressional Research Service, a mass shooting involves at least four deaths in a single incident.[3] There is no such yardstick for a school attack.

To any reasonable person, it doesn't need one. The horror accompanying the death or injury of a child is self-evident. It strikes a deep chord that we instinctively understand as individuals and as a society. Motivated by this knowledge, we have tried to adapt to ongoing tragedies like Sandy Hook. During the Cold War, children practiced "duck and cover" drills in anticipation of nuclear war. Today, they do same in concert with police and emergency medical services to protect schools in "active shooter" scenarios. Educators and clinical psychologists have ongoing discussions about how to help students exposed to a new form of school violence. In the twenty-first century, as Americans welcomed home Iraq and Afghanistan veterans struggling with mental illness, we are also groping with post-traumatic stress disorder (PTSD) appearing among our school children. More chillingly, education professionals are also seeking out strategies to avoid copycat killings for students inspired by an accumulating array of school shooters.[4]

While the vast majority of Americans have tried to find constructive solutions to Sandy Hook and the string of disasters following it, another smaller part of the country took a much different path. They have concocted a scenario that fits the classic definition of a conspiracy, with a network of authority figures in government and media setting about an evil plan designed to expand the power of the state as it takes away freedom of thought and action from law-abiding citizens. It is a complex, multilayered story. And it has managed to make an already terrible situation much worse.

SANDY HOOK CLAIMS:
THE DEEP STATE, FALSE FLAGS, AND CRISIS ACTORS

Conspiracy theories started flowing from Sandy Hook only days after the tragedy. Dozens of claims orbited around the idea that the shooting was a false flag deliberately staged by the government to justify an attack on American freedom and, in particular, gun rights. Moving alongside this core theory was the argument that mainstream media was deliberately manipulating the story as it unfolded, actively falsifying information as it censored citizen activists who tried to tell the truth. Writing for the website *Natural News*, Jon Rappoport noted that "television news people are creating a story line about what happened at the school and in the town, and they are finding people who will corroborate that plot line, or can be convinced by news producers to corroborate it."[5]

There were some variations on main government/media conspiracy that were much more elaborate. Rappoport also saw Sandy Hook as an indictment of both mental health services and pharmaceutical companies "since so many killers have acted under the compelling influence of SSRI (selective serotonin reuptake inhibitors) antidepressants and other brain meds. The drugs are known to induce violence." He followed with the conclusion: "More mental health means more murders."[6]

Much of the remainder of Sandy Hook conspiracy theories tend to spiral around two intertwined threads: identifying inconsistencies in events surrounding the massacre to poke holes in the "official story" and, secondly, seeking out "evidence" of an evil plan. Efforts dedicated to the first goal are similar to the anomaly hunting common in 9/11 Truther conspiracy theories. The many endlessly dissected parts of the Sandy Hook massacre have produced questions about why the emergency medical services response was so slow. Skeptics asked why authorities did not deploy Life Star helicopters to evacuate the wounded from the school. Others focused on the parents of the victims. One, Robby Parker, drew particular scrutiny after he appeared at a news conference and broke down in front of the cameras. On YouTube, this translated into: "Robby Parker Laughing a Day After His Daughter Was Murdered at S H."[7] The apparent conclusion was that he was a "crisis actor" and not a grieving father.

The search for evidence of an evil plot surrounding Sandy Hook included a variety of complicated, overlapping scenarios. Despite the vested faith in a government conspiracy, it appeared that official documents were betraying the plan. One theory offered the idea that no one died at the school because the FBI Uniform Crime Report did not include any victims from the shooting.[8] A website called Chemtrailsplanet claimed that no one died as Sandy Hook because none of their names appeared on the Social Security Death Index.[9] Wolfgang Halbig, a self-styled school safety expert we will discuss in detail later in the chapter, maintained that sixteen Connecticut state police involved in Sandy Hook lied about their investigation.[10] James Fetzer, a University of Minnesota emeritus professor, claimed in his 2015 book, *Nobody Died at Sandy Hook*, that state and county official falsified victims' death certificates.[11]

The internet was both a forum and loudspeaker for this cascade of Sandy Hook conspiracy theories. Before it scoured content for fraudulent conspiracy content after a flurry of defamation lawsuits, YouTube was the primary platform for much of this discussion. One video, titled "The Sandy Hook Shooting—Fully Exposed," appeared in January 2013 and asked: "Wouldn't frantic kids be a difficult target to hit?" It eventually accumulated ten million hits.[12] Websites like *Veterans Today* described Sandy Hook as "psy-op" (psychological operations) designed to "strike fear in the hearts of Americans."[13] Writing for its website, James Fetzer compared the shooting to "terror ops conducted by agents of Israel."[14] Like Halbig, the retired professor quickly became a fixture online. In an eerie echo of the old scapegoating about a global Jewish cabal, Fetzer later doubled down on the claim by repeatedly accusing Leonard Pozner, the father of one of the Sandy Hook victims, of being an Israeli agent.[15]

Perhaps the best-known promoter of Sandy Hook conspiracies is Alex Jones on his Infowars website. Jones repeatedly claimed that the entire event was a government hoax and a false flag. He claimed that families faked their children's deaths. Jones maintained that parents interviewed by television media after the shooting were either coached by unnamed government officials or were crisis actors.[16] Jones's outrageous claims and on-air antics eventually led mainstream media to his doorstep and even greater exposure. Appearing on NBC during a June 2017 interview with Megyn Kelly, Jones found a new audience for his Sandy Hook story: "But then what do you do, when they've got the kids going in circles, in and out of the building with their hands up? I've watched the footage. And it looks like a drill."[17] By 2018, Jones broadcast on sixty radio stations and had 2.3 million subscribers on his YouTube channel. The Infowars website averaged 1.4 million daily visits.[18] In the meantime, Jones made millions, as much as $20 million in 2014.[19] According to a May 2017 BuzzFeed News profile about Infowars's Life health store products:

> Infowars Life now sells a full battery of supplements purporting to solve a vast spectrum of problems, real and imagined; items include Super Male Vitality serum, Brain Force Plus, and Caveman, a $60 mix said to help Infowarriors "rediscover the human blueprint, and experience the power of cutting edge science."[20]

According to one former employee: "It's like QVC for conspiracy."[21]

Wolfgang Halbig was a frequent guest on Infowars and became one of the leading promoters of conspiracy theories about Sandy Hook.[22] A former high school teacher, state trooper, and Florida public school safety administrator, Halbig inserted himself into Sandy Hook issue at first claiming that he was skeptical about the official accounts of the massacre.[23]

In the years that followed, Halbig mounted a one-man investigation of the Sandy Hook shooting. He filed a series of Freedom of Information Act requests with the state of Connecticut, asking for records about the school security system, dash cam footage from responding police vehicles, and even the number of portable toilets on school grounds before the shooting.[24] Halbig eventually visited Connecticut twenty-two times to investigate Sandy Hook. He requested data from United Way offices in Danbury to tabulate charitable giving and attempted to interview volunteer fire fighters stationed near the school. In May 2014, he attended a meeting of the Newtown Board of Education to recite his skepticism about the official account of what happened at Sandy Hook. He told the assembled parents and officials: "Board members, these are your children. We want answers. We want truth."[25]

Halbig's did not provide any radical departures from existing conspiracy theories about the Sandy Hook shooting. His contribution, such as it was, came from the specific culprits named and, more importantly, the perception of expertise his claims carried with them. When a former state trooper named the Department of Homeland Security and the Federal Emergency Management Agency (FEMA) as the parties responsible for a false flag exercise, people listened.[26] When a former school safety administrator claimed in a 2015 interview that the school buildings were dilapidated and uninhabitable, "proving" that they were abandoned prior to the shooting, the theory gained traction.

Halbig did not stop there. He attacked the parents of the shooting victims, asserting as Jones had that some of them were crisis actors. Halbig accused one parent, Jeremy Richman, of faking his daughter's death for financial gain or, as he put it: "to steal money from hard-working Americans." During a May 2014 appearance on Infowars, he expressed his belief that Newtown and victim's families had illicitly received upward of $29 million.[27]

Members of the academic community provided an additional layer of perceived legitimacy to Sandy Hook conspiracy claims. James Fetzer issued his opinions about Leonard Pozner, Israeli secret operations, and faked death certificates as a reputable scholar of philosophy. While he was faculty at the University of Minnesota at Duluth, the school awarded Fetzer a $100,000 "genius" grant, some of which went into his study of conspiracies.[28] Fetzer was joined in his crusade by professor of communication James F. Tracy, who taught a course titled "Culture of Conspiracy" at Florida Atlantic University. Tracy began an ongoing commentary about Sandy Hook on his blog, *Memory Hole*, a few months after the shooting: "While it sounds like an outrageous claim, one is left to inquire whether the Sandy Hook shooting ever took place—at least in the way law enforcement authorities and the nation's news media have described."[29] Like Fetzer, Tracy lent agency and credibility to questions about Sandy Hook by virtue of his position in higher learning. On the face of it, Tracy was simply asking legitimate questions about a tragic event. However, what might have started as an academic exercise soon developed into a series of attacks on the families of Sandy Hook victims, particularly the family of six-year-old Noah Pozner.[30]

MASS SHOOTINGS:
THE CONTEXT OF AMERICAN CARNAGE

In April 2021, *Mother Jones* developed a database that covered mass shootings in America from 1982 to 2021. It tallied a total of 123 incidents that affected 2,439 Americans of whom 987 died and 1,457 were injured.[31] The database is a soul-deadening catalogue of ongoing bloodshed in modern America. Five people killed in a shooting at Watkins Glen, New York, in 1992. Six died in Fort Lauderdale, Florida, in 1996. Five in Columbus, Ohio, in 2004.[32] Today, it almost seems that the list gets longer week by week.

Some mass shootings stand out for their sheer carnage. This was the case in Las Vegas on October 1, 2017, when Stephen Paddock opened fire with an assortment of weapons, primarily AR-15s, some of which were modified with "bump stocks" designed to increase the rate of fire, from his room in the Mandalay Bay Hotel and Casino.[33] His target was the Harvest Music Festival attended by approximately 22,000 people. In a matter of minutes, a total of 58 people died and 869 were wounded or injured, 413 from gunshots and shrapnel and the remainder resulting from the panic once the shooting began.[34] More Americans were injured and wounded in the Las Vegas attack than the entire 1991 Gulf War.[35]

Included in both the data and the human suffering are school shootings. Most Americans tend to identify the April 1999 massacre in Columbine, Colorado, as the starting point for a generation of mass casualty events in schools, although it is clear that they began years earlier. One telling trend has been the increase in such tragic incidents. Between 2010 and 2018, the number of school shootings tripled in America.[36] One of the most recent was when Nikolas Cruz killed seventeen students, teachers, and staff and wounded another seventeen at the Marjory Stoneman Douglas High School in Parkland, Florida, on February 14, 2018.[37]

Following in the wake of mass shootings, Americans engage in a familiar, recurring debate about gun control. For the past generation, the public has moved through a repeating cycle of shock, demands for reform to deal with the latest illustration of the problem before us, and brutal legislative battles between gun rights and gun safety advocates. Yet, there is an irony in this story. Despite all the warnings about false flags and powerful interests emanating from the bowels of the deep state, new national gun reform law remains extremely rare. And there is probably no better illustration of this than what happened after Sandy Hook.

At the time, it seemed like the stunning nature of what had happened would be a final clarion call for action. Speaking in Harford, Connecticut, in April 2013, Barack Obama seemed to capture the moment:

Table 6.1. American School Mass Shootings, 1989–2018

Year	Location	Killed	Injured
2018	Santa Fe High School Santa Fe, TX	10	13
2018	Marjory Stoneman Douglas High School Parkland, FL	17	17
2015	Umpqua Community College Roseburg, OR	9	9
2014	Marysville-Pilchuck High School Marysville, WA	5	1
2012	Sandy Hook Elementary School Newtown, CT	27	2
2012	Oikos University Oakland, CA	7	3
2008	Northern Illinois University DeKalb, IL	5	21
2007	Virginia Tech University Blacksburg, VA	32	23
2006	Amish School Lancaster County, PA	6	5
1999	Columbine High School Littleton, CO	13	24
1998	Thurston High School Springfield, OR	4	25
1998	Westside Middle School Jonesboro, AR	5	10
1992	Lindhurst High School Olivehurst, CA	4	10
1991	University of Iowas Iowa City, IA	6	1
1989	Cleveland Elementary School Stockton, CA	6	29

Source: Mark Follman, Gavin Aronsen, and Deanna Pan, "US Mass Shootings, 1982–2021: Data from Mother Jones Investigation," *Mother Jones,* April 16, 2021, https://www.motherjones.com/politics/2012/12/mass-shootings-mother-jones-full-data/.

So every family in this state was shaken by the tragedy of that morning. Every family in this country was shaken. We hugged our kids more tightly. We asked what could we do, as a society, to help prevent a tragedy like that from happening again.

And as a society, we decided that we have to change. We must. We must change.[38]

The White House took the initiative at the start of the year by presenting a comprehensive program to prevent another Sandy Hook. Titled *Now Is the*

Time, the plan included a ban on military-style assault rifles, more rigorous background checks, and improving mental health care so that individuals like Adam Lanza might get the help they need and never have access to weapons again.[39] Reformers seemed reasonably optimistic about new federal mandates given the fact that Democrats enjoyed majorities in both the House and Senate at the time.

But they failed. Democrats could not muster enough votes for a ban on military-style assault weapons and high-capacity magazines. Bipartisan legislation co-sponsored by Senators Joe Manchin (Democrat, West Virginia) and Pat Twomey (Republican, Pennsylvania) to expand national background checks also failed to gather enough votes to avoid a filibuster. Only a matter of days after Obama's Connecticut speech, Senate Majority Leader Harry Reid (Democrat, Nevada) admitted defeat and halted further work on gun safety legislation. The president angrily lamented: "All in all, this was a pretty shameful day for Washington."[40]

Although some states introduced gun control measures after the Sandy Hook shooting, federal efforts remain gridlocked by partisanship. Seven years after the massacre, mostly Democrat state legislatures addressed expanding background checks, preventing individuals convicted of domestic abuse from having weapons, and "red flag" laws for people "posing a substantial risk" to themselves or others.[41] Legal restrictions have not stemmed American gun purchases. According to a 2018 study, the United States accounted for just under half of the "legal and illicit" civilian firearms in the world. That is 393.3 million weapons.[42] Sales surged during the COVID-19 pandemic and unrest that marked most of 2020. According to one estimate, Americans purchased twenty-three million weapons that year, a 65 percent increase over 2019.[43] In January 2021, the month of the Capitol riot, people bought two million weapons, the third highest monthly total on record.[44]

SEEKING OUT AND NOT FINDING SANDY HOOK EVIDENCE

Before getting into a discussion about Sandy Hook evidence, it is important to understand what happens immediately after a mass shooting. Sandy Hook was like the 2013 Boston Marathon bombing in that it involved a large group of people, a mass casualty situation, overlapping layers of local and state first responders (law enforcement and medical), and national media constantly seeking out new details to feed into the 24-hour news cycle. The early stages are an exercise in chaos as paramedics assess and triage victims and police try to establish control over a large crime scene.[45] This is prime territory for mistakes. Mistakes made because of stress, garbled communications, and wrong assumptions. All of this affects the evidence that outside observers—official authorities or conspiracy theorists—pick over after the fact.

Most Sandy Hook "evidence" offered by conspiracy theorists is, in fact, not evidence at all. Instead, it is a series of claims, guesses, and theories without any supporting facts. At the core of Sandy Hook conspiracy theories, for example, is the idea that it was a massive false flag exercise. According to self-proclaimed experts like Wolfgang Halbig, deep state entities such as FEMA and the Department of Homeland Security are behind the operation. It might also include the FBI, the Connecticut state police, the chief state medical examiner, and the local school board. Yet, when pressed and given the opportunity to provide hard evidence in court (see below), there is none. Which is surprising if you really believe in the Sandy Hook conspiracy. Like the JFK assassination and the September 11 attacks and similar claims about a deep state plot, there should be thousands of people involved, some of whom might have a fit of conscience and spill the details (and documents) behind such a gigantic plan. In 2016, David R. Grimes did a statistical study that estimated how long it might take one of these "megaconspiracies" to become public knowledge. He concludes: "The results of this model suggest that large conspiracies (≥1,000 agents) quickly become untenable and prone to failure."[46] Sandy Hook fits this model perfectly.

The specifics of Sandy Hook "evidence" don't do any better. A common trope among conspiracy circles was that the children killed in the massacre were not actually dead. However, this claim is easily debunked by the availability of a whole chain of documentation, from crime scene pictures, affidavits of eyewitnesses, autopsy reports, and official death certificates.

An adjunct to the crisis actor theory is the claim that Sandy Hook was actually closed when the shooting took place. Basically, theorists believe that the buildings were a sound stage for a false flag theater project. This is an interesting sideline but also easy to research and debunk. Bus drivers transporting hundreds of children to school, parents who dropped off their children, the teachers who greeted them that day are all eyewitnesses. There is also another lengthy paper trail. Public records from the Newtown school district indicate plans and budgets for maintenance projects like roof repairs and window replacement.[47] All of this information is easy to find online.

When Sandy Hook conspiracy theorists acknowledge that the school might have been open, they argue over the finer points of the crisis response, specifically ambulance travel time and the lack of air medical evacuation. The second issue is the easier to address, given the simple fact that ground ambulances could be dispatched to the school more quickly than helicopters. The Sandy Hook Volunteer Fire and Rescue was located less than a quarter mile from the school.[48] Once they arrived at the scene, EMS personnel had to navigate a confusing situation.[49] When the first 911 call went out, dispatchers quickly lost control of the medical responses as dozens of units rushed to what everyone assumed was a mass casualty situation. Once paramedics arrived, they had to wait for police to search and secure the school, a frustrating and time-consuming process. As officers worked their way through the school, they found that the victims, most of whom suffered from multiple gunshots, were beyond emergency care.[50]

The details matter. Whether applied to the big claims or the small ones, any valid evidence to support Sandy Hook conspiracy theories is hard, if not impossible, to come by. The large claims fall apart because evidence simply isn't there. The small ones are easier to research, understand, and debunk in detail. As far as Sandy Hook evidence is concerned, the truth is a sum of many large and small parts. And it is out there.

ANALYZING SANDY HOOK FROM THE OUTSIDE IN

Understanding Sandy Hook takes time. The interval between Adam Lanza opening fire and taking his own life was about ten minutes. Afterward, the FBI, the Connecticut state police, the state attorney general, the governor, and even the Connecticut Office of the Child Advocate all published reports of the incident, a process that consumed thousands of hours of work and produced still more thousands of pages of data and analysis. Like the Warren Commission and the 9/11 Commission before them, officials picked over a catastrophe with literal forensic attention to detail with the hope of answering questions and finding closure. Taken as a whole, the witness statements, interviews, medical records, audio recordings, and crime scene pictures are the proverbial mountain of evidence.

For most people, this was more than enough. However, like their predecessors, these official reports ended up feeding skepticism among outsiders looking into Sandy Hook. Inside the facts, they see deception. Despite the earnestness and professionalism of hundreds of law enforcement officers and other public officials, they see a cover-up. Consequently, the ongoing debate about Sandy Hook conspiracies has taken on the dynamic qualities of the Kennedy assassination and the September 11 attacks. Trying to address every theory is something like squeezing a balloon.

It is not for lack of trying. As one of the higher-profile family members who lost a child at Sandy Hook, Leonard Pozner, founded the HONR Network in 2014. The official website uses a variety of phrases to express the same intent: "protecting the most vulnerable people from online harassment and hate."[51] HONR became a truth squad that followed in the wake of conspiracy theories, rebutting and debunking unfounded claims and answering some of the direct attacks on Sandy Hook families. By 2017, the organization had three hundred volunteers who pursued these tasks and applied them to other victims of harassment beyond Sandy Hook.[52]

At points, Pozner and his wife, Veronique, also took their appeal directly to the media. In a December 2015 editorial for the *South Florida Sun Sentinel*, they focused specifically on Professor James Tracy and his ongoing series of claims about Sandy Hook and the Pozners in particular:

> Tracy even sent us a certified letter demanding proof that Noah once lived, that we were his parents, and that we were the rightful owner of his photographic image. We found this so outrageous and unsettling that we filed a police report for harassment. Once Tracy realized we would not respond, he subjected us to ridicule and contempt on his blog, boasting to his readers that the "unfulfilled request" was "noteworthy" because we had used copyright claims to "thwart continued research of the Sandy Hook massacre event."[53]

Tracy was one of the first Sandy Hook conspiracy promoters ultimately held accountable for his actions. Although tenured, Tracy was still subject to the rules of his contract and employment in a university. As his comments grew more extreme, Florida Atlantic University eventually pushed back, reprimanding Tracy for failing to make it clear that his views were not those of the school. At that point, the issue transitioned into a debate about academic freedom. Tracy raised it on his blog:

> The First Amendment sculpture's spirit and presence at FAU is contradicted by the university administration's recent attempts to coerce faculty and students from publicly addressing controversial subject matter of tremendous public interest and concern.[54]

When the university finally terminated Tracy in January 2016, it had nothing to do with free speech or his conspiracy theories. In a letter made public when he was fired, Florida Atlantic University cited Tracy's refusal to respond to management requests to provide documentation of his outside activities, which included his blog and other media appearances.[55]

In recent years, Sandy Hook conspiracy theorists have been on the receiving end of multiple lawsuits. In one deposition, Alex Jones adopted a variety of defenses. Under the scrutiny of legal action, Jones denied supporting the idea that the Sandy Hook shooting was a hoax; he was simply relating the views of his listeners. Jones also blamed media deception for causing his unwillingness to accept the facts about the massacre. He went on further to say:

> "And I, myself, have almost had like a form of psychosis back in the past where I basically thought everything was staged, even though I've now learned a lot

of times things aren't staged," he said. "So I think as a pundit, someone giving an opinion, that, you know, my opinions have been wrong, but they were never wrong consciously to hurt people.[56]

Pressed by lawyers representing seven Sandy Hook families, he finally did admit the tragedy was real.

Jones's sudden epiphany did not save him. In December 2019, one lawsuit resulted in a $100,000 judgment against the Infowars host.[57] The next year, the Connecticut Supreme Court upheld sanctions against Jones for threatening Christopher Mattei, a lawyer representing one of the Sandy Hook families. Jones suffered an important defeat in January 2021 when the Texas Supreme Court allowed four defamation lawsuits against him and Infowars to move forward.[58]

James Fetzer also found himself in a courtroom in October 2019, subject to a legal action by Leonard Pozner. It took a jury just four hours to render a verdict and award Pozner $450,000 for his defamation lawsuit. Fetzer called the judgment "absurd" after the trial.[59] Four months earlier, when a summary judgment found that Fetzer "acted with actual malice," the publisher of Fetzer's book on Sandy Hook, David Gahary, agreed to stop selling it after meeting with Pozner and went on to "extend my most heartfelt and sincere apology to the Pozner family."[60]

Wolfgang Halbig's crusade eventually caught up with him as well. Not content to air his conspiracy claims online, in public meetings, and media interviews, Halbig took direct action against Leonard Pozner. He was arrested for misdemeanor possession of personal information in January 2020 after repeatedly posting Pozner's Social Security number, birthdate, and credit history to a list of people that included "multiple different law enforcement agencies and news stations," according to the *New York Times*.[61]

CONCLUSIONS

Mass shootings are a terrible and ongoing part of American life. Between the time I write this chapter and when this book is published, we will likely add new names to the long list of people killed and wounded at work, shopping, or trying to go about their normal lives. That sad list may include a school, particularly as the country returns to face-to-face classes after more than a year of COVID-19 sanctions.

The victims of Sandy Hook spent years obtaining some form of justice. The process that started with appeals to reason and then fact-checking and debunking before moving on to a series of lawsuits. As litigation and appeals ground on, exhaustion and other emotional expenses took their own toll. The

Pozners eventually divorced and Leonard Pozner currently lives in hiding, constantly moving his residence to avoid conspiracy-motivated stalkers who seek him out.

Multiple court decisions have not deterred conspiracy theorists from maintaining their narratives despite all evidence to the contrary. Today, James Fetzer's website preserves a long list of articles denouncing his legal problems. One characterized the 2019 defamation verdict as: "The Legal Lynching of a Truth Seeker: Jim Fetzer's Stalinist-Style Show Trial (Expanded)."[62] The website includes other mass shootings—Las Vegas, Marjory Stoneman Douglas High School, and the Orland Pulse Night Club among them—in its main content. For obvious reasons, Alex Jones is more muted about Sandy Hook, but Infowars continues its daily (May 2021) litany of stories about COVID-19, the 2020 election, and collusion with China.[63]

Why? Some answers are obvious. Despite his diminishing popularity, Alex Jones's Infowars store continues hawking products like "Fizzy Magnesium Formula Drink Mix," survival gear, and conspiracy books and videos.[64] Monetizing conspiracies is still a big business. Other motives are much less tangible and harder to identify. True belief motivates some Sandy Hook conspiracy believers. What might also drive them may not be so much the facts as the struggle. When they are rebuffed in the courts or the media or by other fact-checking websites, it plays into a stilted hero narrative where any effort to hold the Sandy Hook conspiracy accountable or ban a speaker for libel is the same as deep state censorship in the current American dystopia. Writing for the *Natural News* website, Mike Adams declared Amazon to be an "Orwellian Big Brother" after it banned James Fetzer's book *Nobody Died at Sandy Hook* in 2015.[65] For too many of these individuals, the facts don't matter. Neither does the deeply felt suffering of thousands who will be affected by tragedies like Sandy Hook for the rest of their lives.

(Public domain via Wikimedia Commons: https://commons.wikimedia.org/wiki/
File:Contrails.jpg.)

Chapter Seven

Chemtrails and Contrails

In 2025, US aerospace forces can "own the weather" by capitalizing on emerging technologies and focusing development of those technologies to war-fighting applications. Such a capability offers the war fighter tools to shape the battlespace in ways never before possible.[1]

—From *Weather as a Force Multiplier: Owning the Weather in 2025*

EVIL ABOVE US

Chemtrails are one of the more recent conspiracy theories that originally appeared in the late 1990s and has been a part of the activist landscape ever since. Interest in the chemtrail phenomena paralleled early and well-publicized scientific attempts to address climate change and then morphed into a freewheeling series of theories about global conspiracies directed against humanity. Chemtrails are everywhere on YouTube. Internet documentaries like *What in the World Are They Spraying?* (2010) are the chemtrail equivalent that *Loose Change* was for September 11. There are many websites dedicated to the issue, like Russ Tanner's *Global Skywatch* and Dane Wigington's *Geoengineering Watch*, which claimed more than 37.4 million visits as of this writing.[2]

Chemtrails are less a reaction to a dramatic historical tragedy (like the JFK assassination or September 11) than an ongoing plot closer to the *Protocols of the Elders of Zion*. The chemtrail movement is dynamic in nature, developing from an original set of claims and correlations that grew more complicated as the conspiracy evolved to meet outside criticism, "moving the goalposts" as fact-checkers began challenge both the evidence and assumptions of their argument.[3]

Chemtrails are interesting because they speak to a lot of issues that dominate the public debate today, from climate change to growing concerns about personal health. Chemtrails also pose a set of questions that attract and deserve attention: Is the story based upon an actual historical chain of events that led concerned citizens to a real conspiracy? Or is the chemtrail conspiracy a series of unrelated correlations that result in a conclusion already made by its advocates? What does the evidence support?

THE CHEMTRAIL CLAIM

According to the people who believe in them, how chemtrails happen is pretty simple. They are part of an active program of high-altitude spraying from civilian and military aircraft. People allegedly discovered this activity because a trinity of elements—aluminum, barium, and strontium—began to appear in abnormally high levels in rainwater, snow, and the soil. According to *What in the World Are They Spraying?* creator, Michael Murphy, geoengineers sprayed between ten and twenty million tons of material into the atmosphere between 2000 and 2010.[4]

The reasons that chemtrails might exist are more complicated and introduce a large group of possible culprits and goals. As noted above, many advocates see trails in the sky and conclude that they represent a military program to weaponize the weather. Others fix their sights on civilian agencies attempting to alter weather patterns to repair environmental damage—otherwise known as geoengineering—or to fix the mistakes of previously failed experiments. Some chemtrail theorists believe that there are much darker purposes at work. They consider chemtrails to be an attempt to control the global population or to be a form of mass mind control. Or both.

Chemtrail advocates apply their claims to a broad array of issues. They attribute temperature extremes, increasing rainfall, hurricanes, and the death of both animal and plant species to man-made geoengineering. Dane Wigington, a long-time promoter of the chemtrail conspiracy, has even gone so far as to say the there is "no natural weather."[5]

Other chemtrail theorists make their claims more personal. While they acknowledge the widespread impact of spraying on the Earth's ecosystems, people like Russ Tanner spend more time talking about chemtrails and individual health. Tanner's website includes a laundry list of ailments that he believes come from aerial spraying, a catalog that includes cancer, strokes, Alzheimer's, asthma, and tinnitus, to name a few.[6] Other maladies are less defined or new diseases not recognized by medical science. These include "brain fog," fatigue, low energy, or, in a more recent addition that carries its own internet origin story, Morgellons disease.[7]

THE HISTORICAL CONTEXT OF WEATHER CONTROL

Like many conspiracy theories, the chemtrail phenomena has some basis in fact. We all understand that humans have been trying to apply science to understand and control nature for centuries. However, the actual historical record of weather modification comes from the twentieth century. One big motivation for research into the idea was drought. We often think of the Dust Bowl in the American Midwest during the 1920s, but this problem was global at the time. The Soviet Union was particularly interested in relieving drought conditions before World War II when it created the Institute of Rainmaking in 1932. Soviet scientists worked on cloud-seeding experiments by using calcium chloride as early as 1934 and continuing until 1939.[8] The United States did not begin experiments on cloud seeding until 1946. Twenty years later, the US federal government sponsored experiments covering a much more expanded scope of activity. In 1965, Lyndon B. Johnson's Science Advisory Committee issued a landmark report, "Restoring the Quality of Our Environment," that warned of the potentially harmful effects of fossil fuel emissions. It was the first high-level government statement on a response to global warming and raised the possibility of "deliberately bringing about countervailing climatic changes," including by "raising the albedo, or reflectivity, of the Earth."[9]

The Cold War is what really spurred on development of weather modification programs in the United States. The race to obtain the hydrogen bomb and project that power into space highlighted only one part of what applied science might do to shift the global balance of power. The 1957 launch of *Sputnik* captured American imaginations as much as it terrified the country about the potential cost of falling behind the Soviet Union. Henry Houghton, who served as the chair of the MIT Meteorology Department, perfectly captured the moment in the wake of *Sputnik*:

> Man's material success has been due in large degree to his ability to utilize and control his physical environment. . . . As our civilization steadily becomes more mechanized and as our population density grows the impact of weather will become ever more serious. . . . The solution lies in . . . intelligent use of more precise weather forecasts and, ideally, by taking the offensive through control of weather.

> I shudder to think of the consequences of a prior Russian discovery of a feasible method for weather control. Fortunately for us and the world we were first to develop nuclear weapons. . . . International control of weather modification will be as essential to the safety of the world as control of nuclear energy is now.[10]

Consequently, both superpowers poured billions of dollars and rubles into weaponizing weather alongside research and development for breakthroughs in nuclear, chemical, and biological warfare.

Records of success are hard to find. One military program declassified in the early 1970s was Operation Popeye. According to a January 1967 State Department memo:

> The objective of the program is to produce sufficient rainfall along these lines of communication to interdict or at least interfere with truck traffic between North and South Vietnam. Recently improved cloud seeding techniques would be applied on a sustained basis, in a non-publicized effort to induce continued rainfall through the months of the normal dry season.[11]

Beginning on March 20, 1967, and continuing through every rainy season (March to November) in Southeast Asia until 1972, US Air Force C-130 aircraft flew 2,602 cloud-seeding missions from Udorn Royal Thai Air Force Base in Thailand.[12] The results, according to the same 1967 memo:

> During the test phase, more than 50 cloud seeding experiments were conducted. The results are viewed by DOD [Department of Defense] as outstandingly successful.
>
> (a) 82% of the clouds seeded produced rain within a brief period after seeding— a percentage appreciably higher than normal expectation in the absence of seeding."[13]

Claims of success aside, when Seymour Hersh of the *New York Times* revealed Operation Popeye, it was something of a bombshell. Framed as it was by the unpopularity of the Vietnam War, the idea of using the weather as a weapon caused a public backlash.[14] In December 1976, the UN General Assembly approved the Environmental Modification Convention, which banned weather warfare and other hostile uses of climate manipulation "having widespread, long-lasting or severe effects." The treaty went into effect a little less than two years later and was eventually ratified by seventy-six countries.[15]

A NEW FOCUS ON HEALTH

When the Cold War ended, the scientific community shifted some of its effort from building super weapons to working on the global consequences of pollution. In 1988, the United Nations formed the Intergovernmental Panel on Climate Change (IPCC) to assess the risk of climate change posed by human activity. The panel focused on fossil fuels that contribute to increases in

One Important Clarification

A common mistake that pops up constantly in the discussion about chemtrails is confusing the terms *weather* and *climate*. They are very different. The National Oceanic and Atmospheric Administration offers this distinction on its website:

Weather

The state of the atmosphere with respect to wind, temperature, cloudiness, moisture, pressure, etc. Weather refers to these conditions at a given point in time (e.g., today's high temperature), whereas climate refers to the "average" weather conditions for an area over a long period of time (e.g., the average high temperature for today's date).

Climate

The composite or generally prevailing weather conditions of a region, throughout the year, averaged over a series of years.

So, the difference regards both time and scale. Weather is short duration and local, while climate covers a much longer time period and geography.

Source: National Oceanic and Atmospheric Administration, National Weather Service. http://w1.weather.gov/glossary/index.php?letter=w.

"greenhouse gases" and significant increases in global temperatures.[16] They concluded that unless global emissions are cut by 60 percent, global temperatures could rise by as much as 5.4 degrees Fahrenheit over the next 110 years, a scenario that poses catastrophic consequences.[17]

At the same time, the discussion about individual health also increased in volume and intensity. As the 1990s started, America was an aging country, a trend led by the graying of seventy-six million Baby Boomers.[18] With advancing age came an increase in physical problems. Diabetes, heart disease, and obesity all rose significantly throughout the country.[19] The same was true with respect to disabilities, particularly autism and learning difficulties. When the United States entered the new millennia, health concerns were at the forefront of most public discussions, a place where they remained as the nation debated health care in the 2020 election.[20]

THE GEOENGINEERING SOLUTION

Despite the dire problems confronting the world, many scientists were optimistic about potential solutions. Whatever dilemma progress might create, they reasoned, progress could fix. In August 2006, Paul J. Crutzen, winner of the 1995 Nobel Prize in Chemistry for his research on ozone, argued that international treaties to reduce greenhouse gas emissions were "a pious wish."[21] What the world needed was direct action. Crutzen published his proposed alternative in *Climatic Change*, where he advocated additional geoengineering research, specifically "albedo enhancement"—the use of artificial materials to reflect sunlight and decrease global temperatures.[22] Crutzen's article was important for two reasons. First, it expressed a division within the scientific community between those in favor of reducing carbon emissions and other researchers who wanted to deal with climate change through "solar radiation management." Second, and probably more importantly, Crutzen introduced the whole idea of geoengineering into the mainstream public debate.

What Is Geoengineering?

The University of Oxford Geoengineering Programme defines it as: "the deliberate large-scale intervention in the Earth's natural systems to counteract climate change."

Source: "What Is Geoengineering?" Oxford Geoengineering Programme (website), Oxford Martin School, University of Oxford, http:// www.geoengineering.ox.ac.uk/what-is-geoengineering/what-is-geoen gineering/.

As the debate over potential solutions continued, private and public research into geoengineering moved forward. Some of the proposed work was a bit odd. In November 2006, at a NASA conference in Silicon Valley, Lowell Wood, a former top weapons designer at the Pentagon, laid out an "instant climatic gratification" scheme to reverse global warming. His plan involved using artillery to fire as much as one million tons of sulfate aerosols into the Arctic stratosphere in order to dull the sun's rays and build up sea ice that could then cool the planet. Science historian James R. Fleming, writing in *Wilson Quarterly*, likened Wood's idea to "declaring war on the stratosphere."[23]

Other ideas were both more rational and more grandiose. Physicist David Keith proposed to have two jets spray one million tons of sulfur dioxide into atmosphere each year, arguing that this action could reflect back 1 percent of the sun's rays. Keith believed that a man-made reproduction of the 1991 Mount Pinatubo eruption could be used to combat global warming. According to his calculations, twenty million tons of sulfur dioxide could reduce global temperature by half a degree Celsius (1.8 degrees Fahrenheit).[24] Keith published these ideas in his 2013 book, *A Case for Climate Engineering*. He eventually became the public face of geoengineering, appearing on popular talk shows like the *Colbert Report*.

CHEMTRAILS APPEAR

The first mention of chemtrails appeared in late 1990s in something that looked more like a political screed than a scientific paper. It came in the form of an email on the mailing list "BIOWAR-L," in September 1997:

> The lines filling our skies are not contrails. The lines are dispersed and may linger for hours . . .

> We now have proof that our goverment [*sic*] is using chemical agents on populated areas they are adding it to military jet fuel. Have you ever looked up at a vapor trail behind military aircraft flying so high a symbol of Americas power. Look again!!

> Commerical [*sic*] jets also leave a lovely (non-toxic) vapor trail when the heat from the turbines come in contact with the cool air condencing [*sic*] the water droplets into steam. Softly the lines defuse into the blue sky. So what is different about the military aircraft, the answer is simple, It's the Fuel JP-8+100 is some really bad stuff.

> When you look up over the skys [*sic*] of New York City on a clear, sunny morning you see the military aircraft making patterens [*sic*] across the sky with their vapor trails. The smoke is thick and does not go away. When it comes in contact with the sunlight it turns to a purple color, then desipates [*sic*] into a over cast Purple Haze. . . .

> this whole thing stinks of a Goverment DePopulation Program [*sic*].[25]

Two years later, an article by William Thomas on the *Environment News Service* website made the correlation between contrails and sickness. In it, Thomas included eyewitnesses who claimed that they experienced diarrhea and fatigue from "high altitude 'crop-dusting' by unidentified multi-engine aircraft."[26] Thomas speculated that the cause of these problems might be toxic residue from military jet fuel.

Thomas also pointed out a few anomalies that later became some of the mainstays of the chemtrail movement. Observers noted strange grid patterns that appeared in the skies above their homes, almost as if the planes were spraying the skies according to an established plan. To this, Thomas added one last important feature:

> Unlike normal contrails, which dissipate soon after a lone jet's passage, video taken by Wallace and Hanford show eerily silent silver jets streaming fat contrails from their wingtips in multiple, criss-cross patterns. But instead of dissipating like normal contrails, these white jet-trails coalesce into broad cloud-bands that gradually occlude crystal clear skies.[27]

Thomas took his story to the Art Bell Show in February 1999. It was an important step given the fact that Bell averaged nine million listeners a week, the fourth highest in the country at the time, right behind radio talk show celebrities like Rush Limbaugh and Howard Stern.[28] A contemporary *Time* magazine article commented: "Bell is a throwback. Unlike other broadcast biggies, he doesn't bully his callers or sensationalize his material. He knows it's sensational enough, so he sells it with a soothing baritone and the coaxing, folksy manner of a modern Arthur Godfrey. He doesn't whine or blurt, even if melodrama is swirling around him."[29] At the same time, they also noted:

> But in a sense, Bell couldn't be more contemporary. For one thing, he practically invented Y2K anxiety by spinning doomsday scenarios since early '98. More generally, his show taps into the millennial malaise; in the wake of Monicagate, it connects with people tired of little adulterous conspiracies and ready for a big interplanetary one. Americans have soured on political haranguing yet find issues like Kosovo too dense or distant. So where do they go? Out There, where The X-Files' Fox Mulder says the Truth is.[30]

So, in a very important sense, the Art Bell show came at a perfect time. Bell gave the chemtrail story gravity and legitimacy, while also neatly folding it into the new wave of conspiracy theories then flowing across the American media landscape.

The internet took it from there. Just as it had with the 9/11 Truther movement, the worldwide web was a perfect place for chemtrail believers to offer what they thought was compelling evidence as they debated cause and effect.

Expertise was not necessary in this arena, only skepticism and belief. Russ Tanner started Global Skywatch in 2009 and immediately picked up the thread that attributed health problems to chemtrails. But there was more to the story than making that one link. Tanner saw himself as a crusader against evil:

> We have one goal, and that is to stop chemtrails. Of course, achieving that goal will require many smaller steps which will only be achieved with your help.
>
> We must first expose chemtrails to the world.
>
> It has been shocking to discover just how blind the world is to the massive spraying activity that is occurring above our heads, nevertheless, exposing chemtrails to the public is the first step.
>
> After this, we must find a way to stop the world's most powerful and well-funded organization from spraying the public with known toxins.[31]

Tanner soon found a few allies from the scientific community. One of them was Frances Mangels, who described himself as "a retired USDA biologist" with a laundry list of related academic credentials that included a bachelor's degree in forestry, a master's in zoology, and thirty-five years in the US Forestry Service.[32] Mangels spoke of specific damage being done to soil and plants and traced the cause back to aerial spraying. Referring, for example, to samples taken around Mount Shasta, California, in 2009, Mangels said: "This rainwater is essentially poisonous."[33] He identified the culprits as aluminum, barium, and strontium, heavy metals he said did not belong in water or the soil.

Frances Mangels added a layer of authority and credibility that people like Russ Tanner and William Thomas lacked. By highlighting the trinity of elements—aluminum, barium, and strontium—Mangels identified specific items easily found on the periodic table. For his audience, he created a veneer of legitimate, specific science for the chemtrail conspiracy.

Cliff Carnicom built his own contribution to chemtrails on this same foundation. Unlike Mangels, his education did not really represent any expertise related to chemtrails. Carnicom earned a bachelor of science in photogrammetry [map-making] from the Civil Engineering Department at California State University at Fresno, California. On his website, Carnicom claims his "education encompasses a wide variety of disciplines, including geodetic science, advanced mathematics, engineering, statistics, physical sciences, accounting, computer science, and the life, environmental, and biological sciences."[34]

Carnicom does not look at the soil like Mangels, but instead focuses on the sky. He began examining what he described as "unnatural cloud formations" as early as 1999.[35] In a 2000 article titled "Contrail Physics" that attempts to explain the difference between a contrail and a chemtrail, Carnicom returned to the idea started by William Thomas about how long a contrail should last:

> Contrails composed of water vapor routinely dissipate, as the physics and chemistry of this model will demonstrate. As a separate and distinct set of events, clouds may form if temperature, relative humidity, and aerosol conditions are favorable to their development. If "contrails" by appearance transform into "clouds," it can be concluded that the material of composition is not water vapor.[36]

Carnicom basically argued that chemtrails were comprised of particles that did not have the same characteristics as water vapor. They were, in fact, made up of a larger, man-made material. To pursue his theory, he founded the Carnicom Institute in 2008. According to its mission statement:

> The purpose for which the corporation is organized is to conduct scientific, educational, environmental, and health research for the public welfare. This corporation shall also provide educational, scientific, legal, and media support for citizens at national and international levels and within local communities, either individually or collectively, with respect to education, environmental, and health issues that affect the general welfare.[37]

In effect, Cliff Carnicom is more than just a scientist. He is an advocate for global truth, addressing a conspiracy affecting the entire world. In some ways, it is the ultimate hero narrative.

Dane Wigington is another self-proclaimed investigator who tries to occupy the same space as an activist. Like Carnicom, Wigington also makes the claim of authority regarding chemtrails. According to a 2012 post on his website:

> Dane Wigington has an extensive background in solar engineering and was a former employee of Bechtel Power Corp. He has devoted the last ten years of his life studying climate change, weather modification, and geoengineering.[38]

Wigington claims involvement in chemtrails starting in 2004, when he began to notice solar panels on his property losing power due to what he explains as aerial spraying. From this basic conclusion, Wigington went on to create Geoengineeringwatch.org in 2009. The website is a clearing house for chemtrail conspiracy theories, offering an archive of local lab tests, notices of anti-chemtrail rallies, weekly broadcasts by Wigington, and a heavily censored message board for people interested in the topic.

Geoengineeringwatch.org has evolved over the years as Wigington faces challenges to his data. Responding to photos of World War II bomber formations producing massive contrail streams over Europe, for example, Wigington moved his timeline backward. When confronted with accumulating criticism of his ideas, Wigington doubled down on the scope and scale of the problem. He has gone so far as to claim, in 2015, that "There is no natural weather at this point" because of geoengineering.[39]

LOOK UP! CHEMTRAIL EVIDENCE

Dane Wigington often explains in interviews that "there's a mountain of data that confirm global solar radiation management programs had been deployed for many decades already."[40] The sources of this "mountain" vary. Some are very simple. They basically follow the chemtrail mantra: "Look up!" As a result, the internet, particularly YouTube, is filled with videos of planes in the sky. Many of these record patterns left by these planes that don't belong in nature. Some highlight trails behind planes with periodic gaps. Other videos show the results of these trails—hazy clouds or irregular cloud formations covering the horizon. Some are simply there to demonstrate how rare a genuine blue sky is today.

Another approach to evidence is following technology and the historical record. Geoengineeringwatch.org, for example, provides a list of 165 patents related to weather modification and climate control. The list goes back all the way to 1891 and continues to 2013.[41]

Table 7.1. Sample of Patents Cited by Geoengineeringwatch.org

Patent	Date	Description
2550324	April 24, 1951	Process for controlling weather
2908442	October 13, 1959	Method for dispersing natural atmospheric fogs and clouds
3534906	October 20, 1970	Control of atmospheric particles
3613992	October 19, 1971	Weather modification method
3899144	August 12, 1975	Powder contrail generation
RE29142	February 22, 1977	Combustible compositions for generating aerosols, particularly suitable for cloud modification and weather control and aerosolization process
5003186	March 26, 1991	Stratospheric Welsbach seeding for reduction of global warming

Source: Geoengineering Watch, "Extensive List of Patents," http://www.geoengineeringwatch.org/links-to -geoengineering-patents/.

Chemtrail advocates dissect the historical record even further by investigating official records related to weather and climate. Keyword searches can unearth dozens, if not hundreds, of documents related to both topics. One of the most often cited plans is *A Recommended National Program in Weather Modification*, published in November 1966. Compiled by NASA administrator Homer E. Newell, the study includes the Department of Defense, the Department of State, the Department of Commerce, and the Federal Aviation Agency, among many other parts of the federal government. This combination of national authority plays into fears of a "power structure" intent to hatch evil schemes against the people.

Weather as a Force Multiplier: Owning the Weather in 2025 presents a similar scenario. Written by seven Air Force officers in 1996, the paper's executive summary makes its purpose clear:

> In 2025, US aerospace forces can "own the weather" by capitalizing on emerging technologies and focusing development of those technologies to warfighting applications. Such a capability offers the war fighter tools to shape the battlespace in ways never before possible. It provides opportunities to impact operations across the full spectrum of conflict and is pertinent to all possible futures. The purpose of this paper is to outline a strategy for the use of a future weather-modification system to achieve military objectives rather than to provide a detailed technical road map.[42]

Later, the authors discuss an array of potential weaponized weather capabilities such as "Precipitation Enhancement, "Storm Enhancement/Modification," "Precipitation Denial," and something called "Space Weather."[43]

Chemtrail advocates also invoke science, particularly when they use complicated jargon to describe the effects of geoengineering. Dane Wigington does this fairly often, peppering his statements with terms like "anthropogenic" (pollution caused by humans), "nanoparticulates" (small particles), or "aluminum in free form."[44] Terminology is another way of using the argument from authority. Words can be used to lend credibility to statements that appear to be hard facts.

Chemtrail believers also cite hundreds of lab tests to make their point. Websites like Geoengineeringwatch.org contain compilations of water and soil samples taken from all around the United States by individual volunteers and sent to labs for testing. Dozens of these tests highlight the chemtrail footprint of aluminum, barium, and strontium. Some tests seem to highlight aluminum oxide that advocates claim is highly toxic and not found in nature. Others interpret lab tests to mean that "aluminum in free form" was present where it never belongs in the natural world.

Some chemtrail evidence is frankly more than a little strange. Russ Tanner argued back in 2016 that chemtrails are being altered to "short non-persistent plumes to fool the public."[45] In other words, the powers that be are fashioning chemtrails to look like contrails. But Tanner doesn't stop there.

Those spraying chemtrails would like nothing more than for you to believe that short, non-persistent plumes coming out of jets are harmless contrails.

If they convince you of this, then, when upgrades in equipment allow them to spray chemtrails which produce only short, non-persistent plumes, you will be convinced that they are perfectly harmless.

These upgrades in equipment are already occurring. Non-persistent chemtrails are now appearing all over the world.

But that's not the end of the story. Now, people in many areas are reporting no visible chemtrails at all. Have they gone away? No. They have only gone high-altitude.

I have personally witnessed chemtrails change from:

(1) Persistent chemtrails, to
(2) Non-persistent chemtrails, to
(3) Non-visible chemtrails (high-altitude chemtrails not visible from the ground),

and because I have a <u>sensitive sense of smell and taste</u>, I have an important story to tell.[46]

Tanner is basically saying that chemtrail conspirators have figured out a way to hide their activity from plain sight. Luckily for us, he can taste and smell their presence anyway.[47]

ANALYZING THE CHEMTRAIL DATA

Let's start with those videos that plaster the internet. What does the eye actually see? The hundreds of YouTube videos chronicling chemtrails moving through the sky actually provide pretty limited information. Distance and picture resolution matter. A smart phone or an old camcorder do not provide much detail on the plane as far its altitude, speed, or direction are concerned. The same is true regarding weather at altitude, specifically air temperature, humidity, or wind speed. Many of the early claims made about the mysterious nature of chemtrail aircraft are rooted in the simple fact that recording devices cannot see tail numbers or any other identifying markings on an object five or six miles above the Earth.

Luckily, the internet is an easy resource to check against these videos. If the time and location are available, we can now find information on flight paths. There are websites like planefinder.net that allow anyone to find a specific commercial plane. The same resource helps us explain all the "strange" patterns—lines that cross, grids—appearing in the sky. Basically, there are more long-haul flights today than there were twenty years ago, producing more examples for people to see.[48] Planes travel through all the points of the compass as they maneuver around the continental United States or any other place on earth.

The claims about patents also deserve some attention. There are two things to always remember about patents. First, most are just proposals or concepts that are legally registered to hinder competition. Second, most patents have never reached even the "proof of concept" stage and are theories or bright ideas rather than reality.

If you look carefully at all the patents featured on Geoengineeringwatch. org, most deal with cloud seeding, which is different from actual geoengineering programs such as solar radiation management or carbon reduction.[49] More importantly, an overwhelming majority of patents cited by Dane Wigington do not contain the trio of elements—aluminum, barium, and strontium—he frequently mentions as one way to identify chemtrails. Strontium appears in only *three of 165* patents listed on the Geoengineering Watch website patents list. All three elements are in only *two of 165* patents.[50]

Next, we should spend some time on chemtrails, geoengineering, and official plans. Having spent much of my life in the archives, I can testify to the fact that there are thousands of file folders filled with government plans. Officials like having options for any number of contingencies, the more the better. Meeting this demand keeps planning staffs busy. The Cold War was famous for this dynamic. Nuclear attack plans with codenames like DROP-SHOT, HALFMOON, or OFFTACKLE are part of the historical record.[51] In some ways, official plans are like patents. They provide a possible proof of concept, an option for any event regardless of how likely, but not proof of action. The 1996 Air Force *Weather as a Force Multiplier* article included a clear disclaimer:

> *2025* is a study designed to comply with a directive from the chief of staff of the Air Force to examine the concepts, capabilities, and technologies the United States will require to remain the dominant air and space force in the future. Presented on 17 June 1996, this report was produced in the Department of Defense

school environment of academic freedom and in the interest of advancing concepts related to national defense. The views expressed in this report are those of the authors and do not reflect the official policy or position of the United States Air Force, Department of Defense, or the United States government.

This report contains *fictional representations* of future situations/scenarios.[52]

Some plans were real and actually implemented, but what did they actually do? A close study of the 1966 *Recommended National Program in Weather Modification* reveals qualifications expressed in its introduction:

Over the past twenty years experiments have been conducted on weather modification, particularly on the effects of seeding clouds with such materials as silver iodide crystals. The results are limited. Under suitable circumstances it has been possible to augment precipitation by ten to twenty percent, and to reduce the frequency of fire-producing lightning strikes. Effects on hail production have been noted, sometimes suppression and sometimes augmentation.[53]

Most of the document addresses mitigation projects for forest fires, such as Project Skyfire, which appeared in 1967.[54] In much the same way, Project Popeye is one of the most commonly cited examples appearing in the chemtrail discussion, but it focused on cloud seeding to affect local weather and had nothing to do with geoengineering.

Lab tests appear to offer solid evidence of chemtrails, but appearances can be deceiving. There are a few ways to approach the reams of tests appearing on Geoengineeringwatch.org and other websites. One is to look at the basic nature of the elements cited. Aluminum oxide appears frequently in *What in the World Are They Spraying?* and online posts as one of the trinity of substances to be found in chemtrails. Michael Murphy and Dane Wigington repeatedly referred to the presence of "toxic" aluminum oxide in air and water.

This is simply not true. A basic search on Wikipedia reveals the following: "Being fairly *chemically inert* and white, aluminum oxide is a favored filler for plastics. Aluminum oxide is a common ingredient in sunscreen and is sometimes also present in cosmetics such as blush, lipstick, and nail polish."[55] In fact, during a 2010 radio interview, Denis Raincourt challenged Murphy on his definition of aluminum with these facts. Murphy ducked and dodged Raincourt and feebly began his own Gish gallop to avoid answering the question.[56] Over the longer term, challenges like these were likely one of the reasons Murphy and Wigington changed their approach by claiming that "aluminum in free form" was being found in chemtrails. It is a classic example of "moving the goalposts" in a debate.

Too many chemtrail theorists also routinely misread lab tests. One of most common mistakes is to confuse the method detection limit (MDL) for a normal limit found in nature. The MDL designates how much of a material is necessary to register on a test. At one point, Dane Wigington claimed extreme levels of aluminum in a rainfall test by comparing what the test found (188 parts per billion) to the MDL (30 parts per billion).[57] He took it to mean that levels were more than six times normal when, in fact, they were higher than the test minimum.[58]

Wigington often ignores basic facts or misrepresents them. Any college geology textbook will indicate that aluminum makes up 8 percent of the Earth's crust. The Environmental Protection Agency allows up to 200 µg/l in drinking water. In other words, by virtue of basic geology and EPA standards, what Wigington found was normal.[59] More recent claims that aluminum in "free form" does not exist in nature is true, but not relevant. Free-form aluminum is rare in nature, but that is not what lab tests find. They are designed to measure trace elements, not types of aluminum.[60]

Lastly, there are serious practical limits to just how metals could be sprayed onto the Earth. Trying to reconstruct such a scenario is similar to figuring out how many demolition charges were placed on World Trade Center 7. In the case of chemtrails, it comes down to working out the basic factors necessary to spray material from an aircraft for hundreds of miles. Except that, taking into account the weight of fuel, the amount of storage space needed for the spray, the displacement of the plane, and a whole lot of important variables, it is impossible.[61] One researcher estimated that it would take something like ten million pounds of aluminum to cover every acre in California with an ounce of the material.[62] People have also tested a more specific claim made by Francis Mangels about increasing the amount of aluminum in Siskiyou County, California, soil. In order to raise the percentage from 1.3 percent to 1.6 percent, the amount Mangels believes to be caused by aerial spraying, it would take 21.92 million tons of aluminum oxide, almost half the total world production.[63]

CONCLUSIONS:
WHAT TO MAKE OF THE CHEMTRAIL PHENOMENA

Chemtrails are similar, in many respects, to 9/11 conspiracies. Advocates seem more vested in who the antagonists are and why they are acting rather than how they accomplish their evil schemes. The chemtrail conspiracy is big, no doubt. The "global power structure," to use Dane Wigington phrase, is the primary culprit and scapegoat.[64] They are responsible for geoengineering programs over the last twenty years, although that timeline and the reasons for the conspiracy are a constantly moving target.

When they press forward to explain just how all this is happening, chemtrail believers fall down hard. In too many cases with respect to basic math, physics, climatology, soil biology, or meteorology, among many complex scientific fields, the facts do not match their claims. Chemtrail advocates do no favors to the study of history either. They constantly rewrite the timeline as they wrestle with the fact that evidence of contrails goes back decades before the scientific community ever considered geoengineering. A number of websites—Metabunk.com and Contrailscience.com—have emerged to provide a constant, factual commentary on chemtrail claims.

Yet even the absence of evidence seems to make no difference. The strange debate about "non-visible" chemtrails and weather patterns is built upon something that can't be seen. This particular rabbit hole is a good illustration of how logic fails the chemtrail community along with their grasp of facts. One writer on the Metabunk website put it this way:

> This long-term observation should be a clue to them that weather causes what they fear, not the other way around.
>
> Instead of incorporating the observation to modify their hypothesis, they conform the observation to fit the hypothesis.[65]

So, it seems to be faith and not facts are what drives this particular conspiracy. Stubborn belief about the machinations of a shadowy global power elite overshadows complicated factual stories. Weather and climate are complex, as are chemistry, physics, and meteorology. What the chemtrails conspiracy offers is a series of shortcuts, a simple scapegoat, and a simplified method.

Current events help chemtrail conspiracy along and give it new life almost every news cycle. We live in a time when tragedy, ushered in by human error or deliberate action, seems to accumulate at an almost daily rate. This is particularly true when news breaks on the latest fires in the Western United States or hurricanes in Florida and the Gulf Coast. On an even more personal level, chemtrails help explain and reinforce modern concerns about health. The number of elderly people accumulates in America with each passing year. Alzheimer's rates follow accordingly.[66] New science helps identify new sicknesses and new threats to our well-being. Much of this work is obviously well intended, but with each newly discovered strain of drug resistant bacteria, is a newly reinforced sense of helplessness and paranoia. For many, the easiest remedy—to connect the dots for all these problems—is to just look up.

(Public Domain via Wikimedia Commons: https://commons.wikimedia.org/wiki/File:Conspiracy_theorist_(48555437426).jpg.)

Chapter Eight

The 2016 Election

People no longer voted for candidates they liked or were excited by. They voted against candidates they hated. At protests and marches, the ruling emotions were disgust and rage. The lack of idealism, and especially the lack of any sense of brotherhood or common purpose with the other side (i.e., liberals and conservatives unable to imagine a productive future with each other, or even to see themselves as citizens of the same country), was striking.[1]

—Matt Taibbi, 2017

REDEFINING UGLY

We can be a pretty ugly country once you get down to it, at least as far as politics are concerned. If you follow many contemporary media accounts, it seems as if the Trump presidency has driven the country off a cliff. His term in the White House was a favorite lightning rod, repeatedly depicted as an ongoing attack on democracy. The discussion often focuses on the decline of democratic norms, the "unwritten rules of toleration and restraint" that define much of how American works.[2] Examples range from the treatment of the media as promoters of "fake news" or as "enemies of the American people," to the seemingly open endorsement of violence against political opponents and a form of hyper-partisanship that allows the wholesale abandonment of facts, or the embracement of "alternative facts" for the sake of hurting a political enemy.[3] Authors Steven Levitsky and Daniel Ziblatt highlight the former president's "reckless attacks on democratic norms" but offer that this danger was offset by the fact that Trump was a "weak and inept leader."[4]

How true is this complaint, both as it applies to the person and his time? The fact of the matter is that political ugliness goes back a long way. In reality, Americans have an extensive history of trashing each other's parties, institutions, and each other. It is part of our tradition, even if most people today think their own time is unique.

Bitter partisanship is as old as America. John Adams used the 1798 Sedition Act against Republican opponents of his administration, indicting fifteen and convicting ten members of the opposing party.[5] When Thomas Jefferson ran for president in 1800, Federalists warned that his election would result in disaster for the young country: "dwellings in flames, hoary hairs bathed in blood, female chastity violated . . . children writhing on the pike and halberd."[6] Anecdotes about Andrew Jackson's stupidity followed him throughout his entire career. When he received an honorary degree from Harvard in 1833, school alumni John Quincy Adams said to the president of the university: "as myself an affectionate child of our alma mater, I would not be present to witness her disgrace in conferring her highest literary honors upon a barbarian who could not write a sentence of grammar and hardly could spell his own name."[7] Abraham Lincoln was regularly savaged by his enemies. The editor of the *Charleston Mercury* described him as: "A horrid looking wretch he is, sooty and scoundrelly in aspect, a cross between the nutmeg dealer, the horse swapper, and the night man, a creature 'fit evidently for petty treason, small strategems, and all sorts of spoils.'"[8] It was a tame reference compared to the commander of the Army of the Potomac, George B. McClellan, who referred to his president as "the original gorilla."[9]

Still, even with all that said, we might have reached a new low in terms of partisan bitterness during the campaign season of 2016. It is interesting to note that conspiracies were an important part of election mudslinging when, for example, the Trump campaign maintained that Ted Cruz's father was involved in the conspiracy to kill Kennedy.[10]

"Pizzagate" did a better job of capturing the essential weirdness of the campaign year. The so-called scandal surfaced online in November 2016 as a story that linked recently released emails from Clinton campaign chair John Podesta to a pedophile ring that was apparently working out of the Comet Ping Pong Pizzeria, a DC area restaurant. The evidence presented was a weird mishmash of pictures of children randomly taken from unrelated internet sites, snippets from Podesta's emails represented as a secret code for sex with minors, and hidden locations in the restaurant itself. The *Washington City Paper* characterized the story this way:

Trump supporters on sites like Reddit and 4chan have long been looking for a stronger connection between Clinton and Jeffrey Epstein, a financial tycoon and sex offender whose plane Bill Clinton sometimes used.

The Wikileaks release of Clinton campaign chair John Podesta's hacked emails inspired a feverish, and mostly hapless, search for salacious scandal evidence, while PolitiFact calls the evidence for a Clinton sex network "ridiculously thin."[11]

For most people, the whole thing was laughable because it was so ridiculous. That is, until Edgar Maddison Welch entered the Comet Ping Pong Pizzeria on December 4, armed with an assault rifle and other weapons. Welch later told police that he was there to "self-investigate" the claims that the restaurant was a front for a child sex ring.[12]

A common denominator shared by many conspiracies in 2016 was Trump himself. In the past, candidates would almost never let the public know what fringe beliefs they embraced, regardless of how deeply felt. Richard Nixon possessed the political discipline necessary to conceal his virulent anti-Semitism when he indulged in his own private conspiracy theories. It was one of the reasons the Watergate tapes were so shocking when they were released in 1974 and exposed the depths of Nixon's hate and paranoia. Donald Trump, in contrast, embraced controversial conspiracies and folded them right into his campaign. His rambling monologues incorporated fringe belief right into the Republican Party platform and became part of the "new normal" on the 2016 campaign trail.

ELECTION CLAIMS AND EVIDENCE (I): THUNDER ON THE RIGHT

The ongoing furor surrounding Hillary Clinton's emails is a good example of a right-wing conspiracy theory with serious legs. The basic premise starts off as fairly simple. The story emerged in 2015 that Hillary Clinton, while serving as secretary of state, used a private cell phone and email server for thousands of official emails. The practice was not officially prohibited when Clinton came onboard in the State Department. But it was a sloppy process that allowed people, who should have known better, to bypass basic security protocols. In other words, it seemed to go against common sense. It didn't pass the smell test.

Clinton's activity triggered a series of internal investigations from the State Department, the FBI, and the intelligence community. In 2014, responding to a request by the State Department, Clinton released almost thirty thousand emails, leaving out personal communications. In August 2015, a special review by the CIA and the National Geospatial Intelligence Agency confirmed that at least five of the documents contained classified information.[13] Over the next six months, Clinton provided thousands of additional emails from her server and, with each new batch, authorities unearthed additional classified information, some of it at the top-secret level. In May 2016, the State Department inspector general reported that

> At a minimum, Secretary Clinton should have surrendered all emails dealing with Department business before leaving government service and, because she did not do so, she did not comply with the Department's policies that were implemented in accordance with the Federal Records Act.[14]

A separate FBI investigation concluded that eighty-one email chains contained classified information ranging from "confidential" to "top secret/special access programs" when they were sent between 2009 and 2013.[15] The Bureau did not find any evidence of outside parties accessing the information by "cyber means." In other words, there was no support for claims that foreign governments had acquired the information.[16]

Unfortunately, these carefully worded official conclusions were a tiny bump in the road to the news industry. The pundits inhabiting cable news had no interest in explaining how or why government agencies decided to retroactively reclassify select documents. The talking heads also had no patience for the time it took agencies to process thousands of emails before they could be made public. They jumped to conclusions that fed our frantic news cycle. What made this worse was Hillary Clinton's habit of treating the email issue like a lawyer, constantly parsing her role in the official investigations. It did not help when she said, in a 2015 interview:

> Well, let's start from the beginning. Everything I did was permitted. There was no law. There was no regulation. There was nothing that did not give me the full authority to decide how I was going to communicate. Previous secretaries of state have said they did the same thing. And people across the government knew that I used one device—maybe it was because I am not the most technically capable person and wanted to make it as easy as possible.[17]

FBI director James Comey delivered the final punctuation mark on the story in a letter to Congress literally at the end of the 2016 presidential campaign. Comey's actual language is pretty bland: "Although the FBI cannot yet assess whether or not this material may be significant, and I cannot predict how long it will take us to complete this additional work, I believe it is important to update your Committees about our efforts in light of my previous testimony."[18] There are no bombshells or major revelations in the Comey letter. However, what the FBI director did, from his position of authority in the American power structure, was very publicly resuscitate the issue of emails only days before the general election.

Throughout 2016, Donald Trump used the email controversy to promote his "Crooked Hillary" meme during the campaign:

To cover up her corrupt dealings, Hillary Clinton illegally stashed her State Department emails on a private server.

Her server was easily hacked by foreign governments—perhaps even by her financial backers in Communist China—putting all of America in danger.

Then there are the 33,000 emails she deleted.

While we may not know what is in those deleted emails, our enemies probably do.[19]

Trump very effectively used the email controversy to challenge Clinton's legitimacy by exploiting doubts about her judgment and trustworthiness. Although none of his claims were based on facts, the constant refrain was enough to undercut support among potential Clinton voters, particularly in key battleground states like Michigan, Ohio, Wisconsin, and Pennsylvania. According to a September 2016 Gallup poll, more voters saw Trump (35 percent) as more honest than Clinton (33 percent).[20]

The conspiracy theory regarding illegal voting also plagued the 2016 presidential contest. Only days after the election ended, internet sources, particularly Alex Jones's Infowars, claimed that three million illegal immigrants cast ballots in November.[21] Jones was basically repeating a claim already made by Greg Phillips at VoteFraud.org. After his inauguration, Trump picked up the thread from Phillips in a tweet, "Look forward to seeing final results of VoteStand. Gregg Phillips and crew say at least 3,000,000 votes were illegal. We must do better!"[22] It was a big claim that demanded big proof. However, when mainstream outlets started looking into Phillips' assertion, they found out that he never provided any evidence of it.[23]

To answer the question of voter fraud once and for all, President Trump signed an executive order in May 2017 that created the Presidential Advisory Commission on Election Integrity. Vice President Mike Pence chaired the commission, launching an official federal investigation into allegations made on Infowars six months earlier. It was an interesting, somewhat surreal and familiar moment where a conspiracy theory guided officials in Washington. In some respects, it was an echo of probes into the Kennedy assassination conducted in the mid-1970s.

Funded at a cost of $500,000 and with a mandate for a two-year investigation, the commission ran into trouble early and often.[24] Statisticians questioned the claimed extent of voter fraud, which was very rare, according to multiple studies on the subject. Most states simply refused to comply with requests from Pence's commission because they were required to protect private information (e.g., Social Security numbers) on voter rolls.[25]

The commission finally disbanded at the end of 2017, its mission unfulfilled and no evidence of three million illegal votes uncovered. None of this has stopped new claims from resurfacing after every election since. When Democrat candidate Doug Jones defeated Republican Roy Moore in a 2017 Alabama special election, *Breitbart* ran multiple stories on the issue, one maintaining that George Soros had funded a campaign to register convicted felons in the state.[26] In the aftermath of the 2018 congressional midterms, the claim resurfaced yet again. The David Harris website promoted a story that one hundred thousand illegal aliens were registered to vote in Pennsylvania, one reason that Republicans suffered serious losses in the rustbelt swing state.[27]

In most of these cases, the truth was the least important element of the story. Whether applied to State Department emails or illegal votes, it was the audience that mattered more than the evidence. The idea of private servers stuffed with classified information and millions of votes made by illegal aliens played to the confirmation bias of people who distrusted the system and disliked both Hillary Clinton and immigrants. Looking back on the 2016 election year, many commentators attributed these tendencies to a political base that lacked education and diversity.[28] As we will see in chapters 10 and 11, reducing an election to white, "low information" voters barely scratched the surface of the problem.[29]

CONSPIRACY CLAIMS AND EVIDENCE (II): LIGHTNING ON THE LEFT

If conspiracy theories were deeply embedded among conservatives, the same was true among Americans who skewed to the ideological left. Scandals given political oxygen at the national level tend to have a long shelf life. That was true during the Red Scare of the 1940s and 1950s. It was also true after the 2016 general election when, strangely, Russians re-entered the conspiracy sphere to a degree probably not witnessed since the glory days of Joe McCarthy.

The Russia story is actually a series of complicated, overlapping stories. The first culprit to surface was Michael Flynn, a retired three-star general who joined his son's consulting firm in 2014 and served as a paid lobbyist for the Turkish government prior to the US election. Flynn received more than $500,000 for his effort.[30] In 2015, he spoke at a Russia Today (RT) conference. RT is a news outlet funded by the Russian government.[31]

None of this would have particularly mattered if Flynn had continued a career as a well-paid lobbyist. Unfortunately, he did not. Flynn was sworn in on January 22, 2017, as Trump's national security advisor. Flynn's real problems began at that point, when the news emerged that he had met with Russian ambassador regarding a UN resolution on Israel, something he had not disclosed before returning to government service. Barely three weeks into his new job, Flynn was forced to resign on February 13 over the issue and later pleaded guilty to making false statements to the FBI about his Russian contacts.[32]

The Flynn resignation turned out to be just the tip of the Russian iceberg. Ongoing media stories about Russian dealings with Trump businesses began to appear after his inauguration and illustrated years of corrupt business practices. The *New Republic* revealed that convicted Russian mobster David Bogatin admitted to purchasing condos in the New York Trump Towers in the 1980s to launder money.[33] Business ventures between Trump properties and Russian investors continued and expanded over the next twenty-five years. In 2015, the Trump Taj Mahal was fined $10 million—the highest penalty ever levied by the federal government against a casino—and admitted to having "willfully violated" anti-money-laundering regulations for years.[34]

The term "collusion" became the new watchword as more and more information about Trump and Russians came to light. It applied to series of alleged economic, political, and foreign policy relationships. As these revelations began to appear, conspiracy theories kept pace with them. Louise Mensch, for example, wrote a March 2017 editorial in the *New York Times* that listed a cabal of Russian operatives active in the US government. In the article, Mensch, a former member of the British Parliament, posed a series of hypothetical questions to a host of Republican politicians and political operatives dealing with not just corruption but deliberate interference with elections.[35]

The election angle gave the Russia story legs. Corrupt business dealings are almost an American tradition, easy to delegate to background noise. Stories about manipulating American democracy were different. They tapped into a deep well of political paranoia stoked by the 2016 presidential run. In a strange historical twist, the Russia allegations also forced Republicans, the party of red baiters like Joe McCarthy and Richard Nixon, to defend themselves against charges of treason.

As political operatives and media pundits flocked to the story, the intelligence community weighed in. Two weeks before Trump's inaugural, the Office of National Intelligence (ONI) assessed the election:

> Russian efforts to influence the 2016 US presidential election represent the most recent expression of Moscow's longstanding desire to undermine the US-led liberal democratic order, but these activities demonstrated a significant escalation in directness, level of activity, and scope of effort compared to previous operations.

> We assess Russian President Vladimir Putin ordered an influence campaign in 2016 aimed at the US presidential election. Russia's goals were to undermine public faith in the US democratic process, denigrate Secretary Clinton, and harm her electability and potential presidency. We further assess Putin and the Russian Government developed a clear preference for President-elect Trump. We have high confidence in these judgments.[36]

At approximately the same moment, the prestigious Center for Strategic and International Studies published the *Kremlin Playbook*, an in-depth examination of Russian efforts to reassert its influence after the Cold War.[37]

Prompted by rising concerns, the Justice Department authorized a special counsel "to investigate Russian interference with the 2016 presidential election and related matters."[38] Led by former FBI director Robert Mueller, the investigation rapidly developed a series of indictments, plea agreements, and convictions that reached directly into the White House. By the end of 2018, the list included Michael Flynn, former campaign manager Paul Manafort, staffers who worked on the campaign or personally for Trump, fourteen Russian nationals, three Russian companies, and twelve Russian GRU (military intelligence) officers.[39]

Even though a redacted version of the Mueller Report became public in April 2019, a series of questions echoing the Watergate conspiracy and the downfall of Richard Nixon remain: How much did the president know? How involved was he in all of this activity?

Despite all of the hype surrounding the Mueller investigation, it provided few complete answers. A December 2018 court document submitted by Mueller indicates that President Trump was directly implicated in campaign finance violations.[40] However, according to Mueller's original mandate, these were "related activities" not directly tied to Russia. The wording in the final report is sometimes painfully obscure and framed by legal language. For example, in the introduction to volume two, the report states:

> if we had confidence after a thorough investigation of the facts that the President clearly did not commit obstruction of justice, we would so state. Based on the facts and the applicable legal standards, however, we are unable to reach that judgment. The evidence we obtained about the President's actions and intent present difficult issues that prevent us from conclusively determining that no criminal conduct occurred. Accordingly, while this report does not conclude that the President committed a crime, it also does not exonerate him.[41]

Reading this statement, both sides claimed victory. A number of Senate and House Democrats vowed to pursue impeachment, while the party leadership attempted to hold them back. Senator Elizabeth Warren of Massachusetts was the first to include impeachment in her 2020 presidential campaign.[42] For his own part, the president celebrated "complete and total exoneration" after the Mueller Report went public.[43]

FINAL ANALYSIS: MAINSTREAM CRAZY?

Trump's inauguration seems to have ushered the country into a post-information era. Our "new normal" allows any accusation to morph into a conclusion. Confirmation bias drives a lot of our debates. Many authors have urged caution. As Colin Dickey pointed out in a *New Republic* article about conspiracies coming from the left: "But a shell company does not automatically mean money laundering. This form of internet sleuthing is little more than garden-variety inductive fallacy: While the underlying premise is true, the conclusion could well be false."[44] *Rolling Stone* writer Matt Taibbi argued for caution regarding stories about Russian collusion. The joint intelligence report about Russian interference in the election established links to the Putin government but not to Trump or his campaign staff. To assume more, was to "connect the dots" without proof.

> The notion that the president is either an agent or a useful idiot of the Russian state is so freely accepted in some quarters that Beck Bennett's shirtless representation of Putin palling with Alec Baldwin's Trump is already a no-questions-asked yuks routine for the urban smart set.
>
> And yet, this is an extraordinarily complex tale that derives much of its power from suppositions and assumptions.[45]

Taibbi's point is well taken. As much as we assume conspiracy theories live in the minds of the political right wing and that liberals could never fall into the rabbit hole, both sides seem equally open to them.[46] In his political autopsy of the 2016 election, *Insane Clown President*, Taibbi observes that neither party seemed willing to accept responsibility for its failures. This was true of mainstream Republicans as well as Clinton Democrats.[47] Colin Dickey's conclusion was more pointed: "As it turns out, though, the left wasn't smarter than the right; it simply wasn't terrified enough."[48]

They are now. And angry. And retaking legislative seats in state and federal governments. The slow blue wave eventually brought Joe Biden to the White House. Where it leads from there is an open question. But the history we know highlighted some potentially troubling trends. One example appeared in a December 2018 *New York Times* story covering a speech made by Elizabeth Warren at Morgan State University:

> "The rules are rigged because the rich and powerful have bought and paid for too many politicians," Ms. Warren said. "And if we dare to ask questions, they will try to divide us. Pit white working people against black and brown working people so they won't band together and demand real change. The rich and powerful want us pointing fingers at each other so we won't notice they are getting richer and more powerful.
>
> "Two sets of rules: one for the wealthy and the well-connected. And one for everybody else," she said. "Two sets of rules: one for white families. And one for everybody else. That's how a rigged system works. And that's what we need to change."[49]

A great deal of what Warren said is true. As a country, we still struggle with racism and ongoing problems of wealth, opportunity, application of the law, and a long list of other factors shaping daily American life.

Problems begin when politics are applied to the truth. Donald Trump ran in 2016 as a populist. As Warren prepared for her 2020 presidential run, she touched on similar themes, waging class war and frequently using the "system is rigged" catchphrase in her speeches.[50] Her rhetoric could be the start a meaningful policy debate that might begin a new era of productive policy. Or her words could simply be pandering to our fears, triggering yet another round of name-calling, scapegoating, backlash, and additional self-inflicted wounds to American politics. We will discuss where and how these ideas landed as part of the 2020 campaign in chapter 11.

(Public domain via Wikimedia Commons: https://commons.wikimedia.org/wiki/
File:COVID-19_Slogan.png.)

Chapter Nine

The 2020 "Plandemic"

It's going to disappear. One day, it's like a miracle, it will disappear.[1]

—President Donald J. Trump, February 28, 2020

Well, the way you get ahead of it is that as—as I try to explain to people, that I want people to assume that I'm over—or that we are overreacting, because if it looks like you're overreacting, you're probably doing the right thing.[2]

—Dr. Anthony Fauci, March 15, 2020

FORCES OF NATURE

There are points in time when a generation experiences a once-in-a-lifetime disaster. Some, like a category 5 hurricane or a rampant wildfire, can occur naturally, although more often in the recent past. Other catastrophes are man-made. War and its consequences—death, wounds, social dislocation, economic calamity—plague the human race and show no signs whatsoever of disappearing any time soon.

Disease is another constant threat. Beyond the regular undercurrent of chronic problems coming from poor diet, nonpotable water, new strains of insect-born maladies, and the like, are recurring epidemics and pandemics, which are happening with greater frequency than most people realized before 2020. A little more than ten years earlier, the H1N1 swine flu pandemic killed an as many as eighteen thousand Americans.[3]

The COVID-19 pandemic that struck the world was on an order of magnitude worse than swine flu. At the time of this writing in May 2021, global cases surpassed 167.4 million, with more than 3.4 million deaths. Total cases in the United States stood at 28.3 million and approximately 594,000 dead.[4] Cold weather brought with it a predicted surge in sickness that touched nearly every corner of the country. Rural areas, which largely escaped the first wave of sickness, were particularly hard hit. A national vaccination program has made a significant impact on COVID-19, although global access remains limited.

To just about any reasonable person, the moment called for cool heads, national planning, and a consensus on how best to address a threat to millions of lives and the basic underpinnings of the country. And yet, as 2020 ground relentlessly forward, none of this happened. Instead of finding common cause, the United States was overwhelmed and divided by dissent, at times informed by older antivaccination sentiments, in other cases by virtue of new conspiracy theories linking medical authority to corrupted government power. Collectively, they moved conspiracy belief from the fringe firmly into the mainstream of public debate.

It was a direction propelled and sharpened by an unprecedented degree of political partisanship and social division left over from the 2016 presidential election. Bitter arguments seemed to seep into every part of American life. It all made for great cable television and supplied late-night comedians with a seemingly endless stream of material. But there was a cost to this endless cycle of ridicule and reaction at a moment when literally millions of lives hung in the balance.

THE "PLANDEMIC" ARRIVES

The year started with news of an outbreak in the province of Wuhan, China. Initial reports noted what appeared to be a variation of a "pneumonialike illness," although exact details were unclear at the time. News organizations indicated that the disease was not "readily spread" between humans.[5] However, within a matter of weeks, COVID-19 reached Japan, South Korea, Thailand, and western Europe. The first official COVID-19 case in the United States appeared on January 21 in Washington State.

At first, the official US response was cautious and tempered by a lack of information. Despite multiple attempts to render assistance to Chinese health officials and share information with the Centers for Disease Control and Prevention (otherwise known as the CDC), Beijing initially kept a close hold on the nature and spread of the virus, something that became the source of significant frustration among American health professionals. On January 31, the Trump administration announced a travel ban on foreign nationals from China. It did not include family members of American citizens or permanent residents.[6]

In a relatively short period of time, it was clear that the situation was worsening. By March 26, there were a total of 81,321 COVID-19 cases in the United States.[7] State governments, particularly in New York, which was hardest hit in the early stages of the pandemic, implemented a series of measures designed to mitigate the spread of COVID-19. Individual governors began coordinating a response at the regional level. On March 20, Andrew Cuomo said in an announcement: "We remain in constant communication with our neighboring states to ensure we are establishing a set of uniform rules and regulations for the entire region. These temporary closures are not going to be easy, but they are necessary to protecting the health and safety of New Yorkers and all Americans."[8] As restrictions multiplied, they triggered a ripple effect throughout the country. Businesses shuttered and a predictable surge in unemployment followed soon after. In just four days in March, the Dow Jones Industrial Average plummeted 6,400 points, losing 26 percent of its total value.[9]

These early state actions provoked a significant backlash from some Americans. Mass rallies against new state health mandates followed in Texas, Missouri, Pennsylvania, and Michigan. Dozens of protestors came armed with civilian versions of assault weapons, body armor, and other military paraphernalia.[10] While many people turned out to register their complaints about the economic hardships caused by new restrictions, a vocal contingent rejected the whole concept that COVID-19 even existed. At a "You Can't Close America" rally in Austin, Texas, Infowars conspiracy pundit Alex Jones promoted two contradictory positions, denouncing the pandemic as a: "Chi-Comm globalist bioweapons attack," but also proclaiming that "America knows it's a hoax."[11] Matters did not improve when President Trump entered the fray, tweeting messages like: "LIBERATE MICHIGAN!" and "LIBER-ATE MINNESOTA!" on April 17.[12]

* * *

Slightly more than two weeks later, a twenty-six-minute video titled "Plandemic Movie" entered into this tumult on social media. Most of it is an interview of Dr. Judy Mikovits by "filmmaker/humanitarian" Mikki Willis.[13] The first part of "Plandemic" establishes Mikovits's credentials and offers a teaser about the heart of the conspiracy: "Dr. Judy Mikovits has been called one of the most accomplished scientists of her generation. . . . So, you made a discovery that conflicted with the agreed-upon narrative."[14] For all intents and purposes, Mikovits is the hero of the story. After establishing her authority, Willis goes on further to say: "At the height of her career, Dr. Mikovits published a blockbuster article in the journal *Science*. The controversial article sent shock waves through the scientific community, as it revealed that the common use of animal and human fetal tissues was unleashing devastating plagues of chronic diseases."[15]

The film then pivots to characterize Mikovits as a victim who was punished for her research breakthroughs. She describes herself as a "fugitive from justice" who was arrested without charges and then issued a gag order to both retaliate against her groundbreaking research and silence her challenge to the status quo.[16] At this moment, Mikovits specifically identifies the villain in the story, the director of the National Institute of Allergy and Infectious Diseases, Dr. Anthony Fauci. Mikovits claims that Fauci: "threatened her with arrest if she visited the National Institutes of Health to participate in a study to validate her chronic fatigue research."[17] She goes on to add the bombshell that Fauci financially benefitted from a career of mishandling responses to disease at the cost of millions of lives.

Mikovits finishes out her story with a number of claims about the COVID-19 virus, specifically that it was the result of "manipulation" in military and civilian laboratories, not nature.[18] Following her earlier line of argument, she went on to say that, like HIV, current research into COVID-19 was dedicated to profit and not public health.[19] Regarding mask use, the biochemist noted: "Wearing the mask literally activates your own virus. You're getting sick from your own reactivated coronavirus expressions, and if it happens to be SARS Cov-V-2, then you've got a big problem."[20]

In Mikovits's narrative, she is a crusader, a lonely voice fighting against what she portrays as systemic corruption in the medical profession and government. From her perspective, the stakes involve millions, if not billions, of lives in America and around the world: "If we don't stop this now, we can not only forget our republic and our freedom, but we can forget humanity because we'll be killed by this agenda."[21]

HISTORICAL CONTEXT: STRANGE DAYS REDUX

In many respects, the contentiousness emerging in the earliest days of the pandemic simply was a continuation of the angry stew bubbling out of the 2016 presidential election. Conspiracy-tinged conflict broke out literally on the day of Donald Trump's inauguration as pundits encamped on both sides of the political divide entered into a pitched battle over just how big the crowd was around the US Capitol Building. It continued into immigration, tax cuts, and, in the final days before COVID-19 appeared, made its grand finale with President Trump's first impeachment.

An array of contemporary media outlets channeled and reinforced a constant stream of animosity. Speaking about cable television in 2019, Matt Taibbi was typically blunt when he observed: "We sold anger, and we did it mainly by feeding audiences what they wanted to hear. Mostly, this involved cranking out stories about people our viewers loved to hate."[22] Liberal viewers gravitated to CNN and MSNBC, while conservatives flocked to Fox News. It was an almost perfect example of confirmation bias come to life in electronic form. Both sides—viewer and broadcasters alike—fired off rhetorical broadsides, vested in the belief that they were not only better informed than the other side but also simply better people. This cleavage came to shape how Americans discussed politics, culture, faith, and a seemingly endless array of issues.

One particular flashpoint involved modern disease and vaccinations against it. A growing body of Americans challenged the basic legitimacy of inoculations. Many more still portrayed vaccinations as a threat, directly linking them to childhood developmental disabilities. Celebrity "anti-vaxxers" like Jim Carrey and Jenny McCarthy and highly visible activists such as Robert F. Kennedy Jr. generated a great deal of attention to the cause, which appeared to be more than a fringe movement.[23] According to an October 2020 article published in the prestigious *The Lancet*, as many as thirty-one million Americans follow anti-vaccination groups on Facebook. Another seventeen million are subscribed to YouTube channels covering the topic.[24]

The anti-vax movement rested, to a large part, on scientific conclusions promoted by gastroenterologist Dr. Andrew Wakefield in a 1998 article in *The Lancet* that connected the measles-mumps-rubella (MMR) vaccine with childhood autism. Wakefield provided an extremely useful service to vaccination conspiracy believers. As a medical doctor, although without a specialization in virology or epidemiology, Wakefield's perceived authority gave agency to anti-vaxxers and their ongoing criticism.

But it was a flawed authority. By 2010, it came to light that Wakefield had conducted his research with a prohibitively small number of test subjects—twelve in total—while violating basic medical ethical standards. Wakefield subjected children to unnecessary medical procedures, like spinal taps, demonstrating a "callous disregard" for his patients. This was the conclusion of the British General Medical Council, which denounced Wakefield and stripped him of his medical license in England.[25] *The Lancet* retracted his article. Further investigations revealed that Wakefield was paid approximately $750,000 as an expert witness in a lawsuit against MMR manufacturers and that his published research was derived directly from preparations for litigation.[26]

Wakefield gained a second lease on life in 2016 when he directed the movie *Vaxxed: From Cover-Up to Catastrophe*. *Vaxxed* accomplished a number of important tasks all at once. Rather than again assume the scientific burden of proof linking vaccination to autism, where the facts had failed him, Wakefield moved the discussion away from the rarified air of *The Lancet* to a movie, transforming a complex story about medicine into something easily digestible for a layperson. Images mattered more than hard evidence. The film seemingly corroborated Wakefield's initial claims by linking them to the testimony of CDC "whistleblower" Dr. William Thompson, who revealed an alleged plot to deny the link between autism and the MMR vaccine.[27]

Wakefield's message was just as controversial but in a different context. Within the medical community, it cost him his license. As art, controversy was (and is) an incredibly useful promotional tool, particularly in the internet age. New rounds of celebrity endorsements and criticism created a media cycle that subsequently amplified Wakefield's message. *Vaxxed* was initially featured in the Tribeca Film Festival and publicly defended by Robert De-Niro. Additional figures familiar to the anti-vax movement—Jenny McCarthy, Jessica Biel, and Jim Carrey—endorsed the movie and generated national publicity.[28] Even though DeNiro eventually pulled the film from the festival, he defended its premise afterward. Appearing on the *Today* show, DeNiro noted: "As a parent of a child who has autism, I'm concerned, and I want to know the truth. And I'm not anti-vaccine. I want safe vaccines."[29]

The anti-vaccination effort received one additional, important endorsement from an unexpected source in 2016: Donald Trump. Interestingly, Trump had a long record regarding vaccines. His statements supporting the anti-vax cause appeared as early as 2007, when Trump said: "When I was growing up, autism wasn't really a factor. And now all of a sudden, it's an epidemic. . . . My theory, and I study it because I have young children, my theory is the shots. We've giving these massive injections at one time, and I really think it does something to the children."[30] He returned to the same theme as a presidential candidate in 2015: "Just the other day, two years old, two and a half years old, a child, a beautiful child went to have the vaccine and came back, and a week later got a tremendous fever, got very, very sick, now is autistic."[31]

Trump's years of endorsements seemed to add even more momentum to a growing anti-vaccination movement. In 2017, Sara and Jack Gorman published *Denying to the Grave: Why We Ignore the Facts That Will Save Us*, a study that pointed out that despite the vast majority of scientific evidence to the contrary, more and more Americans are jumping on the anti-vax bandwagon. In fact, as *Denying to the Grave* points out, some of the strongest opponents of vaccinations are the well-educated and affluent.[32]

But just how much does the anti-vaccination crusade impact medical practice in the contemporary United States? A review of CDC data indicates that vaccination rates for measles, mumps, and rubella (MMR), polio, and other diseases have remained relatively stable.[33] Domestic cases of tuberculosis dropped by half between 1991 and 2018.[34] The country has experienced measles outbreaks, although overall numbers are relatively small, increasing from 375 cases in 2018 to 1,282 in 2019.[35]

These trends and this national debate provided the framework for COVID-19 when it began to emerge in America during the spring of 2020. Old conspiracy theories added momentum to a new array of American problems and anxieties. Uncertainty defined the early months the pandemic. Few people had a firm grasp on how the disease was transmitted, its infection rates, or likelihood to result in death. Anxiety also came with the prospect of getting sick and the potential costs. COVID-19 testing, which was usually free, sometimes cost people thousands of dollars after the fact.[36] COVID treatment, although it varied according to the severity of the disease, the patient's age, and preexisting conditions, was a daunting prospect. One estimate early in the pandemic placed the cost between $10,000 and $20,000.[37] At a time when businesses across the country where being shuttered by state restrictions and unemployment rates were spiking (at 14.7 percent in April), new medical calamity risked personal bankruptcy for thousands of people.[38]

National COVID policy responses did not help and, in some cases, compounded the crisis. Test kits released by the CDC for use in public labs proved to be defective. Although officials initially blamed contamination during the production process, an internal review determined that "process failures, a lack of appropriate recognized laboratory quality standards, and organizational problems related to the support and management of a laboratory supporting an outbreak response" had all contributed to the problem.[39] The mistakes affected approximately a hundred labs across the country. Although more reliable tests eventually appeared, precious weeks, and public trust, were lost.

When it gradually focused on the COVID crisis, the White House added little clarity. President Trump repeatedly framed the pandemic using terms like "China virus" as early as March 2020, a practice that both politicized the issue and added an unnecessary racist element to a discussion about public health, neither of which helped address the fundamental challenge of a rapidly increasing national case load.[40] As president, Donald Trump projected even more authority than his earlier incarnations as a real estate developer and a political candidate. His daily White House press conferences on COVID, provided a bully pulpit for misinformation, distractions, and unproductive tangents that led the country away from the core problem at hand.

COVID-19 conspiracy theories rapidly spread throughout the spring and summer of 2020, very effectively preparing the way for the "Plandemic" video. Some were grandiose. One theory, a modern update to old paranoia about the Illuminati or the *Protocols of the Elders of Zion*, posited the idea that a vaccine would alter human DNA or introduce hidden microchips, making the public "programmable" by dark global forces. Bill Gates seemed to be a popular culprit, according to this school of thought. A number of social media platforms established a false correlation between the locations of 5G cell towers and the spread of COVID.[41] Other conspiracy theories were more benign, but also more dangerous. The claim that COVID-19 was the same as seasonal flu, an assertion repeated by both the White House and conservative media for months, prompted many Americans to disregard warnings and ignore social distancing and masking standards.[42] Sadly, it was easy to measure the actual impact of this misinformation. Although the United States contains only 4 percent or the world's population, it had accumulated 25 percent of the world's COVID cases and 20 percent of its total deaths by the beginning of March 2021.[43]

"PLANDEMIC" EVIDENCE: CONCEPT WITHOUT PROOF

The foundation of Mikovits's argument is her authority as a scientist. She worked at both the National Cancer Institute and later as director of the Whittemore Peterson Institute for Neuro-Immune Disease. Mikovits received a doctorate in biochemistry and molecular biology from George Washington University in 1991.[44] For all intents, she is a bona fide scientist with strong credentials and a research record that is easy to find and scrutinize. Mikovits's main breakthrough was the link she established between chronic fatigue syndrome and the xenotropic murine leukemia virus retrovirus (XMRV). She published her findings in the peer-reviewed journal *Science* in 2009.[45]

Over the next two years, Mikovits's research in XMRV became embroiled in controversy. Independent labs found that they could not replicate her findings, something that pointed to flaws in the original work. Consequently, portions of the paper were removed in 2011, and eventually, *Science* retracted the entire article. Mikovits undertook a $2.3 million effort to provide proof of her original concept but was forced to admit in September 2012 that there was "no evidence that XMRV is a human pathogen."[46]

Many of Mikovits's basic scientific claims regarding COVID-19 were also quickly debunked by the scientific community in 2020, even before her video appeared on YouTube. A main point promoted in "Plandemic" was that COVID resulted from man-made "manipulation" in secret military or civilian laboratories. However, a detailed study published in March indicated that "The virus's genetic makeup reveals that SARS-CoV-2 isn't a mishmash of known viruses, as might be expected if it were human-made."[47] Similarly, after Mikovits asserted that previous flu vaccines included the coronavirus, the CDC noted that treatment for influenza A, influenza B, and other viruses had no such ingredient.[48] Amazingly, as of March 2021, the official "Plandemic" website contained a section titled "The Case against Masks," despite the avalanche of published studies that prove their utility in a public health crisis.[49]

Some of the other "Plandemic" claims about vast political and professional conspiracies directed against Mikovits herself were easy to debunk because they completely lacked evidence. The video may have offered dramatic assertions about planted evidence or paid-off investigators, but it never provided one shred of proof that any of these elaborate machinations actually occurred. In response to the film, Fauci's office issued a simple statement: "The National Institutes of Health and National Institute of Allergy and Infectious Diseases are focused on critical research aimed at ending the COVID-19 pandemic and preventing further deaths. We are not engaging in tactics by some seeking to derail our efforts."[50]

A few statements were simple distortions. Mikovits was not jailed in 2011 for expressing unpopular political or scientific views. In simple fact, she was briefly arrested for stealing research material from the Whittemore Peterson Institute.[51] The original warrant, her arrest record, and subsequent court filings are easy to find, even for an amateur researcher with basic internet access.

There is an obvious irony to the vulnerability of "Plandemic" to basic fact-checking. For all her talent as a credentialed research scientist, Dr. Judy Mikovits broke an unbreakable rule of basic logic: claims require proof. A series of accusations, accompanied by dramatic music, long, slow-motion tracking shots, and sincere narration, are no substitute for hard evidence. The further Mikovits moved from her original academic training, the less viable her position became.

ANALYZING THE MANY LAYERS OF THE PLANDEMIC

Yet, millions still believe Mikovits, and it is important to understand why. One explanation might be that it is easy to believe that official authority is inherently evil. At the start of the COVID-19 outbreak, the Chinese government went to extreme, often cruel, lengths to both suppress information and limit the spread of the disease. It is possible to believe that the pharmaceutical industry and the American health care industry, in general, are at best indifferent or, in many well-documented instances, a system designed for profit and not human dignity. Viewed with these perspectives in mind, it is much easier to understand how a lifetime public servant like Dr. Anthony Fauci was rebranded as a criminal bent on power and profit. Whether evil informed the motives or defined the outcome doesn't matter. The core of Markovits's "Plandemic" is a textbook definition of a conspiracy theory.

COVID-19 also invited many Americans to indulge in the old practice of crafting scapegoats to vent their anger on. In practice, the "China plague" shared many of the same features as the 1919 "Spanish flu" in that it was a powerful magnet for nativism and xenophobia. The term, like the "China virus" or even the "kung flu," became a familiar device for Donald Trump on the campaign trail.[52] In October 2020, he tweeted that China would pay a "big price" for sending the virus to the United States.[53] At one point, the president combined his ongoing campaign to expand the US border wall with the government's efforts to combat COVID, claiming that illegal immigrants were a threat to American health. By building a wall, the United States could somehow keep the pandemic at bay.[54] Despite the fact that cases were actually skyrocketing as he made these proclamations, 78 percent of Republican voters still approved of his treatment of the pandemic in the summer of 2020.[55] Most Americans disliked the president's handling of the crisis, but his most important constituency overwhelmingly endorsed Trump's methods and results.

Throughout the COVID-19 crisis, political partisanship encroached on science. Members of the White House Coronavirus Response Task Force, which included CDC director Dr. Robert R. Redfield, NIH director Dr. Francis Collins, Department of Health and Human Services secretary Alex Azar, and task force coordinator Dr. Deborah Birx, tread lightly around the president, risking public criticism if they departed too far from his approach to the disease. Anthony Fauci, who sometimes criticized the administration in carefully couched terms, drew fire from White House economic advisor Peter Navarro in a July 2020 editorial that portrayed the doctor as wrong on a host of issues from mask use and the therapeutic value of hydroxychloroquine, to the early ban on travel from China.[56] Fauci, who began to regularly receive death threats for his positions on health policy, required beefed-up security for himself and his family. In relatively short order, he was also displaced in White House circles by radiologist, Hoover Institute senior fellow, and Fox News commentator, Dr. Scott Atlas.

In 2020, it became increasingly obvious that our politics defined how we understood, or even tolerated, science. A Pew Research Center survey of Americans in September unearthed a wide gap between Republicans and Democrats regarding COVID-19 and sources of information. When asked if the CDC "gets the facts right almost all or most of the time when it comes to the coronavirus outbreak," 70 percent of Democrats agreed, while only 48 percent of Republicans took that position. In contrast, 48 percent of Republicans answered yes when the question applied to the president, with only 10 percent of Democrats agreeing.[57]

During the pandemic, the severe politicization of official science had an immediate and negative impact on both formerly venerated institutions like the CDC, the National Institutes of Health, and public health in general. Prompted by the White House, the Food and Drug Administration (FDA) briefly authorized emergency use of the anti-malaria drug hydroxychloroquine for COVID-19 treatment, before reversing the decision after an outcry regarding its potentially dangerous side effects.[58] The same official tug-of-war broke out over policy regarding the use of masks. Dr. Anthony Fauci and an overwhelming majority of public health officials consistently touted their importance to reducing the spread of COVID-19, while simultaneously, Republicans at the state and federal level downplayed or simply denied their value. On October 17, 2020, White House medical advisor Dr. Scott Atlas tweeted:

> Masks work? NO: LA, Miami, Hawaii, Alabama, France, Phlippnes, UK, Spain, Israel. WHO:"widesprd use not supported" + many harms; Heneghan/Oxf CEBM:"despite decades, considerble uncertainty re value"; CDC rvw May: "no sig red'n in inflnz transm'n"; learn why https://t.co/1hRFHsxe59[59]

Rather than focus on social distancing and masks, which Republicans equated with a loss of personal freedom, Atlas instead stressed the need to rely on "herd immunity" to COVID, which he argued would happen when between 20 percent and 40 percent of the population were infected with the disease.[60] For his own part, Fauci denounced the whole idea, noting that the subsequent death toll would be "enormous and totally unacceptable."[61]

As the pandemic continued onward into its severe spike during the winter of 2020–2021, both sides continued to invoke the argument from authority. Medical professionals like Fauci, speaking from their positions within government agencies, made the rounds on talk shows and other media, and continued their appeal for caution and compliance with good scientific practices. Directly paralleling their efforts, the White House, friendly Republican governors like Brian Kemp (Georgia), Ron DeSantis (Florida), and Kristi Noem (South Dakota) and their medical surrogates worked conservative outlets like Fox News, Newsmax, and the One America News Network. The message remained muddled while COVID-19 cases and deaths surged to alarming levels.

Despite this constant battering, public trust in medical professionals remained strong. Before the pandemic, doctors were among the most respected figures in the country. A 2019 Pew Research poll recorded an 87 percent positive rating, higher than the military (82 percent), religious leaders (57 percent), or business leaders (46 percent).[62] Well into the first months of the pandemic, this support was largely unmoved. According to a *New York Times*/Siena College poll conducted in June 2020, 84 percent of registered voters still trusted medical professionals. Democrats were more positive (90 percent) than either Independents (86 percent) or Republicans (75 percent).[63] Among well-known medical figures, Anthony Fauci earned high marks from the public. In one July 2020 poll, 62 percent of Americans rated his handling of the pandemic positively, more than double the president's approval rating.[64]

Even though medical science seems to have withstood 2020's constant controversy, there is an important and lingering impact on America's health in the present day. One of the great successes of the pandemic year was Operation Warp Speed, the government program dedicated to fostering a vaccination for COVID-19. Most Americans were relieved to find out that deliveries of Pfizer's version of the drug would be delivered in mid-December. It was a remarkable feat, accomplished in a matter of months, something that stood in contrast to the many time-consuming difficulties involved in a normal drug development process.[65]

Unfortunately, not all people celebrated the good news. As was the case with masks, social distancing, and an array of public health policies, interest in obtaining COVID-19 vaccination varied significantly according to political affiliation. At the start of the vaccination campaign in December, 69 percent of Democrats indicated that they would get the shot, compared to just 50 percent of Republicans, according to the Pew Research Center.[66] A Monmouth University poll conducted two months later noted that the gap had widened with 72 percent of Democrats responding that they were eager to get vaccinated versus 51 percent of Republicans. More alarmingly, 42 percent of Republicans said that they would actively avoid getting the COVID-19 vaccine.[67] The individual implications of this split are obvious. However, with the increasing incidence of coronavirus mutations and variants, the long-term impact of missing the vaccination threshold necessary for effective herd immunity are far more ominous.

CONCLUSIONS

At the heart of controversies surrounding vaccinations and COVID-19 is a collision between our understanding of science and a competing perception of personal freedom.[68] The obvious complexities involved in fields like immunology and virology, among many others, are far outside the reach of most people, including the author. The same is not true with respect to what the average American wants as far as work, travel, social interactions, or entertainment are concerned. We are an impatient country with modern technologies that put convenience literally at our fingertips.

Scientists who have to follow the hard rules of human biology cannot provide the fast and simple solutions that we crave. Many of these same scientists who work in public health have to be cautious as they contemplate worst-case scenarios resulting from a whole array of threats to hundreds of millions of people. For years, we tolerated these scientists' dire warnings when the worst-case scenario never came to be or were so small that they had virtually no impact on our normal lives. This was true of SARS (2002), swine flu (2009), MERS (2012), the avian flu (2013), and Ebola (2013–2016).[69] We became used to tuning out science and enjoying our routines. For obvious reasons, COVID-19 was different, but old habits die hard.

Enter Dr. Andrew Wakefield and Dr. Judy Mikovits. Both earned professional credentials at the start of their respective careers. However, both abandoned their chosen professions for better access to a public audience with far less accountability. It is a classic case of "moving the goalposts" with respect to the medium, not the message. Professionals have to submit their work through the time-honored filter of peer review. YouTube and the Tribeca Film Festival have a far lower bar.

None of this is new. For years, television personalities like "Dr. Phil" (Phil McGraw) or "Dr. Oz" (Mehmet Oz) have dispensed medical advice as a form of entertainment, much in the same way "Judge Judy" has performed on a television set designed to look like a courtroom. None of it is real. Yet, people follow medical personalities not just for entertainment but for advice. Mehmet Oz started his medical career as a cardiothoracic surgeon but earned a fortune with eight *New York Times* bestsellers devoted to topics like alternative nutrition.[70]

For millions of Americans, the line between information and entertainment is blurry at best. In 2020, this led to bizarre instances where celebrity medical personalities, like Dr. Phil, became an ongoing counterpoint to doctors like Anthony Fauci. What mattered in these exchanges was not credentials but relatability or, as an April 2020 *Washington Post* story observed, "to speak in sound bites, and to opine confidently and comfortably on camera, regardless of expertise."[71] These pundits are living examples of a false equivalency that exercises a powerful influence on American life.

The damage this discourse has caused is significant and not yet complete. Before COVID-19, arguments about measles, mumps, and rubella vaccinations involved sickness and potential death, but nowhere near the magnitude of the current pandemic. In 2020, the CDC reported just thirteen individual cases of measles in the entire country.[72] The last death was in 2015.[73] Our current situation may be prolonged by a plurality of Americans who simply will not trust science. These millions of people will impact current COVID vaccination efforts and will almost certainly affect a national response to the next inevitable outbreak.

Vice President Mike Pence poses with a SWAT team, 2018. The officer on the left is wearing a QAnon symbol on his uniform. (Public Domain via Wikimedia Commons: https://commons.wikimedia.org/wiki/File:Pence_posing_with_QAnon_police_crop.jpg.)

Chapter Ten

QAnon: Enemies inside the Gates

When does the benefit of informing people about an emerging piece of misinformation outweigh the possible harms? It's a hard balance to strike, and a judgment call every time. Give too much attention to a fringe conspiracy theory before it's gone viral, and you might inadvertently end up amplifying it. Wait too long, and you allow it to spread to millions of people with no factual counterweight.

—*New York Times* technology reporter Kevin Roose, October 2020

THE QANON PHENOMENA

There is a large, sprawling conspiracy theory that believes the world, including the US government, is controlled by the "deep state," a shadowy group comprised of pedophiles and child-eating Satanists bent on world domination through their control of intelligence agencies, government offices, banking, and the mainstream media.[1] Originating in the United States, it is, as *New York Times* reporter Kevin Roose wrote in October 2020, equal parts a "massively multiplayer online game and an internet-based religion."[2]

As QAnon belief grew and spread, official authority began to take note. The FBI identified the type of extremist theories promoted by QAnon as a domestic security threat as early as May 2019. In September 2020, before the House Homeland Security Committee, FBI director Christopher Wray assessed QAnon "as less of an organization and more of a complex set of conspiracy theories." In the weeks leading up to the general election, Wray believed the problem was not right- or left-wing threats, "but rather lone actors, largely self-radicalized online who pursue soft targets using readily available weapons."[3] Events in January 2021 proved Wray wrong.

Today, millions of Americans subscribe to QAnon conspiracy theories. Believers included dozens of congressional candidates in 2020 and at least two current serving members of the House of Representatives. According to a September 2020 Daily Kos/Civiqs poll, 56 percent of Republicans responded that QAnon theories were "mostly" or "partly" true. Only 13 percent of Republicans said that QAnon conspiracy theories were not true at all compared to 72 percent of Democrats.[4] At the end of 2020, 39 percent of Americans agreed that there was a deep state actively working against President Trump.[5]

Some of the elements—its vastness and the cast of characters involved—of QAnon may sound familiar and they should be, as this chapter will discuss. Other portions are quite unique. Perhaps more perplexing is the fact that in our modern information age, so many people do believe what appear to be on the face of it a series of outrageous claims about the current state of the world. All of this begs a few obvious questions: Why now? How did we get here?

QANON ORIGINS IN HISTORICAL CONTEXT

The origins of QAnon can be traced back to October 2017 when references on 4chan—an anonymous internet image board—identified an individual using the code name "Q," who supposedly was working from inside the corrupt, deep state, government-within-the-US government. His/her mission: to save Americans from this conspiracy in plain sight by sending coded messages and warnings about its activities.[6] Many QAnon advocates came to believe that Donald Trump was actually "Q" and was working inside the deep state to fight against its machinations. In effect, the president, as commander-in-chief, was a mole inside his own administration, the first to break free from a line of "slave presidents" working for the secret cabal. In this narrative, Trump was a hero who would eventually lead a countercoup against the shadow government, smash pedophile deviants, and save the children as well as the country.[7]

Some parts of QAnon belief resemble the virulent anti-Semitism prevalent more than a hundred years ago in documents like the *Protocols of the Elders of Zion* and Nazi Party propaganda.[8] QAnon invokes a familiar range of antagonists: corrupted elites bent on hollowing out public institutions while they undermine the bedrock principles of faith, family, and democracy that constitute accepted norms of American life.

But QAnon is also distinct from the *Protocols* for a number of reasons. The most obvious is the fact that the older conspiracy theory never considered a civil war within the deep state. QAnon rests on the belief that a select group with "Q-Level" security clearances [an actual term taken from the Department of Energy] fights an ongoing battle from within against its evil counterparts.[9] Possibly led by President Trump, their goal is to retake legitimate authority and restore the American way of life.

QAnon is fundamentally different than the *Protocols* for another, more important reason. Rather than simply make pronouncements, QAnon invites believers to become part of an interactive experience. As they look through posts on a variety of news and social media sites, QAnon followers are encouraged to seek out clues to the truth. There is a utility to being a member of this process. People who pursue QAnon conspiracy theories are in the story and not just passive bystanders. They will be rewarded for their efforts when they finally pierce the veil of secrecy and find hidden secrets. In that important sense, they are all "Q." It is the ultimate hero narrative.

From its obscure 2017 origins, QAnon quickly developed a much broader appeal in conspiracy circles. Inside its big tent are any number of old and existing grievances. QAnon appeals to Republicans upset about opposition to Trump during and after his 2016 election victory, particularly at the hands of the mainstream media and the Democratic Party, elites they consider a key part of the conspiracy against their country. QAnon includes Christians intent on fighting a perceived deep moral decline evident everywhere in American society and culture. The movement is also attractive to libertarians constantly on the lookout for abuses committed by the deep state in America and around the world.[10]

In relatively short order, QAnon conspiracy theories escaped the internet and found their way into mainstream society. We discussed the 2016 Comet Ping Pong Pizzeria incident in chapter 8.[11] It was followed by lesser-known instances, such as in June 2018, when Matthew Wright briefly commandeered the Hoover Bridge with an armored truck and demanded that Robert Mueller release his report on the Trump investigation. After a brief chase, police discovered two handguns, two rifles, and nine hundred rounds of ammunition in his vehicle.[12] QAnon resurfaced again after the December 2019 arrest of Cynthia Abcug, a Colorado woman who believed "evil Satan worshippers" and "pedophiles" were involved in her dispute over custody of her son. Colorado authorities acted after learning that she was planning to take him back by force.[13]

It was becoming increasingly clear that QAnon was evolving from internet chat to action. Like the monster in *The Ring*, it had stepped through the screen and into reality. The QAnon hero narrative, along with the whole shared experience, was finding its way into daily American life. All of this was before the COVID-19 crisis arrived and the 2020 election rhetoric really began to increase in intensity.

QANON EVIDENCE: LIKE A SNAKE EATING ITS TAIL

When it comes to evidence, the QAnon movement follows an almost perfectly circular path. Because it deals with a civil war within the deep state, there is no obvious evidence to explain the many QAnon conspiracy theories. On the one side, evil pedophiliacs cover their tracks using all the mechanisms of the elite establishment at their disposal. On the other side, the "good" Q forces within the deep state, including Donald Trump and his allies, are forced to transmit messages to followers in code to preserve and continue their fight. It is a seamless, almost elegant thought process.

Instead of having clearly delineated evidence, QAnon followers are engaged in the constant search for signs or "Q-Drops" on the internet. Originally, this led them to image boards on 4Chan and 8kun, but it has expanded over the years to include Twitter, videos of speeches, and virtually every available media platform.[14] Before his account was suspended, QAnon followers pored over Donald Trump's tweets, attempting to draw correlations between their time stamps and suspected Q-Drops.[15] Whenever Trump spoke during press conferences and speeches, they tried to decipher his hand gestures. One woman attending a January 2020 rally in Milwaukee, Wisconsin, was convinced that Trump was tracing the letter "Q" through the air as he spoke to the crowd.[16] A few days before the January 6 assault on the Capitol, many QAnon followers saw a call to action when one of the president's supporters tweeted: "The calvary [*sic*] is coming Mr. President!" and Trump responded: "A great honor!"[17]

But again, all of this is part of the attraction for QAnon conspiracy theorists. A game developer interviewed in October 2020 by *Wired* magazine noted that the whole process resembled an "alternate reality game" (ARG):

> ARGs are designed to be clue-cracking, multiplatform scavenger hunts. They're often used as a promotion, like for a movie. A studio plants a cryptic clue in the world around us. If you notice it and Google it, it leads to hundreds more clues that the gamemaker has craftily embedded in various websites, online videos, maps, and even voice message boxes.[18]

The subsequent hunt for QAnon clues is personal, passionate, and endless. Followers share discoveries, begin discussions about what they mean, and embark upon a whole new process of debate, interpretation, and dissemination. After a point, what begins to matter most is the process and not the end result.

ANALYZING QANON BEYOND THE SHAMAN:
NEW AGE BELIEF AND SPIRITUALISM

One of the most common images associated with QAnon in 2021 is of Jacob Anthony Chansley, the bearded, tattooed protestor sporting a horned head-dress, otherwise known as the "QAnon Shaman." Standing and shouting from the speaker of the house's podium, he presented a jarring, absurd image that drew a steady stream of snarky comments from late-night talk show hosts. In his "Seditionist Round Up Roundup," Steven Colbert referred to Chansley as an "endangered dumbass" in one of his opening monologues.[19] Although dozens of stories following the January 6 unrest focused on his arrest, his subsequent protests regarding vegan food options in prison, and his eventual expression of remorse, there was a larger story at work.[20]

A strong thread of spiritualism lives within QAnon. As the movement migrated from fringe imageboards inside 4Chan to a broad array of social media platforms including Twitter, Instagram, and Facebook, it drew an increasingly diverse group of supporters. This expanding circle includes: "lifestyle influencers, mommy pages, fitness pages, diet pages."[21]

Women are clearly part of this new constituency. One, for example, was a member of the Free Birth Society, a collection of people that promotes at home, unassisted childbirth. Others belonged to Informed Mothers, an anti-vaccination Instagram group. Many followed Dr. Christiane Northrup, who promoted natural childbirth and had 146,000 Instagram followers. Regularly embedded in her posts were both COVID-19 conspiracy theories and links to QAnon topics.[22] As Marc-André Argentino observes, "These influencers provide an aesthetic and branding to their entire pages, and they, in turn, apply this to QAnon content, softening the messages, videos, and traditional imagery that would be associated with QAnon narratives."[23]

Journalists began to refer to this as the "Pastel QAnon" phenomena.[24] In terms of branding, internet posts literally include pastel blue and pink memes. More importantly, however, Pastel QAnon messaging keys in on meaningful issues that concern parents, but particularly resonate with women. This was especially so regarding the protection of children. The appeal of a QAnon mainstay theory, like elite promotion of pedophilia, seems obvious. *Slate* author Lili Loofbourow framed the issue simply: "Who doesn't want to protect children and restore order?"[25]

Consequently, QAnon crusades against subjects like sex trafficking regularly appear in women's online user groups. In a 2020 echo of Pizza-gate, QAnon believers speculated that the Wayfair home furnishing company website was a place that was marketing children using an elaborate series of code names.[26] In a classic application of QAnon methodology, they corelated specific items in the Wayfair catalogue, like the "Neriah Swivel Bar & Counter Stool," with names of missing children (in this case, Neriah), and coming to the conclusion that it was all an elaborate system promoting child slavery.[27]

Other portions of Pastel QAnon conspiracy theories associate the deep state with vaccination efforts and COVID-19 public health policies in particular. Anti-vax sentiments that follow the logic of "protecting the children," regularly appear on these social media platforms. Not surprisingly, the same groups almost immediately gravitated to the deep-state conspiracy theories promoted by Dr. Judy Mikovits in the May 2020 video "Plandemic."[28] It was a short trip—bridged by outright suspicion of medical elites like Dr. Anthony Fauci—from measles, mumps, and rubella vaccinations to the origins of the coronavirus. Many QAnon posts portrayed the pandemic as a classic false flag exercise. For them, it was a contrived event created by evil authority to impose a dictatorship. QAnon conspiracy theories applied to all parts of the public health response to COVID-19. For example, rather than see masks as a commonsense way to mitigate risk, QAnon proponents believed they were a device to ensure obedience to a false doctrine that had no medical value. As early as August 2020, both Twitter and Facebook began removing posts attributed to QAnon followers regarding the pandemic.[29]

Pastel QAnon's fixation on health conspiracies tends to overshadow one of its most important features, an aspirational quality that allows it to be "authentic enough to allow for relatability" among women.[30] This version of QAnon focuses on female empowerment and assertiveness in the face of a system that simultaneously threatens women's health and their personal freedom. The conspiracy theory promotes a "you-go-girl argot," as one writer put it. "The appeal is morally unambiguous, simultaneously frightening and reassuring, and perfectly crafted to draw in a certain slice of suburban women."[31]

Men can be attracted to QAnon for exactly the same reasons. Its main message resonates with an important part of the contemporary, New Age men's movement. For some converts, QAnon is a means to combat modern social forces that place traditional male roles and norms under increasing scrutiny, at points crowding men out of their former status and marginalizing them. QAnon offers a way to defend the male identity as leader and protector. By following its narrative, a man is transformed back into a defender of children against dark conspiracies of pedophiles. At the same time, he can also restore his own identity. It is a hero narrative that is a combination of both altruism and narcissism.[32] Chansley, the "QAnon Shaman," is a case study of this process. He is the founder of the "Star Seed Academy," which promises: "Star Seed Academy creates leaders of the highest order! We help people to awaken, evolve and ascend! Are you ready to be a leader? Are you ready to ascend?"[33]

By crafting a world of stark contrasts between good and evil, by identifying culprits and crusaders, and by pointing the way toward personal restoration and fulfillment, QAnon has spread far beyond its original fringe constituency. Further amplified by an array of platforms and algorithms, it is today embedded in millions of lives and conversations. As one author noted in August 2020: "There's no warning—just a warm, glamorous façade, and then the rabbit hole."[34]

ANALYZING QANON AND THE 2020 ELECTION

There are points in American history where the public and not their leaders define politics. In times of peace and in times of crisis, the public's likes, wants, fears, and priorities sometimes set the stage for electoral contests. As QAnon spread throughout America, the conspiracy theory found its way into the mainstream political system. At one official 2018 stop in Broward County, Florida, Vice President Mike Pence unknowingly posed for a photo with members of a local SWAT team, one of whom was wearing the "Q" symbol on his uniform.[35] Throughout the 2020 election season, QAnon was increasingly woven into the Republican Party under President Donald Trump and a surprisingly large number of congressional candidates. The optics were everywhere: "Q" signs, shirts, and slogans which included obscure abbreviations like "WWG1WWA" ("Where we go one, we go all").

QAnon gained significant momentum when Trump not only refused to distance himself from the movement but also periodically retweeted posts that amplified its conspiracy theories. During his four years in office, Trump indulged QAnon followers on at least ninety occasions. On July 4, 2020, alone, he retweeted posts from QAnon accounts fourteen times.[36] When the issue came up at an October town hall meeting, Trump initially denied any knowledge of QAnon conspiracy theories but reversed himself moments later by saying, "Let me just tell you what I do hear about it is they are very strongly against pedophilia and I agree with that."[37]

Other segments of the Republican Party appeared to have the same muddled relationship with QAnon. During the summer of 2020, Texas Republican Party state chair Allen West adopted the slogan "We Are the Storm," a move that immediately prompted criticism regarding its similarity with QAnon rhetoric, which frequently features the word "storm" in its messaging. Allen defended his decision, attributing the slogan to one of his favorite sayings: "The devil whispers to the warrior slyly, can it withstand the coming storm. The warrior responds, 'I am the storm.'"[38] The national GOP headquarters defended Allen, claiming that the quote was derived from Psalms 29.

Other notable Republican officials, operatives, and candidates, like former National Security Advisor Michael Flynn and longtime Trump political advisor Roger Stone, publicly embraced QAnon. Flynn went so far as to take the QAnon "pledge of allegiance" on July 4, 2020.[39] During the 2020 campaign season, dozens QAnon believers represented the Republican Party on ballots around the country. Some of the best-known included Jo Rae Perkins, who prevailed in a four-way race during the Republican Senate primary in Oregon by obtaining almost 50 percent of the total vote. In a January 2020 interview, she stated that there was "a very strong probability/possibility that Q is a real group of people, military intelligence, working with President Trump." During her primary victory speech, Perkins again directly invoked QAnon: "Where we go, we go all. I stand with President Trump, I stand with Q and the team. Thank you, Anons, and thank you patriots. Together, we can save our republic."[40]

Perkins was joined by a host of fellow QAnon proponents in the Republican Party. Lauren Boebert successfully ran for a seat in Colorado's Third Congressional District and said in a May 2020 interview with the podcast *Steel Truth* that:

> Honestly, everything I've heard about Q, I hope this is real. Because it only means America is getting stronger and better and people are returning to conservative values. And that's what I'm for. And so, everything that I have heard of this movement is only motivating, and encouraging, and bringing people together stronger, and if this is real, it could be really great for our country.[41]

Georgia Republican Marjorie Taylor Greene, who prevailed in that state's "Fourteenth Congressional" District, believes in all of the concepts promoted by the QAnon conspiracy. In a thirty-minute video she posted in November 2017, Greene said:

> I don't know how much you guys know about Q. It's an anonymous person all right? So, Q is a patriot. We know that for sure, but we do not know who Q is, okay? So now the question is, I'm going to talk about this and I'm gonna tell you I don't know who Q is, but I'm just going to tell you about it because I think it's something worth listening to and paying attention to. Okay and the reason why is because many of the things that he has given clues about and talked about on 4chan and other forums have really proven to be true.[42]

Greene goes on to say that "Q has put out there that many high-level officials will soon be arrested and it will actually be the drain the swamp scenario that we have we have always been wanting to happen." She believed that the Mueller investigation might expose "satanic worship" and "child pedophilia" and would lead to what "Q" called "The Awakening" in America.[43] Following this same reasoning is Republican Angela Stanton King, who won the 2020 primary in Georgia's Fifth District in an attempt to fill the position vacated by the death of Georgia Democrat John Lewis. Stanton King repeatedly tweeted the QAnon slogan: "THE STORM IS COMING" during her unsuccessful campaign in the general election.[44] Before her Twitter account was suspended, she used the platform to forward a number of QAnon posts and sites.

The nonprofit Media Matters for America compiled a list of ninety-seven candidates who supported QAnon in 2020. The group is overwhelmingly Republican, who comprised eighty-nine of the total. One was a Libertarian, one represented the Independent Party of Delaware, and four were independents. Two were Democrats.[45] One of the things made clear by the Media Matters survey was that existing party mechanisms were not adequate filters for the QAnon conspiracy. Along with Perkins, Boebert, Taylor Greene, and Stanton King, a total of twenty-seven candidates (twenty-five Republicans) won in primary contests.[46] None were Democrats. Although Jo Rae Perkins was soundly trounced in her Senate contest against Democrat Jeff Merkley (57.0 percent to 39.4 percent), she still gained 912,814 votes in the end, a startlingly significant number.[47]

Granted, some Republicans did attempt to hold back QAnon's growing influence in the party and openly denounced the movement. Days after Joe Biden's inaugural, Senator Ben Sasse of Nebraska called on his colleagues to "repudiate the nonsense that has set our party on fire."[48] Three months before the election, Representative Liz Cheney, the Wyoming Republican and daughter of party icon Vice President Dick Cheney, was blunter: "QAnon is a dangerous lunacy that should have no place in American politics."[49] These were rare exceptions. In the Georgia congressional race, key members of the Republican Party leadership, specifically the president, House minority leader Kevin McCarthy, and other members of the Georgia delegation publicly supported Marjorie Taylor Greene regardless of her unhinged embrace of QAnon.[50]

The endpoint of the 2020 election was a classic QAnon moment. Or two, to be more accurate. The country held its breath when people went to the polls in November, expecting widespread interference with the process, although no major problems were in evidence. The final certification of the election was a different story. Although we will take a detailed look at the events of

January 6, 2021 in the next chapter, it is worth discussing here. On that day, Congress met to simply recognize the final result of both the popular vote and the Electoral College.

Unfortunately, the crowds that converged on the nation's capital that day, many in full QAnon regalia, had different ideas. For any careful observer, organizing efforts leading to the mass rally held in front of the White House were a case study in "Q" messaging. Advertised by the president as the "SAVE AMERICA RALLY" on Twitter, it was a literal call to action, a message repeatedly echoed by state and national Republican Party leaders.[51] Pennsylvania State Senator Doug Mastriano spent thousands in campaign funds for charter buses for the event.[52] Former Pennsylvania state representative Rick Saccone was also present at the riot and preceded it with multiple Facebook posts openly endorsing a series of conspiracy theories that included QAnon.[53] In August 2020, he posted a video (since removed) titled "Why Is the Left So Afraid of Q?"[54] In all, fifty-seven state and local Republican officials were present at the rally, and many were subsequently identified as part of the Capitol riots, some by their own social media posts.[55] "The Storm" had arrived.

In contrast, QAnon rallies planned for the March 4 "inauguration" were a textbook case of an anti-climax. The entire premise behind the gatherings was odd. Although the Twentieth Amendment changed the date of presidential inauguration to January 20 in 1933, QAnon conspiracy theorists simply chose to ignore the constitution. In its place, believers seemed convinced that Donald Trump would return to assume his rightful place as the re-elected president of the United States on March 4.

It was easy to dismiss this movement as a fringe fantasy. However, polling provides a disturbing counterpoint to the next round of anticipated QAnon action. A February 2021 American Enterprise Institute report indicated that 15 percent of Americans agreed with the statement "Donald Trump has been secretly fighting a group of child sex traffickers that include prominent Democrats and Hollywood elites." Although it was an obvious minority, the prospect that it might include as many as fifty million Americans is alarming. More important was the fact that an additional 41 percent of people surveyed were simply uncertain about the claim.[56]

In the days leading up to March 4, police agencies tasked with security in the nation's capital expressed deep concerns that protests might be even larger than the one in January. Precautions put in place after the riot—fencing, traffic barriers, and thousands of National Guard—remained in place as authorities anticipated possible clashes with armed protestors. Yet, no protests appeared in Washington, DC, or anywhere else in the country. The actual reasons are unclear, although some QAnon internet posts, not surprisingly, thought that the event might be a deep state trap.[57] Once again, the snake appeared to be eating its own tail. People breathed a sigh of relief, at least for the moment.

ANALYZING AND UNDERSTANDING QANON

On one level, the QAnon phenomena is consistent with other historical conspiracy theories. It offers certainty in a time of social, political, and economic anxiety, a state of affairs that pre-dated COVID-19 and was exponentially increased by it. QAnon contains a world with clearly delineated good and evil. From this structure will come justice. Ali Breland observes: "QAnon adherents also share with traditional conservative culture warriors a vivid eschatology in which judgement will at last be rendered against liberals, and the nuclear family will be restored to its proper place."[58]

Although QAnon sees dangers in dark corners throughout American society, its focal point is the threat to children. Again, this is a very old narrative, a story that goes back to medieval Europe and tales of "Blood Libel," where Jews murdered Christians, particularly children, and drained them of their blood for rituals for the Passover meal.[59] It is timeless because there is nothing more visceral for an adult to understand than a threat to the lives and well-being of children. It is a concept that also resonates in the present day, given years of public awareness campaigns that first focused on rape and later included child abuse. Support for these causes entailed a "refusal to disbelieve," as one historian put it.[60]

If the same vein, QAnon conspiracy theorists see skepticism as a vindication of their beliefs. The harder media fact-checkers, academics, or even friends and family members push back, the more righteous the cause appears to be. Responding to a media inquiry, a member of a Facebook group, The Unmasked Home Schoolers of Collier, replied: "We are believers. We question things. You don't have to like us, but tattling to a news reporter is comical. It means we are worthy to be talked about and not sheep."[61]

Lastly, it is clear that QAnon conspiracy advocates think of themselves as part of a larger event. In some respects, the movement hearkens back to religious revivals in that it not only incorporates a stark moral understanding of events but also identifies believers as morally superior to non-believers. Followers of QAnon are "chosen people" in their own minds and destined for some type of spiritual reward. QAnon also vests a great deal of faith in the idea that society is on the verge of a major shift.[62] It may take the form of a political coup against deep state enemies or a much broader version of an end of days that resembles millenarian movements that popped up in the 1990s.

In other words, QAnon believers are preppers, ready for the sudden collapse of society and their vindication and ascendance in a new world order.

CONCLUSIONS

Without question, the QAnon conspiracy is a spreading problem, a point driven home in part by the January 6 riot. Unfortunately, this event did not illustrate just how far QAnon extends around the world today. By the spring of 2021, followers could be found in seventy countries. In England, QAnon gained traction among the 17 percent population that believes COVID-19 is part of a depopulation plan, according to one survey.[63] QAnon has even appeared in Japan, although some commentators have cast doubt on its impact because of the amateurish nature of the conspiracy.

Efforts to reduce QAnon's spread online resemble squeezing a balloon. Fact-checking is too often overwhelmed by the sheer volume of posts on a variety of platforms. As noted above, QAnon articles and links are now woven into an ever-increasing variety of groups that, at first glance, have no relations whatsoever to world-building, global conspiracies. When they are unearthed, fact-checked, or banned, users are also simply migrating to alternate locations. After a crackdown on Facebook and Twitter, QAnon moved to Parler. Once that site came under scrutiny, they congregated around Telegram and MeWe.[64] The end result is a social media industry "whack-a-mole strategy" that is becoming an exercise in futility.[65]

QAnon believers also appear undeterred by repeated failures. When Donald Trump did not return to power as expected on March 4, it led some to doubt the cause, but it did not cause the movement to fall apart. Although many of the individuals who were arrested after they stormed the Capitol eventually expressed public fits of remorse, a disturbingly large number of Americans remain vested in the use of violence to promote their ideology. According to the February 2021 American Enterprise Institute poll cited earlier, 56 percent of Republicans supported the idea of using force "to arrest the decline of the traditional American way of life."[66]

Without a clear protagonist in the White House, QAnon has since shifted to new targets, primary among them is COVID-19 and the ongoing federal vaccine roll out. The massive campaign to inoculate the country against the pandemic fits into already well-worn grooves comprised of anti-vax conspiracies, New Age philosophy regarding holistic healing, and libertarian political ideals.[67]

In practice, it is likely that the surge in federal programs sponsored by the new Biden administration may foster a concurrent growth in QAnon. From their perspective, big government is only a short step away from a revised, constantly evolving vision of what the "deep state" means. This, combined with access to a constantly evolving array of internet platforms and a pre-vailing sense of mission and narcissistic self-importance, translates into a conspiracy movement that will remain a part of our social and political dis-cussion for years to come.

The January 6, 2021, Capitol Riot. (Public domain via Wikimedia Commons: https://commons.wikimedia.org/wiki/File:DC_Capitol_Storming_IMG_7951.jpg.)

Chapter Eleven

Stop the Steal! The 2020 Election

We respect the law. We were good people. The government did this to us.
We were normal, good, law-abiding citizens. And you guys did this to us.
We want our country back.[1]

—Capitol rioter speaking to a British journalist, January 6, 2021

The year 2020 was, in many ways, a perfect storm of problems. It was an election year and, as American political history held, it was full of the usual partisan broadsides fired by both parties. Mudslinging and baseless accusation are, after all, part of the traditional American process.

Yet, there was a particular edge to politics in 2020 that made older conflicts look almost quaint by comparison. Vicious debates left over from 2016 ricocheted through the country and the halls of Congress and were daily amplified by cable news and social media. Old norms continuously fell away under the weight of it all. President Donald J. Trump remained the undisputed master of Twitter, and his daily posts prompted a constant stream of commentary and criticism. Younger, media-savvy politicians like Representative Alexandria Ocasio-Cortez (Democrat, New York) joined the fray in 2019 and added their own substance and snarkiness. When newly elected Democrat Rashida Tlaib (Michigan) promised to go to Washington and "impeach the motherfucker," it raised barely an eyebrow.[2]

This was all before COVID-19, before almost six hundred thousand Americans died as of this writing. The global pandemic is the greatest American public health crisis in a century. As the country struggled with measures necessary to fight it, COVID-19 added to widespread economic uncertainty, racial tensions, and violence; it took an already angry and bitter election year and increased the momentum powering a vortex of savagely ugly rhetoric and escalating paranoia.

The end result was anything but routine. Part of the background noise of 2020 was the constant claim that the election was about to be stolen and, when it was over, the same claim only grew in volume. Most of this fury came from Trump, who had a long history of attacking the democratic process. In 2012, he referred to Barack Obama's 2012 re-election victory as a "total sham." When Ted Cruz won the Iowa primary in 2016, Trump called foul, tweeting: "Ted Cruz didn't win Iowa, he stole it. That is why all of the polls were so wrong and why he got far more votes than anticipated. Bad!" Before the general election that year, he again took to social media: "The election is absolutely being rigged by the dishonest and distorted media pushing Crooked Hillary—but also at many polling places—SAD."[3] The same mantra appeared again in 2020 as part of his regular campaign speeches. In Wisconsin, Trump told an assembled crowd: "The only way we're going to lose this election is if the election is rigged."[4] When Trump lost the popular vote by a margin of seven million, 81.2 million to 74.2 million, and in the Electoral College 306 to 232, accusations rapidly escalated in the subsequent weeks and months.[5]

The consequence was the January 6 insurrection, an event that horrified most outside observers.[6] Condemnation rippled around the country and the world. A British journalist reporting for ITV said as he watched the riot, "This is exactly what was feared, but in no way is this a surprise. It has been fueled by the president's rhetoric, and it's increasingly clear, this election has not healed the wounds, it has simply amplified them."[7] Many world leaders joined in on the commentary. British Prime Minister Boris Johnson tweeted on the day on the attack, "Disgraceful scenes in US Congress. The United States stands for democracy around the world and it is now vital that there should be a peaceful and orderly transfer of power."[8] Spanish President Pedro Sanchez tweeted, "I am following with concern the news that are coming from Capitol Hill in Washington. I trust in the strength of America's democracy. The new Presidency of @JoeBiden will overcome this time of tension, uniting the American people."[9] Other countries were less supportive. In a statement made a day after the riot, the Chinese Foreign Ministry took the opportunity to highlight American hypocrisy: "If you still remember how some US officials, lawmakers, and media described what's happened in Hong Kong, you can compare that with the words they've used to describe the scenes in Capitol Hill."[10]

ELECTION CLAIMS: FROM THE LEFT AND RIGHT

It is important to remember that claims about the integrity of the US election came from both political parties in the years leading up to the 2020 contest.

For many Democrats and the political Left, the specter of Russian interference in 2016 carried forward right into the Trump administration, particularly after the Office of National Intelligence (ONI) issued its official assessment in January 2017. As the country digested the ONI report, an ongoing FBI investigation into Russian influence on the election and the new administration was about to move to another level. The bureau originally started its inquiry under the codename "Crossfire Hurricane" in July 2016 and specifically identified Republican operatives George Papadopoulos, Carter Page, Michael Flynn, and Paul Manafort. Given its potential impact, the issue was political dynamite, even more so since the target of the investigation had won the election.[11]

The White House's handling of the matter quickly generated more controversy. Newly appointed Attorney General Jeff Sessions earned the president's public wrath in March 2017 when he recused himself from any election investigation to avoid a conflict of interest over his role in Trump's political campaign.[12] After he failed to provide adequate assurances that the FBI was not pursuing the president, Trump fired director James Comey on May 9. The following day, in a meeting with Russian Foreign Minister Sergey Lavrov and ambassador to the United States, Sergey Kislyak, Trump called Comey "a real nut job" and said, "I faced great pressure because of Russia. That's taken off."[13]

The Justice Department intervened a week later, when former FBI director Robert Mueller was appointed as a special prosecutor to investigate the Russian influence on the 2016 election. Because Attorney General Jeff Sessions had recused himself, the task fell to his deputy, Rod Rosenstein.

> Considering the unique circumstances of this matter, however, I determined that a Special Counsel is necessary in order for the American people to have full confidence in the outcome. Our nation is grounded on the rule of law, and the public must be assured that government officials administer the law fairly. Special Counsel Mueller will have all appropriate resources to conduct a thorough and complete investigation, and I am confident that he will follow the facts, apply the law, and reach a just result.[14]

Trump never appeared in the official announcement, although it was obvious from the start that he would be a focal point of the Mueller investigation.

What followed over the next two years was an often partisan and poorly defined discussion of real and suspected crimes committed by the Trump administration. Throughout, media commentators consistently failed to articulate the difference between a criminal conspiracy and the vague term "collusion," which gained constant traction as the Mueller investigation ground onward. Overheated rhetoric was a constant part of the backdrop as well. Senate Majority Leader Mitch McConnell came under fire for blocking efforts to reform both campaign finance practices and election security, an effort that earned him the title "Moscow Mitch." The insult became an instant internet meme. Ironically, even when the administration attempted to protect McConnell's political flank, the efforts sometimes backfired. Trump said at a July 2019 press conference: "Mitch McConnell is a man that knows less about Russia and Russian influence than even Donald Trump. And I know nothing."[15]

Cable news pundits like Rachel Maddow spent months speculating on the federal convictions that might follow the conclusion of the Mueller investigation. Reflecting on the presidential election, Maddow said in March 2017: "We are also starting to see what may be signs of continuing influence in our country. Not just during the campaign, but during the administration. Basically signs what could be a continuing operation."[16] None of this speculation hurt Maddow's ratings. Her MSNBC show bested top-rated Sean Hannity in March 2018 with more than three million viewers.[17]

However, when Robert Mueller finally released his report in March 2019, it contained no judgments regarding collusion and no indictment of Trump, although in its elliptical wording, the report also did not completely clear the president. Maddow cried foul and began to indulge in language that sounded suspiciously like a conspiracy theory: "Well, why did Mueller make that determination and was it, in fact, a choice?"[18]

The Mueller investigation did produce tangible results. While it lacked clear linkages between Donald Trump and Russia, a total of thirty-five individuals (twenty-six Russian) eventually plead guilty and were convicted or indicted for a variety of felonies. This was true of a number of highly visible American actors: Michael Cohen, Paul Manafort, Roger Stone, and Michael Flynn. The most common charges were obstruction of justice (Manafort, Stone), lying to the FBI (Flynn), campaign finance violations (Cohen), lying to Congress (Cohen and Stone), and witness tampering (Stone). Former Trump campaign manager Paul Manafort and his aid Richard Gates were also charged with "conspiracy against the United States."[19] Although some of these charges were obviously serious, none of them were directly related to treason or collusion. In fact, the charge of "conspiracy against the United States," which resulted in a guilty plea from Paul Manafort, was not as serious as it seemed on the face of it. It related to Manafort's crimes against parts of the US government, specifically the Departments of the Treasury and Justice for money laundering, tax fraud, and perjury. It had nothing to do with overt espionage.[20]

The problem for the American political left is something we have covered repeatedly throughout the book: confusing correlation for corroboration. For more than two years, the series of allegations linking Trump advisors back to the president followed the logic of Watergate, but without its "smoking gun" evidence. Cable media pundits speculated endlessly about potential links, at points aided by leaks from former American law enforcement and intelligence officials—Jim Comey (FBI), John Brennan (CIA), and James Clapper (DNI), among others—that were tantalizing and gave the veneer of credibility because of the authority of the source, but still lacked that final, critical connection to the White House.[21]

Although a great deal of criticism is clearly justified, it is also equally clear that critics missed some important points. The Mueller report established official Russian interference in the 2016 election. These efforts included information operations on American social media platforms, hacking the Democratic National Committee database, and some actual links between Russia and Trump campaign staff like George Papadopoulos.[22] While there was no evidence of Trump's direct complicity in any of these issues, not everyone's hands were completely clean either.

Republicans and the American conservative establishment generated accusations about the election that covered a much broader array of actions and actors in 2020. They were also different in that there was a constant drumbeat of claims regarding election fraud in the weeks and months before November. These culminated in a predictable claim on election night that Trump won the election.

All of this was plain to see when the president held a 2:30 a.m. meeting with his family and inner circle and gave a short speech denouncing the election: "I want to thank the American people for their tremendous support. Millions and millions of people voted for us today and a very sad group of people is trying to disenfranchise that group of people and we won't stand for it."[23] As he spoke, the results in Pennsylvania, Wisconsin, Georgia, Arizona, and Michigan were too close to call.

Trump repeated these same claims on November 5 in another televised speech from the White House. He added an interesting detail that polling was a form of election interference. According to the president, pollsters had gotten their results "knowingly wrong." He went on further to say:

> As everyone now recognizes, media polling was election interference, in the truest sense of that word, by powerful special interests. These really phony polls—I have to call them phony polls, fake polls—were designed to keep our voters at home, create the illusion of momentum for Mr. Biden, and diminish Republicans' ability to raise funds. They were what's called "suppression polls." Everyone knows that now. And it's never been used to the extent that it's been used on this last election.[24]

Literally dozens of claims flowed into the national debate from these starting points. Among them was the accusation, resurrected from 2016, that millions of voters were illegal. Trump and a rotating group of conservative politicians and their media surrogates accused the Democratic party of conducting "vote dumps" by adding paper ballots after polling places closed. In a variation on that theme, Republican pundits singled out Dominion Voting Systems for manipulating software used in voting machines to either add votes for Joe Biden or delete votes for Trump. Sydney Powell, a key member of Trump's legal team, which we will discuss below, claimed foreign interference, after two whistleblowers with apparent connections to the Hugo Chavez regime in Venezuela came forward.[25] Some claims were specific to states. In Arizona, it was what Fox News called "Sharpiegate," where election officials gave Republican voters Sharpies to vote so that their ballots could not be read by computer scanners.[26] Republicans attacked a March 2020 agreement in Georgia, claiming that it blocked state officials from verifying voter signatures.[27]

Texas Republican Congressional Representative Louie Gohmert offered one of the most bizarre and all-inclusive conspiracy theories that followed the election. In an interview held only a few days after the polls closed, Gohmert claimed that he had learned from "former intel people" that "US Army forces" had raided the Frankfurt offices of Scytl, a software company that had manipulated US election results.[28] Convicted former Trump staffer George Papadopoulos jumped on the bandwagon almost immediately, if not accurately, tweeting: "Breaking: Congressman Louie Ghomert [*sic*] has stated that The US Army has seized servers for Dominion in Germany."[29] Thomas McInerny, a retired three-star Air Force general, took to social media to claim that American special forces operatives died in an attack on what was actually a CIA computer facility in Germany. When the *Military Times*, which publishes news for the US armed forces, asked him for evidence, he responded: "President Trump won in a landslide and the Dems left so many footprints that this TREASON must be stopped!!!"[30]

THE HISTORICAL CONTEXT
OF ELECTION FRAUD AND IRREGULARITIES

Election fraud is as old as democracy. Political intrigue and machine politics are American institutions that go back as far as Aaron Burr and Tammany Hall. There are almost too many modern examples to count. Some are famous. When Lyndon Johnson challenged the popular governor of Texas, Coke Stevenson, for a senate seat in 1948, the race was neck-and-neck until Precinct Box 13 suddenly turned up late on election night. In the box were two hundred previously uncounted votes, all delivered in alphabetic order for Johnson.[31] Precinct Box 13 was on display for years in the Johnson presidential library, along with a picture of the men who stuffed it.

Better known are the last-minute ballots cast for John Kennedy during the 1960 presidential election. In an extremely close contest with Richard Nixon, Kennedy won Illinois by only 8,800 votes. More than a few Republicans believed that some of the late returns from Cook County, controlled by Democrat machine boss Richard J. Daley, were likely fake.[32]

The 2000 presidential campaign between Al Gore and George W. Bush is memorable for its sheer mayhem and the deep scars it left on the body politic. In an election year defined by how best to spend projected budget surpluses—tax cuts versus Social Security—and a bipartisan consensus on bringing American troops home from peacekeeping commitments abroad, decision time came down to Florida, where 5.9 million people voted but the initial margin of "victory" for Bush was just 1,784 votes.[33]

What followed was a toxic combination of voter confusion, technical problems, protests, and legal battles, all covered in a thick layer of partisanship. The infamous "butterfly" ballot proved a challenge for many voters, who mistakenly cast their ballots for Pat Buchanan instead of Al Gore or who failed to make a completed hole through the punch card for an optical scanner to later read. Making matters worse, as county election boards attempted lengthy hand recounts, they were besieged by lawyers and protestors who flooded offices and began chanting "Stop the count! Stop the fraud."[34] The fact that the governor of Florida at that moment was the Republican candidate's brother did absolutely nothing to calm concerns.

In the end, the US Supreme Court settled the matter in a 5-4 decision that finally halted the Florida recount. At that moment, Bush won the state by a total of 537 votes and with that, the Electoral College, and the presidency.[35] Speaking of the court, Vincent Bugliosi scathingly claimed:

> The stark reality . . . is that the institution Americans trust the most to protect its freedoms and principles committed one of the biggest and most serious crimes this nation has ever seen—pure and simple, the theft of the presidency. And, the perpetrators of this crime *have* to be denominated criminals.[36]

Bugliosi's anger was palpable, understandable, and masked some important distinctions that would come back to haunt the country in 2020. First among them is the difference between a voting "irregularity" and outright fraud. For example, the ancient optical scanners used to tabulate ballots in Florida and many other states at the time were there because of neglect and not fraud. When older voters failed to punch the right hole for Gore, it was not for lack of help from local election officials, who routinely posted examples of the ballot at polling places.[37] When protestors flocked to county offices in Florida, the action was orchestrated by long-time Republican operatives like Roger Stone. Harassment of election officials might have been intimidating and technically illegal, but it did not amount to stealing votes. Yet all of these things taken together, whether accidental, deliberate, or the product of neglect, infuriated Americans and set the stage for even more ugliness in the future.

THE CONTEXT OF A COVID-19 ELECTION

When the COVID-19 pandemic appeared, the country was already well into the 2020 primary season. As far as the political process was concerned, coronavirus presented unique questions regarding how voters might access polling places. In states where voting by mail was already established, it was not a problem. For most of the rest of the country, long lines and crowded local precincts were the "congregate settings" that the Centers for Disease Control were constantly warning Americans against.[38] Was voting worth the health risk? How would it impact turnout in a hotly contested election year?

One of the first test cases was Wisconsin, which held its April primary as the pandemic was beginning to accelerate. Democrats lost bids in court to extend absentee voting and postpone the primary date.[39] Voters waited in long, socially distanced lines, although two-thirds voted by mail. Despite Democrat concerns, voter turnout was 34 percent, higher than average for primaries since 1984.[40]

Other states adapted according to existing law or adapted as best as they could. Colorado had automatic registration and allowed vote-by-mail for all elections. Florida had early mail-in and in-person voting and started counting ballots before the general election.[41] States like Pennsylvania allowed mail-in voting but restricted in-person access to election day. Other states modified existing standards to address COVID-19. Lawsuits blanketed the election year, with Democrats attempting to increase voting flexibility, while Republicans opposed the idea, with the justification that it hurt election integrity. In Georgia, both sides reached a compromise that allowed for early notification of rejected mail-in ballot applications and provided procedures for signature verification.[42]

Change was the constant for 2020. It applied to deadlines for mail-in votes, the locations of drop boxes and their security, the overall number of polling places available for people who wanted to vote in person, and any number of things voters needed to know. Only weeks before the November election, state officials decided that Pennsylvania voters who received mail-in ballots could surrender them at polling places if they wanted to vote in person.[43] Between policy revisions, court challenges, and ongoing partisan accusations, voters were, not surprisingly, confused on election day. It was a situation where irregularities promised to be the rule rather than the exception.

THE ACID TEST: ELECTION ALLEGATIONS, EVIDENCE, AND THE COURTS

Debunking election claims became an ongoing cottage industry before, during, and after the final vote tallies ended in November. Confronted by Louie Gohmert's fantastic story about an Army raid on German computer servers, Madrid-based Scytl issued a press release stating that it had no offices in that country and had no role whatsoever in the American election. Similarly, US Special Forces Command also issued a formal statement denying any raid took place.[44]

The real test of election claims came when a group of lawyers, the self-proclaimed "elite strike force team," took fraud claims to dozens of courts in the United States. The public face of the team was comprised of three individuals: Jenna Ellis, Sydney Powell, and Trump's personal lawyer, Rudy Giuliani. Ellis was a former deputy district attorney from Weld County, Colorado, whose primary focus there was theft, assault, prostitution, and domestic abuse. After leaving public office, she taught undergraduate pre-law at Colorado Christian College and became a Fox News commentator, where she was rechristened as a "constitutional law attorney."[45] Sydney Powell started her career as a US attorney in Texas. By the time of the 2020 election, she was best known for representing former national security advisor Michael Flynn.[46] Rudy Giuliani was clearly the most famous of the trio. As "America's Mayor," he presided over New York City during the September 11 attacks and unsuccessfully attempted to translate his fame into a presidential run in 2008. When the "elite strike force team" went to work, Giuliani was Donald Trump's personal attorney. He had not practiced law in a court since 1992.

As fraud claims worked their way through the court system, a number of official institutions verified the integrity of the election. The Cybersecurity and Infrastructure Security Agency (part of the Department of Homeland Security) issued a statement on November 12 which said simply: "The November 3rd election was the most secure in American history. Right now, across the country, election officials are reviewing and double checking the entire election process prior to finalizing the result."[47] Trump fired Christopher Krebs, the director of the Cybersecurity and Infrastructure Security Agency five days later.[48] The move backfired when Krebs took to national media to elaborate on his agency's original assessment. At the beginning of December, Attorney General William Barr stated that "To date, we have not seen fraud on a scale that could have effected a different outcome in the election."[49] A few weeks later, in a news conference following his resignation, Barr said that although he was "sure there was fraud in this election," he did not believe that it was "systemic or broad-based." Barr went on to further note that the Justice Department had no plans to seize voting machines or appoint a special counsel to investigate the election.[50]

In the meantime, court challenges proceeded in Wisconsin, Georgia, Pennsylvania, and other key battleground states. Ellis, Powell, and Giuliani discovered that the affidavits they were touting on nightly cable talk shows did not automatically translate into plausible or concrete evidence. For example, documents submitted by two Venezuelan whistleblowers attempting to connect election interference with the deceased Hugo Chavez contained the identical misspelled phrase: "I am an adult of sound mine."[51] Sydney Powell's intelligence "expert," code-named "Spyder," turned out to be Army veteran Joshua Merritt, who had never worked in military intelligence.[52]

An array of Republican- and Democrat-appointed judges ravaged the lawsuits that came before them. Diane Humetewa, federal district judge for Arizona, wrote:

> Plaintiffs append over three hundred pages of attachments, which are only impressive for their volume. The various affidavits and expert reports are largely based on anonymous witnesses, hearsay, and irrelevant analysis of unrelated elections. Because the Complaint is grounded in these fraud allegations, the Complaint shall be dismissed.[53]

In response to a portion of a lawsuit that Republican voters' Fourteenth Amendment rights had been violated, Michigan Federal Judge Linda V. Parker said: "With nothing but speculation and conjecture that votes for President Trump were destroyed, discarded, or switched to votes for Vice President Biden, Plaintiffs' equal protection claim fails."[54]

In all, Ellis, Powell, Giuliani, and a host of litigators filed a total of at least sixty-three lawsuits regarding the 2020 election. The results were less than spectacular. In one state, Pennsylvania, litigants were able to limit the number of days (three) allowed for voters to confirm their identities.[55] Unfortunately, despite repeated failures to negate the election outcome, conspiracy theories continued forward. As did plans to "stop the steal."

AFTERMATH (I): JANUARY 6, 2021

Even as legal challenges to the presidential election fell apart, the White House, Republican leaders, and thousands of their followers continued efforts to stop Joe Biden's inauguration. Trump pressured Vice President Mike Pence to reverse the election when it came for its final confirmation before a joint session of Congress in January. At a Georgia political rally on January 4, he said: "I hope Mike Pence comes through for us, I have to tell you. I hope that our great vice president, our great vice president comes through for us. He's a great guy, because if he doesn't come through, I won't like him quite as much."[56] He inaccurately tweeted on the next day that "The Vice President has the power to reject fraudulently chosen electors."[57] Representative Louie Gohmert attempted a new lawsuit that would grant Pence the "exclusive authority and sole discretion under the Twelfth Amendment to determine which slates of electors for a State, or neither, may be counted." US District Court Judge Jeremy Kernodle rejected the claim in a ruling at the start of the new year, and Trump's own Justice Department opposed the lawsuit on the grounds that "the Vice President is not the proper defendant to this lawsuit."[58] This reversal did not deter Representative Mo Brooks, an Alabama Republican, from announcing that he would oppose verification of the election. He was eventually joined by 146 Republicans in the House and Senate.[59]

The center point of opposition soon shifted to a rally at the Ellipse in front of the White House, planned for January 6, the day that Congress would meet to accept certification of the election. A collection of Republican officials, corporate leaders, and private groups pitched in to help plan for the event. It included Mike Lindell, CEO of the MyPillow company, the Global Vision Baptist Church, the political action committee Turning Point Action, and right-wing radicals such as the Proud Boys, Oath Keepers, and the Three Percenters.[60] Former Tea Party activist Amy Kremer and Women for America First put together a multi-state bus tour that made twenty-five stops in Arizona, Louisiana, Kentucky, Georgia, and Tennessee before arriving in Washington. Throughout the tour, Kremer called on crowds to join her on January 6 to stop the election certification.[61] In-person events ran concurrently with a call for support on a variety of social media platforms. A "Stop the Steal" Facebook group began on election night and rapidly accumulated 320,000 members before it was shut down.[62] The Red-State Secession Group encouraged its 8,000 members to share an "enemies" list that included members of Congress, judges, and well-known progressives before it was also banned on Facebook.[63] Thwarted by one platform, organizers simply shifted to Parler and Gab, or started their own websites.[64] While he was still on Twitter, the president messaged his millions of followers on December 19: "Big protest in DC on January 6. Be there. Will be wild!"

On the day of the January 6 rally, a dozen speakers addressed the crowd, numbering as many as ten thousand, although it may have been higher. Amy Kremer told the assembled: "It is up to you and I to save this Republic. We are not going to back down, are we? Keep up the fight!"[65] When Rudy Giuliani took his turn at the podium, he shouted: "If we're wrong, we will be made fools of. But if we're right, a lot of them will go to jail. So, let's have trial by combat."[66] Republicans from more than a dozen states were also present. Two guest speakers were serving members of Congress; Mo Brooks (Republican, Alabama) and Madison Cawthorn (Republican, North Carolina). Cawthorn claimed that "our constitution was violated" in the 2020 election.[67] Brooks noted that America was based upon sacrifice for "foundational principles" that were under attack from "socialist Democrats." He went on to say: "We are not going to let socialists rip the heart out of our country. We are not going to let them continue to corrupt our elections and steal from us our God-given right to control our country's destiny."[68] Former Trump 2016 campaign spokesperson and liaison with January 6 protest groups Katrina Pierson said, "Americans will stand up for themselves and protect their rights, and they will demand that the politicians that we elect will uphold those rights, or we will go after them."[69]

The main attraction of the January 6 rally obviously was President Donald Trump. Although the content of his speech would be picked over by political commentators and a second impeachment process in weeks to come, both the spirit and the wording basically continued the same belligerent themes evident throughout 2020. From the very start, Trump made his point clear:

> Our country has had enough. We will not take it anymore and that's what this is all about. And to use a favorite term that all of you people really came up with: we will stop the steal. Today I will lay out just some of the evidence proving that we won this election and we won it by a landslide. This was not a close election.

Peppered throughout the speech, Trump used the words "fight" or "fighting" at least twenty times.[70] If the certification proceeded, Trump told his audience, "You will have an illegitimate president. That is what you will have, and we can't let that happen." He added: "When you catch somebody in a fraud, you're allowed to go by very different rules." He finished by encouraging the crowd to march down Pennsylvania Avenue and give Republicans "the kind of pride and boldness that they need to take back our country."[71]

Mayhem followed immediately after thousands marched to the Capitol, tossed aside barriers, attacked police, and smashed their way into the building. In the process, according to an account by *Reuters* after the riot, 140 police were injured by "a makeshift arsenal that included metal pipes, wooden poles with embedded nails, aluminum baseball bats, a hockey stick, a wooden door ripped off its hinges, and a coffee table."[72] On the day of the violence, police fatally shot Air Force veteran Ashli Babbitt as she attempted to break into the House chamber. Three other rioters also died that day, Benjamin Phillips and Kevin Greeson from "natural causes from cardiovascular disease," according to the District of Columbia's chief medical examiner. Roseanne Boyland succumbed to "acute amphetamine intoxication."[73] Officer Brian Sicknick suffered a stroke and died after being spray with a chemical agent. Two other police officers committed suicide shortly after the riots.[74]

AFTERMATH (II): VOTING RIGHTS IN 2021

An important and long-term consequence of 2020 election conspiracy claims has been a nation-wide Republican effort to restrict voting rights. Even before the Capitol riot, lawmakers softened their claims of fraud by reframing the issue as a general concern about voting "irregularities" and "election integrity."[75] The same claims continued into the new year. At the Conservative Political Action Conference in February 2021, Donald Trump repeated the same messaging he uttered four months earlier: "This election was rigged, and the Supreme Court and other courts didn't want to do anything about it."[76] By March 2021, according to the Brennan Center for Justice, legislators in forty-seven states had introduced 361 bills to curtail voting rights.[77]

Georgia was one of the first post-election voting rights battlegrounds for reasons that don't seem to make sense at first glance. In the decade before the election, population trends marked a state moving past its traditional southern roots. During that time, the population grew by 30 percent, bolstered by increasingly diverse numbers of liberal, out-of-state transplants. A political shift was also apparent. Organizers like Stacy Abrams and the New Georgia Project spent years on voter registration drives, particularly among African Americans, and door-to-door efforts to engage voters. The result was a substantial jump in voter turnout from 40 percent in 2016 to in 74 percent 2020.[78] Demographic and political changes increasingly pointed to a future where Georgia might become a blue state. That was true in the US Senate where Democrats Jon Ossoff and Raphael Warnock unseated two incumbent Republicans.

For the Republican Party, however, these changes represented a threat to the old political status quo, and they responded accordingly. When Georgia Governor Brian Kemp signed new voting legislation on March 25, 2021, he cited concerns regarding election integrity: "Georgia will take another step toward ensuring our elections are secure, accessible, and fair."[79] While most critics focused on the provision that made it a misdemeanor to provide food or water to voters waiting in line, the legislation also added a long list of new restrictions. The law made it illegal for the state to send out absentee ballot applications to all voters. It set the maximum number of drop boxes for the state at twenty-three, down from ninety-four in 2020. The law also allowed the state legislature greater control over the State Election Board as well as county election officials.[80]

Republicans in Georgia defended the changes. In an April 2021 *Washington Post* editorial, Gabriel Sterling, the chief operating officer for the Georgia Department of State, took President Biden to task for mischaracterizing elements of the new law as "Jim Crow in the 21st century."[81] He noted that previous legislation had banned "gifts" to voters waiting in line and added that poll workers could hand out donated water. Sterling was upbeat about severe cuts in drop boxes, saying that the legislature was writing them into the law for the first time. He did agree that removing the Georgia secretary of state from the State Election Board was "ill-conceived," but pushed back on the idea that restrictions on local elections boards amounted to voter suppression.[82]

It is easy to argue that voting integrity requires constant attention and periodic reform. Everything from changing technologies that improve voter access to foreign cyberthreats justifies constant vigilance. However, Republican claims regarding massive, systemic, national voter fraud are simply not supported by the facts, as dozens of court cases have proven. Beneath all the layers of rationalization, there is a simpler goal at work, something Michael Carvin, a lawyer representing the Republican Party in Arizona, revealed in open court: "Because politics is a zero-sum game."[83] The objective is not protecting democracy. It is to win.

CONCLUSIONS:
POSTMORTEM ANALYSIS OF THE 2020 ELECTION

Although American democracy proceeded to a legal and stable conclusion in 2021, signs of trouble were everywhere. Surveys taken in the wake of the January riot noted that although most (68 percent) Americans believe the election was legitimate, a more careful examination of the data revealed a striking divide in the country. Democrats overwhelmingly (98 percent) endorsed the election outcome as did a smaller (73 percent) but still significant number of independents. However, only 32 percent of Republicans share their view.[84]

Some of the key players targeted by 2020 election conspiracies fought back in its aftermath. Dominion Voting Systems embarked on a series of lawsuits against both news networks who broadcast unsubstantiated claims of fraud and the individuals who made them. The company launched multibillion dollar lawsuits against Fox News and Newsmax. Dominion also individually sued Sydney Powell and Rudy Giuliani for $1.3 billion each.[85]

Powell's defense was an interesting postscript on the election year. She argued that "no reasonable person" should believe her claims to be literally true. Basically, Powell's counterclaim was that her speech in 2020 was political and not necessarily factual.[86] She cited case law in her response that "[A] statement of opinion relating to matters of public concern which does not contain a provably false factual connotation, or which cannot reasonably [be] interpreted as stating actual facts about an individual, continues to receive full protection."[87] It was a difficult, if not impossible, argument to sustain given the fact that she had officially represented the president of the United States in litigation about the election. Yet, as legislative efforts to restrict voting rights across the country move forward, it appears that at least part of America has found a way to do so.

(Public domain via Wikimedia Commons: https://commons.wiki
media.org/wiki/File:North_America_from_low_orbiting_satellite
_Suomi_NPP.jpg.)

Conclusions

Finding a Way Forward

We're going to need a bigger boat.

—Chief Brody, *Jaws*

WHERE TO BEGIN?

At the end of a discussion about the September 11 terrorist attacks in a spring 2021 class, one of my students asked if education could be the best way to solve the ongoing problem of conspiracy belief in America today. The answer is yes and no. We can teach facts and timelines, logic and the rules of debate, but we can't guarantee success. There are many complex parts of human nature to think about that have nothing to do with just academics or education. To be effective, we have to consider ivory tower theories, common sense that might guide the average person, and the limits of both. There are a few things to think about that overlap and affect each of these qualities in any conversation.

THE 80/20 RULE

Working as a union activist, I attended many different training sessions dedicated to organizing people. During these sessions, we learned about the 80/20 rule, which basically divides up time into the percentage you should listen (80 percent) and the percentage you should talk (20 percent). It is a goal that seems like common sense, but it is not. A lot of people, especially academics, are not good at listening or, more importantly, giving themselves the time and mental space to consider an alternative viewpoint. Teachers lecture and too often don't take enough time to learn from their students. They talk, sometimes to captive audiences in giant survey classes. The same is true for people who troll each other online in a format that is badly suited for a constructive debate.

That is not to say all sources of discussion are equally bad. I very explicitly talk about civil discourse in my classes and moderate conversations accordingly. Many of my faculty colleagues do the same. There are good websites—Metabunk.org is among them—where posted rules are clear and consistently enforced by moderators.[1] Podcasts, like *Conspirituality*, supplement this work by trying to understand the current trend toward conspiracy thinking before criticizing it. Its goal is "to bring understanding to this landscape," and it starts by counseling patience with the process.[2]

These are good starting points. Unclench your fists. Be prepared to listen.

KNOWING THE CONTEXT

It is extremely important to know the context of events and never build your understanding on a single piece of information. I like to ask my students when the counterculture really began, for example. The "school answer" usually puts it around 1967, when the Summer of Love arrived in a psychedelic swirl of the Beatles *Sgt. Pepper's Lonely Hearts Club Band* album, hippies, free love, drugs, and teenaged Baby Boomers.

Frankly, I don't think that answer comes even close. Tom Wolfe pointed out more than forty years ago that many different generations of Americans joined in the free-for-all we called American society after World War II. Blue-collar types did not want to live in planned workers' housing. They left for the suburbs. Older folks bought "recreational vehicles" and took to the roads. As Wolfe noted, hippies were only the most "flamboyant" example of a larger social movement. From all these groups, actively seeking their own personal freedom, the "Me Generation" came.[3]

Conspiracies are part of this story. As I mentioned in chapter 3, Joe McCarthy took a hammer to the pillars of authority in the 1950s, be they cabinet officials like Dean Acheson, a five-star general, and war hero like George C. Marshall, or a respected playwright like Arthur Miller. Few people, great or small, escaped his ham-fisted crusade. After John F. Kennedy died, the Warren Commission banked on a level of public trust in federal power that was already seriously eroded by 1964. The Vietnam War, Watergate, and a long list of other events each added new layers of doubt, distrust, and suspicion. This is important to think about. Conspiracies have a tendency to accumulate.

As the pile gets higher, it becomes harder and harder to recover the old relationship between average people and the ones in power.

In this vacuum of trust live conspiracies. They tempt us by taking away the need for the hard work of recovery. Instead, they move us in the opposite direction. Conspiracies make complicated reality simple and manageable. We don't need to know how all the moving pieces fit together. Historian David Wrone described it as the "assassination syndrome" and applied it to John F. Kennedy's death:

> To my mind, this assassination syndrome, this terrible collapse of the critical people—witness Lane, and Lifton, and Garrison and the rest—it's a suggestion that we are really in trouble as a society. These theorists take us away, fly us away to this unknown land of Oz, wherever they take us. They divert our attention from the reality.[4]

The hard part for educators, or anyone trying to move another person along a difficult path strewn with facts and dates, is motivating them to stop, contemplate what they know, and test their assumptions against new information. All along the way, we fight the temptations offered by click-bait, pundits pandering to the lowest common denominator, and oversimplified solutions.

HAVING A FEW MODELS

As we have seen, there are some real conspiracies in American history. The Nixon White House engaged in a conspiracy against the public interest during Watergate. By itself, Watergate is a real conspiracy. However, one bad act is not evidence of conspiracy theories that followed afterward. The Latin phrase *post hoc, ergo propter hoc*, which means "after this therefore because of this," applies here. It points out a basic mistake that people make about cause and effect. They assume that if one action occurred earlier in a timeline it was the cause of a later event. That is to say, if Watergate was a conspiracy that involved the government, then the Sandy Hook shooting was also caused by a government conspiracy. Except it doesn't. This is a good model of an assumption, otherwise known as a false correlation.

Anyone navigating through the conspiracy world needs to keep this model in mind to avoid a pretty common mistake. Good researchers who really connect the dots must build anchor points that link cause to effect with documents and facts that are both relevant and corroborated. Simple, but painstaking, rules apply to how it all gets done.

Operation Northwoods comes up repeatedly in the conspiracy world. In 1962, the joint chiefs of staff concocted a plan to provoke a war with Cuba.

It was a classic example of a false flag operation. However, the archives are stuffed full of plans that come out of civilian and military organizations. When they are not planning to do something real, the Pentagon and its civilian counterparts are usually planning for an unexpected contingency. That is what conspiracy believers tend to forget. The Centers for Disease Control and Prevention actually had a "Zombie Preparedness" page on its website.[5] The CDC is not expecting a zombie attack and its plans are not evidence of one. The government is simply trying to find a way to get people to prepare for problems with a pop culture meme. It is clever marketing, not evidence of a conspiracy.

The same is true with the patents constantly cited by the chemtrail community as evidence of a conspiracy. Some offer fairly vague ideas, for example, Patent #2550324 "Process for controlling weather" (April 24, 1951). Others seem overly precise, like Patent #5003186, "Stratospheric Welsbach seeding for reduction of global warming" (March 26, 1991).[6] The larger point here, something we discussed in chapter 6, is that these are only ideas, not evidence. Regardless, it is important to repeat. Theory is not reality. Neither is an intention without an action. Something has to exist before it can even be considered as evidence.

Then there is a phenomena I define as *parallel conspiracies*. There are points in time when real conspiracies give credibility to suspected ones. They travel alongside each other and coexist on the timeline, creating layers of real and suspected history. The first attack on the USS *Maddox* in the Tonkin Gulf is a good example. The United States clearly was engaged in a conspiracy against North Vietnam through a series of covert military operations. The CIA and American naval forces supported OPLAN 34A commando raids against a sovereign nation in its territorial waters. Technically, the United States was committing an act of war, something the Johnson administration denied outright in 1964. It is also highly likely that the second Tonkin Gulf clash never happened, although administration officials—particularly Robert McNamara—used evidence of the first clash to convince the world that the second battle had.

The linkage between the first and second Tonkin Gulf incidents illustrates the dilemma for both citizens and historians. The US government knowingly violated international law, causing a conflict with North Vietnam. American officials misrepresented facts to obtain public support and a congressional resolution to escalate the war in Vietnam. Basically, our foreign policy was built on a series of bad acts, some real, some not. It would take years for declassified documents to separate truth from fiction.

The September 11 attacks are a better example of parallel conspiracies. The first layer is straightforward. Al-Qaeda terrorists hijacked four planes in 2001 with the intent to destroy political, military, and economic targets, and cause massive loss of life. The Bush administration subsequently manipulated intelligence reports and public fury to justify a war against Iraq, creating a second layer of conspiracy. In the aftermath of the terrorist attacks and war in the Middle East, the 9/11 Truther movement emerged, weaving together a third layer of complicated LIHOP and MIHOP scenarios from facts, revealed deception, bad science, and speculation.

Trying to separate out the different layers of truth and falsehood is exhausting and almost never conclusive. As I mentioned in chapter 1, I often tell the students in my conspiracy class that the best way to treat history is to pretend that your audience is a jury. Your best hope is to apply useful models and pile up enough evidence to convince them full well knowing that finding the complete truth is impossible. Reaching that critical mass, that tipping point where the proof is adequate, might have to be enough.

Sometimes it is not enough. The unknown is frustrating. Filling gaps with intuition and speculation can be incredibly tempting. That is why conspiracy gurus like Dane Wigington or David Icke pack auditoriums with people craving a simpler world, one where the shadowy power structure concocts "crisis-response" operations that move the unenlightened masses. It is equally easy to denounce scientists, engineers, the medical profession, professional diplomats, or any other perceived part of the power structure as "disinformation shills." The seamlessness of this simplicity is often too tempting to overcome.

BREAKING THROUGH TO THE OTHER SIDE

Logic and carefully constructed arguments will only get you so far. Today, some of the best debunkers are experts with a sense of humor. There are more than a few types of these people out there. Neil deGrasse Tyson is one of the better examples of a scientist who has been woven into popular culture to translate complex ideas into understandable terms. Tyson appears at academic conferences and late-night television with equal ease, articulating the mysteries of the universe with infectious enthusiasm.

Tyson also has successfully bridged the increasingly fuzzy divide between information and entertainment. That boundary is a permanent feature of how we learn. When Jon Stewart left the *Daily Show* in 2015, analysts commented on the impact that a comedy show had on how people, particularly young ones, get their news.[7] For Stewart's audience, the message was just as important as the messenger. John Oliver continues the tradition on *Last Week Tonight* combining, like Stewart, satire with current events to produce "investigative comedy."[8] Dozens of podcasts follow a similar formula. For the last four years, two former stand-up comedians have followed the rise and fall of Alex Jones on their podcast *Knowledge Fight*. They are asking a good question, namely: "How did we disrespect information and the conveying of information so much that we ended up where we are in 2021?"[9] Their answers come in the form of humor, when *Knowledge Fight* picks apart the flaws and inconsistent logic that is everywhere in Infowars. With a smile.

The results are highly entertaining, but there is the risk of obscuring the line between information and entertainment. Matt Taibbi's point about reducing a complex story to a late-night talk show punchline is worth remembering. Humor, however intended, might either oversimplify the subject or alienate part of an intended audience.[10] The infotainment approach also cannot escape the basic principles of market economics. As popular as Stephen Colbert might be, his content is still ultimately responsible to corporate sponsors and ad buys. Smaller venues can't escape this reality any more than Colbert. Although *Knowledge Fight* started on a shoestring budget, by April 2021, it had more than 2,700 Patreon contributors. Unfortunately, in a weird example of a marketing domino effect, *Knowledge Fight's* revenue stream is currently threatened as Infowars declines in a crowded conspiracy media landscape now dominated by personalities like Tucker Carlson.

LIMITS AND THE IMPORTANCE OF BELIEF

It is hard for any educator to admit that learning has its limits. As I said at the start of the chapter, not every poorly informed idea crumbles under more facts, more data, or painstakingly crafted, rational arguments. There is a point where we can't just reason our way out of a problem. There are limits to what education can do.

Sara and Jack Gorman reflect on this dilemma in *Denying to the Grave: Why We Ignore the Facts That Will Save Us*. Their basic point is straightforward. People respond to information both emotionally and intellectually. In practice, we tend to believe things that have a strong emotional association. In other words, we cannot separate our animal brains—where fear, outrage, and survival instincts live—from our higher mental functions.[11] Ideas gain traction if they begin on this type of emotional foundation. According to the Gormans, charismatic conspiracy pundits are masters at manipulating emotions, not just facts.[12]

We are right to have fears about dangers to the Earth's environment, or threats to our children, or wrongful acts committed against the public and its leadership. As discussed in the chapter on QAnon, these types of fears are often a gateway to conspiracy theories, which start building an elaborate architecture of fantasy around the original concern. It serves the purpose of establishing control over a fear that strikes at the very core of who we are and how we live each day.

Lastly, there are spiritual or moral elements to conspiracy theories that we should consider before every conversation. Studying the "Pastel QAnon" phenomena taught me that many people start off with a desire for a positive outcome that might be as simple as self-improvement or more broadly applied to helping with a social problem. What motivates them is a clear choice between right and wrong.[13] A moral or spiritual pursuit obviously is not the same as an intellectual argument based on principles. Core beliefs occupy a unique place that are always subject to logic but still vulnerable to the same mistakes addressed about throughout this book. In the end, the same methods apply: listening, patience, persistence, and unclenched fists. The result may well be worth the effort.

Afterword

June 2024

Education takes for granted that sight is there but that it isn't turned the right way or looking where it ought to look and tries to re-direct it appropriately.[1]

—Plato, *The Republic*

INTRODUCTION

Arthur Mann warned me, but I didn't listen.

Dr. Mann was a storyteller in the best sense of the word, who taught a popular class on twentieth-century American social history at the University of Chicago. When he talked about Progressives and the Settlement House Movement, or the Red Scare, I would lose track of time, caught up in the personalities and details of a hundred years ago. But I remembered many of his lessons to graduate students and someday historians, one of which was to avoid researching and writing about events that happened during our lifetimes. Perspective is important. More so, as I tell my students today, new evidence almost certainly become available over time, and the story will quite naturally evolve. It is easy to be overcome by events.

I didn't listen, but Arthur Mann was right. This new chapter is the result.

History today reminds me of the "once in a generation" storms that used to strike parts of our planet. They were rare disasters that we remembered because they were so unique and terrible. Hurricane Agnes (1972), with its sudden school closings, power outages, and general mayhem, was that event in my own life. My father, who worked at the Philadelphia Electric Company, did not come home for a week.

As we all know, these "once in a generation" events now happen in rapid-fire succession each year. History seems to have also accelerated at the same tempo as Mother Nature. COVID-19 set the stage for both the writing and the publication of this book, but it did not, and does not, occupy the world stage alone. The 2020 election devolved into open sedition, a term that I can use now after the court system had its chance to unpeel the crimes committed by many January 6th participants.[2] Russia invaded Ukraine in 2022 and nuclear saber-rattling, in an unsettling callback to the bad old days of the Cold War, is back. The dual humanitarian disasters in Israel and Gaza have destabilized the Middle East.

This list is long and ready to grow.

What do the times say about us? A crisis can be an honest mirror for us to stare into. People seek out acceptance and friendship. They want to be well-liked in the same way Willy Loman did in *Death of a Salesman*. Yet, moments of profound stress can take away our public personas and reveal who we truly are. This can be true for individuals and countries. In 2020, COVID was our national stress test and the best in people came out. We rightly celebrated nurses, parents, and teachers (for a while) as they struggled to care for the sick, pay the rent, educate our children, or simply stay one step ahead of the next day's catastrophe. Hard times produced heroes, just they always have.

But the opposite can also be true. Crisis too often unearths the worst in us, where the first response, sometimes made from the deepest well of belief, is also the most truthful for all the wrong reasons. Public polling tells us a consistent and disturbing story. In June 2020, one in four Americans thought that COVID was the result of a conspiracy. A quarter of respondents surveyed by the Chicago Project on Security and Threats in September 2021 believed that "the 2020 election was stolen from Donald Trump and Joe Biden is an illegitimate president."[3] At the beginning of 2022, the Pew Research Center indicated that 25 percent of Republicans and 16 percent of people in general believed the core ideas of QAnon.[4]

Why are we here? Partly because we always have been. Arthur Goldwag predicts the demise of QAnon in *The Politics of Fear* (2024), with the caveat that "the underlying structure of its narrative will abide. Much older than Trump and Trumpism, it is almost infinitely adaptable."[5] The foundation for conspiracies like QAnon is ancient. As many authors, me included, have noted, it is a compilation of fear, hatred, paranoia, racism, a "sense of dispossession," and a dozen other factors.[6]

But modern times have also augmented and adapted to deeply ingrained bad habits. Conspiracies today exist in a toxic "Iron Triangle" of media outlets, elites, and their audiences.[7] The days of the big three networks—ABC, CBS, NBC—are a fading Boomer memory. In their place are layers of cable news networks, websites, blogs, YouTube channels, and social media platforms. The situation is a modern update of something sociologist Doug

McAdam said about the Baby Boomers; when the current generation takes the stage today, it is custom built.[8]

Politicians, celebrities, and academics, "influencers," populate these platforms, lending their authority and credibility to the discussion.[9] Dan Coats and other highly placed former intelligence officials speculated about Trump's relationship with Russia during the Mueller investigation.[10] Hundreds of retired senior military leaders, organized as "Flag Officers 4 America," characterized the 2020 election as "a conflict between supporters of Socialism and Marxism vs. supporters of Constitutional freedom and liberty" and denounced Biden's victory.[11] During the Super Bowl buildup at the beginning of 2024, we were treated to conspiracies about Taylor Swift being in cahoots with the Democrats.[12]

The audience for the panoply of platforms and elite influencers has broken into warring tribes at the moment. Confirmation bias is so deeply embedded in who we listen to and what we believe, it is a key part of the new norm. A 2022 survey by the Public Religion Research Institute (PPRI) noted that people who watched Fox were twice as likely to believe in QAnon as regular news outlet consumers. However, if Fox was too "moderate," there were other spaces available. The same PPRI study reported that Americans who followed Newsmax and One America News Network were five times as likely to accept QAnon beliefs.[13] Many of these individuals are well-meaning and sincere as they draw their information from unreliable internet sources and social media platforms. But they are vulnerable to other actors who use these same venues to amplify conspiracies for their own ends. As Republican strategist and bomb thrower Steve Bannon once put it: "The Democrats don't matter. The real opposition is the media. And the way to deal with them is to flood the zone with shit."[14]

The story of "Twitter Files" is one case in point. At the end of 2022, journalist Matt Taibbi published a long piece on one of the most influential social media platforms in the world and its impact on American politics. Specifically, Taibbi suggested that Twitter executives deliberately censored information about Hunter Biden's laptop, a fall 2020 story that had the potential to influence the upcoming presidential election.[15] In his December 2, 2022, preliminary "Note to Readers," Taibbi offered: "It's about to get weird in here."[16]

From that point, however, the story broke along our political/tribal lines. Were the Twitter Files a matter of "a systemic violation of the First Amendment, the largest example of that in modern history," according to Tucker Carlson? Or did the Twitter Files simply illustrate "a group of executives earnestly debating how to deal with an unconfirmed news report that was based on information from a laptop that appeared to be Hunter Biden's," as one reporter for the *New York Times* commented?[17]

There are glimmers of a very old story in the back-and-forth about the Twitter Files.

The whole discussion recalls the Protocols of the Elders of Zion in that global forces are manipulating our ability to think and make decisions on our own. Twitter is a combination of Protocol No. 12 Control of the Press, Protocol No. 15 Ruthless Suppression, Protocol No. 16 Brainwashing, and so on. Adding a modern-day social media platform simply updates suspicions cultivated more than a century ago. One of Taibbi's December 2022 tweets straddled the issue of old versus new: "The 'Twitter Files' tell an incredible story from inside one of the world's largest and most influential social media platforms. It is a Frankenstein tale of a human-built mechanism grown out of the control of its designer."[18]

Are the Twitter Files a matter of technology truly out of control? Or are they an example of a shadowy, corporate cabal pulling strings behind the scenes? Many people will not learn the answer for a very simple, contemporary reason. Most of Taibbi's writing live behind a paywall and are only open to subscribers.

There are more examples that we will examine in the following passages. In truth, a continuing stream of new analyses and sources makes it possible to revise and reinterpret almost all the chapters in this book. For example, the 2021 Dominion Voting Systems lawsuit against the Fox Network revealed many documents illustrating the gap between election fraud, TV programming, and what Fox management and television personalities understood as fact. However, for the sake of focus and keeping this chapter reasonably short, we will return to this story while revisiting three recent conspiracy theories that continue to have a serious impact on America: COVID-19, QAnon, and the 2020 election.[19]

COVID-19

When I was wrapping up the final draft of this book in May 2021, global cases of COVID stood at 167.4 million, with more than 3.4 million deaths. There were 28.3 million total cases in the United States and approximately 594,000 had died of the disease.[20] Three years later, times have changed and not for the better. At the end of May 2024, worldwide cases had advanced to a staggering 775.4 million. Global deaths had doubled to over 7 million. The United States alone accounted for 103.4 million of these cases and almost 1.2 million deaths.[21]

At the start of 2023, there was a strong sense of the COVID déjà vu. China was again in a full-scale health crisis. However, this time, Beijing's "Zero

COVID" policy had provoked a serious public backlash. Throughout the country, citizens openly protested the severe COVID policies taken by the communist regime. In response, Beijing pivoted and rolled back many of the restrictions in place for almost three years. As COVID cases began to rise rapidly, Chinese public health officials retreated behind official censorship. Between November 1, 2022, and January 13, 2023, the Chinese Center for Disease Control and Prevention reported fewer than fifty deaths in the whole country.[22] Although the Chinese government cooperated more fully with the World Health Organization and other institutions, the lack of transparency cultivated old suspicions about the origins of COVID-19.

February 2023 saw yet another COVID callback. In an updated multiagency intelligence report, the U.S. Department of Energy revisited the idea that the pandemic originated in a Chinese lab. Although other members of the intelligence community challenged this assessment and Energy Department officials admitted there was "low confidence" in the conclusion, it restarted an old debate about blame and official coverups.[23] Three House Republicans—Cathy Rodgers (R-WA), Morgan Griffith (R-VA), and Brett Guthrie (R-KY)—released a statement within days of the breaking news:

> This report affirms our belief that the substantial circumstantial evidence favors COVID-19 emerging from a research-related incident. These revelations also further strengthen the need to uncover why high-ranking government officials, with help from Big Tech and the media, sought early on to silence any debate into a plausible theory of a lab incident while the Chinese Communist Party stonewalled investigations by the global scientific community.[24]

Federal officials actually in charge of public health policy were more philosophical. Anthony Fauci, the public face of the U.S. COVID response and the ongoing target of partisan attacks, was nearing the conclusion of his long tenure in government service at the end of 2022. He was in a reflective mood in November: "As a public health official, I don't want to see anyone suffer and die from Covid. I don't care if you're a far-right Republican or a far-left Democrat, everybody deserves to have the safety of good public health and that's not happening."[25]

Fauci was pointing out a fundamental flaw of America's COVID response. It was as much, or perhaps more so, a topic of politics than it was of medicine. As a physician, he looked at the problem as a matter of identifying a disease and a medical response. Unfortunately, Fauci was and remains a right-wing lightning rod. "Fire Fauci" chants are a fixture at Republican rallies. In the lead-up to the 2020 presidential election, Donald Trump constantly threatened to fire the head of the National Institute of Allergies and Infectious Diseases in front of cheering crowds.[26] Florida governor and presidential hopeful

Ron DeSantis joined the bandwagon in August 2022: "I'm just sick of seeing him! I know he says he's going to retire. Someone needs to grab that little elf and chuck him across the Potomac."[27] Elon Musk added himself to the scrum shortly after taking over Twitter in early December 2022, when he tweeted: "My pronouns are Prosecute/Fauci."[28]

Even after his retirement, conspiracy-minded Republicans were not done with Fauci. When he appeared before the House Oversight and Accountability Subcommittee on the Coronavirus Pandemic in June 2024, years of accumulated claims saw the light of day again.[29] Presented with the notion that he had worked with the intelligence community to suppress the truth about the pandemic, Fauci jeered: "I was parachuted into the CIA like Jason Bourne and told the CIA that they should really not be talking about a lab leak."[30] Marjorie Taylor Greene, a leading light among conspiracy mongers in the GOP, asked: "You know what this committee should be doing?" She then cut right to the chase: "We should be recommending you to be prosecuted. We should be writing a criminal referral because you should be prosecuted for crimes against humanity. You belong in prison, Dr. Fauci."[31]

Over the last four years, rhetoric like this has set a tone that directly affects the publics' perception of COVID. A March 2022 Pew Research Center report noted a clear correlation of voting patterns, COVID infections, and deaths. In its earliest stages, before vaccines were available, COVID hit counties that voted Democrats hardest. This was the case in New York, which suffered significantly in the spring of 2020. Later, COVID Omicron and Delta variants, emerging after public vaccinations began, took a much different route. During the third wave of infections, starting in the fall of 2021, the death rate among Republicans was more than three times that of Democrats.[32] As of January 2023, vaccination rates remained lowest in Alabama, Louisiana, Mississippi, Tennessee, Idaho, Wyoming, Ohio, and Indiana. All of these states voted for Donald Trump in 2020.[33]

One unfortunate consequence of politics and its influence on public health is a body of unvaccinated people, approximately 20 percent of the country, who are serving as an environment for a steady stream of new COVID mutations.[34] At the start of 2023, there were thirteen versions of the Omicron COVID variant infecting Americans.[35] Each new variant tested the effectiveness of vaccinations. The crossover point came in August 2022 when 58 percent of COVID deaths were among vaccinated Americans, an increase from 42 percent in February and more than double the rate (23 percent) in September 2021.[36] There were some reasonable explanations for the trend. More Americans are vaccinated, and an increasing proportion are likely to be part of mortality statistics. However, the data also speaks to the declining impact of vaccines, especially in the wake of new variants like BA.5 Omicron, which dominated new COVID cases in the summer of 2022.

As I write this, it seems as if the country is enjoying a hopeful break from COVID. Last spring, only .84 percent of counties (27 total) were experiencing high (red) rates of infection. In May 2024, the red, orange, and yellow zones were gone. As far as the CDC was concerned, America was literally in the green.[37]

The Biden administration has also adopted a number of measures to bolster readiness for the next pandemic. In October 2022, the White House issued a *National Biodefense Strategy and Implementation Plan* that tasked twenty federal agencies to "protect the American people and its global interests from biological threats, regardless of origin."[38] As part of his 2023 budget, the president requested $88 billion over the next five years to support these efforts.[39] In July 2023, the administration formally created the White House Office of Preparedness and Response Policy.[40]

Regardless, warning signs still flicker. The start of 2024 saw a surge in respiratory illnesses that included influenza, RSV (Respiratory Syncytial Virus), and COVID-19.[41] More to the point, given the current state of Congress, neither funding nor coherent policy seems to be a given. American health lives between opposing forces: "the safety of good public health," as Dr. Fauci said in 2022 and constant partisan attacks on medical authority that erode its public legitimacy. In the end, our success or failure in fighting COVID will not be only a matter of technology, or supply chains, or government funding. Success or failure belongs to us.

QANON

The misguided, paranoid crusade that emerged from internet message boards only a few years ago has morphed, ironically, into a movement now living openly inside the national government itself. Indiana Republican Jim Banks made this clear in a January 2023 statement:

> We no longer live in a normal America. The issues that Congress used to take up, like healthcare, the economy, or our withdrawal from Afghanistan, all regrettably pale in comparison to the creeping tyranny which nearly all Americans now feel.

> The nation's most powerful forces—our intelligence agencies, corporations, the press, our universities, and even our military—are all pressing further and further into uncharted territory from which it's not clear America can return.

> For the time being, saving America rests in the House of Representatives.

> The most toxic part of this tyranny is its doctrine—"wokeness." Everyone has by now heard this word but it means something very specific. It means that all the

so-called oppressor groups must be punished for their past and present alleged sins. There are many steps to punishing them: inducing self-hatred through indoctrination, stripping away their rights by not enforcing the laws on their behalf, public humiliation, hatred, expropriation, and ultimately violence. That's what the Left has done so far. It's not exactly clear yet how far this can go.[42]

In many respects, Banks' statement follows the same path of the omnipotent, evil threat articulated by Richard Hofstadter in the "Paranoid Style of American Politics" sixty years ago.[43] More to the point, then as now, according to the QAnon universe, the enemies threatening America are no longer outside the gates defended by a cohort of right-minded patriots. They are inside now and in charge.

Representative Banks' use of the word "woke" is also a modern update to a very old idea. Reading through his statement is like taking a trip in a time machine. His accusations about the "woke" Left "inducing self-hatred through indoctrination, stripping away their rights by not enforcing the laws on their behalf, public humiliation, hatred, expropriation, and ultimately violence" would have fit well into the angry exchanges of the First Red Scare (1919), McCarthyism (1950), Watergate (1972), or the 2016 election.

Or it could be right now. Minutes after his conviction in New York on thirty-four felony counts, Donald Trump denounced "a rigged, a disgrace." He went so far as to single out the "Soros-backed DA" who prosecuted him.[44] Death threats against jurors, the trial, judge, and prosecutors followed in the wake of the verdicts. One post read: "1,000,000 men (armed) need to go to Washington and hang everyone. That's the only solution." Wrote another user, "This s--- is out of control."[45]

More important to our time right now is how this anger has percolated down into our communities. It is a constant at school boards, libraries, and local polling places. This is particularly true in my home state of Pennsylvania. For example, "activists" that are part of the so-called Project Veritas are promoting a campaign to have grade schoolers record their teachers using hidden cameras.[46] Another group that calls itself the Pennsylvania Family Institute publishes a "School Incident Report" and justifies it by stating: "Public Schools are not to be used for taxpayer funded political, sexual, or racist ideological indoctrination."[47]

State Republican politicians have taken up these causes and amplified them with their authority and well-funded election campaigns. While running for governor of Pennsylvania in 2022, Doug Mastriano made the pointed accusation:

"This is disgusting to me, where bureaucrats and Tom Wolf—and Josh Shapiro—thinks it's okay to come in and threaten parents and therapists because their kids might be confused and confused because of what's going on in the schools where they have graphic pornographic books laid out in elementary schools, teachers . . . or some who are out of control there and they're using their platform to confuse kids on gender."[48]

He went on further to say: "These people want to take over your kids and indoctrinate them and take away any power you or a medical professional has in helping or assisting them and rather use this opportunity here as a tool to strip your rights away."[49]

School boards are now ground zero for the "woke" version of QAnon. Bucks County, Pennsylvania, gained national attention for vicious, combative public debates often on display. At a November 2021 school board meeting, the *New York Times* recorded: "Parents and other residents took turns standing before the board, speaking about Zionism, Maoism, slavery, freedom, the Holocaust, critical race theory, the illegality of mask requirements, supposed Jewish ties to organized crime and the viral falsehood that transgender students were raping people in bathrooms."[50] School officials and board members soon began receiving death threats. The district canceled an August 2021 special meeting on masking policy after social media indicated a group with alleged ties to right-wing militias might attend.[51] Police became a regular feature at Bucks County school board gatherings.

In 2021, several Republican candidates joined the contest for the Central Bucks School Board. Some conservatives, like Jim Pepper, moderated their language, promising "a strong voice for children, parents and taxpayers."[52] Other candidates did not. Debra Cannon declared during a May 2021 public meeting that "demonic adults are recruiting, brainwashing, and participating in unconscionable behaviors with our children, and every one of you know it."[53] Both Pepper and Cannon were elected in November and joined the Central Bucks School Board as part of a new 6-3 Republican majority.[54]

In just a few short years, QAnon has transformed from what we assumed was a small, cultish group of fringe believers who popped up on message boards and political rallies in their conspiracy march, to a movement deeply embedded in our local communities. QAnon themes are central to discussions regarding education, library holdings, LGBTQ rights, public protest, candidates' political affiliation, and a dozen other issues. These ideas were constantly on display at the March 2023 Conservative Political Action Conference (CPAC) by an array of Republican presidential hopefuls. Florida governor Ron DeSantis, who did not attend, made the current culture war central to his candidacy, declaring that his state was a place where "woke goes to die."[55] Clearly, whether we use the term "QAnon" or not, it will be a fixture in America, from top to bottom, for the foreseeable future.

THE BIG LIE

Almost two years to the day after Joe Biden was officially certified as the winner of the 2020 election, Lycoming County, Pennsylvania, held a ballot recount to contest the truth of that decision. Over a three-day period, that is exactly what local officials did. After processing nearly 60,000 ballots by hand, Joe Biden lost fifteen votes and Donald Trump gained eight. In a deep red county where the former president won with 69.98 percent of the vote, the recount did not discover any evidence of fraud.[56]

High-profile Republicans made the mantra of the "stolen" election a constant feature of 2022 and continue to do so. In public rallies and a constant stream of statements, Donald Trump repeated a series of debunked claims about the 2020 election. In an October 2022 Texas gathering, Trump denounced the January 6th Committee and what he called for an investigation into "the cooked, stolen election."[57] On December 3, 2022, the former president went so far as to say on his Truth Social account that "A Massive Fraud of this type and magnitude allows for the termination of all rules, regulations, and articles, even those found in the Constitution. Our great 'Founders' did not want, and would not condone, False & Fraudulent Elections!"[58]

Many candidates took up Trump's banner throughout 2022. Doug Mastriano, who was present during the Capitol riot, constantly raised the issue, something that has been extensively documented by the Pennsylvania press.[59] Speaking about his home state of Pennsylvania in a December 28, 2020, letter to the Justice Department, Mastriano asked: "Why is the very state where the light of liberty was lit in 1776 is unable or unwilling to have elections as free and safe as war torn Afghanistan? Something is seriously wrong in this Commonwealth and unless this is corrected, our republic cannot long endure."[60] In Arizona, Kari Lake doubled down on the same claims. During a June 2021 Fox News interview, she flatly stated: "We had a fraudulent election, a corrupt election, and we have an illegitimate president." Lake went on to say: "There's a mountain of evidence, and I wish that the corporate media would start covering it instead of putting their head in the sand and acting like it didn't happen."[61]

If the Lycoming County recount and a barrage of 2022 election claims demonstrated the persistence of a myth, the January 6th Committee investigation revealed its depth, complexity, and danger.[62] An estimated 20 million Americans watched the first day of hearings in June 2022. In the days following, the committee addressed a host of issues, from the range rioters' motives—some of whom had sincere beliefs about an open threat to democracy to often bizarre and repeatedly debunked theories still lingering on social media and courtrooms even today—to direct evidence about the day itself.[63]

The January 6th Committee report is a massive 845-page tome that we will spend years unpacking. The committee's due diligence produced an array of detail that speaks to the real threat present that day. Police radio traffic revealed firearms among the crowd outside the Ellipse, where Trump encouraged the assembled to "fight like hell." Secret Service reports detail a brutal array of weaponry—knives, tasers, brass knuckles, and blunt instruments—confiscated from people passing through metal detectors to cheer the president.

Under oath before the committee, some of the loudest voices encouraging rioters to descend upon the Capitol backtracked or outright rejected their earlier advocacy. Ginni Thomas, wife of Supreme Court Justice Clarence Thomas, was a prominent actor before the riot. In the weeks following the 2020 election, she peppered officials with texts. One, sent to White House chief of staff Mark Meadows, exclaimed: "Help This Great President stand firm, Mark!!! . . . You are the leader, with him, who is standing for America's constitutional governance at the precipice."[64] She went on further to say: "The majority knows Biden and the Left is attempting the greatest Heist of our History."[65] However, when called to testify before the January 6th Committee, she offered that it was an "emotional" time and expressed her regret about sending texts.[66] In a separate deposition for the Dominion Voting Systems $1.6 billion lawsuit against Fox News, Sean Hannity denied any belief in 2020 election fraud claims despite promoting them for months on television.[67]

Department of Justice investigations added another strata of disturbing detail. In the three years since January 6th, a total of 1,265 individuals have been arrested. Of these, 452 were charged with "assaulting, resisting, or impeding officers or employees, including approximately 123 individuals who have been charged with using a deadly or dangerous weapon or causing serious bodily injury to an officer."[68] One hundred and thirty-nine people took their cases to trial and were found guilty. Another 718 took plea deals on a variety of federal charges.[69]

Although detailed accounts of violence at the Capitol are chilling enough, it was not a one-off spasm perpetrated by easily duped citizens. There was a darker, premeditated plan at work. Evidence unearthed by the January 6th Committee and a series of investigations revealed dozens of local, state, and congressional Republicans networking in a campaign to reverse a legal election. Seven states launched probes of what was an orchestrated campaign to interfere with the 2020 election and substitute false electors for the people legally designated by voters. By April 2024, dozens of Republican operatives in five states—Arizona, Georgia, Michigan, Nevada, and Wisconsin—faced a range of charges related to forgery, attempts to file false documents, fraud, and conspiracy, among many others. Nationally known Republican figures like Rudy Giuliani, Mark Meadows, John Eastman, Jenna Ellis, Sydney Powell, and Kenneth Chesboro faced a variety of indictments.[70] In Georgia, Trump was charged with thirteen counts, to include racketeering, "overt acts in furtherance of a conspiracy," and making false statements.[71] In Arizona, Trump was not charged but named as an unindicted co-conspirator.

Legally, this story seems very clear cut, although juries will get the final word, as one did in New York. But what about the politics of January 6th? Short-term signs were encouraging. The results of the 2022 election indicated a consistent failure among conspiracy candidates at virtually every level.[72] In Pennsylvania, gubernatorial candidate Doug Mastriano was spectacularly unsuccessful in his run against Josh Shapiro by 56.5 percent to 41.7 percent.[73] Failing at her own bid for governor, Kari Lake denounced the process and took her claims to court. In his December 2022 decision, Judge Peter Thompson noted technical problems on election day Arizona but no evidence of fraud, going on further to say: "Every single witness before the Court disclaimed any personal knowledge of such misconduct. The Court cannot accept speculation or conjecture in place of clear and convincing evidence."[74]

National surveys are more ambiguous. Over most of 2022, pollsters maintained that the January 6th investigation had little impact on public opinion. Between June and July, the percentage of Americans who described events at the Capitol as a "riot" hovered between 64 and 65 percent, according to a Monmouth University poll. People asked if January 6th was an "insurrection" increased from 50 percent to 52 percent.[75] In contrast, it looked like Republicans were tracking in the opposite direction. Between June 2021 and June 2022, the number of Republicans who saw January 6th as an insurrection declined from 33 percent to just 13 percent. On the other hand, the percentage who described the event as a "legitimate protest" grew from 47 percent to 61 percent.[76]

Trump was not politically unscathed from his relentless promotion of January 6th conspiracy theories, at least initially. A Quinnipiac University poll published at the end of 2022 indicated that the favorable opinion of Trump (31 percent) among registered voters was its lowest in seven years.[77]

Two years can be a long time in politics, however, and polls can be problematic. The website FiveThirtyEight maintains an ongoing record of polls related to political figures, Trump included. When the FBI executed a search warrant at Mar-a-Lago in August 2022, Trump's average approval was 40.1 percent. In May 2024, right before the New York verdict, it stood at 41.6 percent.[78] In comparison, Joe Biden's average approval on June 6, 2024, was a meager 37.6 percent.[79]

The new 118th Congress, which convened in January 2023, understands these numbers very well. This is the case in the House of Representatives, where the so-called "Freedom Caucus" has relentlessly deployed a rotisserie of conspiracy theories in committee meetings, speeches, and interviews. Writing for the *New York Times*, Michelle Goldberg succinctly evaluated this new crop of law makers: "They don't want policy; they want airtime."[80]

WITH A LITTLE HELP FROM MY FRIENDS

When my wife and I watch the nightly news, we often refer to it as the "daily bummer," a term borrowed from Hunter S. Thompson's *Fear and Loathing on the Campaign Trail* (1973). Thompson dove headfirst into the worst parts of American political arena during the age of Watergate. In hindsight, those days seem naïve, almost quaint.

Today is a different story. Today, we can read from *Project 2025*, the Heritage Foundation's template for a return of Republican power. Think tank projects being what they are, I anticipated the usual bland, careful language of seasoned political consultants.

I was wrong.

Mandate for Leadership: The Conservative Promise: Project 2025: Presidential Transition Project starts off like any of the paranoid conspiracy tracts that I have read over and over for this book: "The long march of cultural Marxism through our institutions has come to pass. The federal government is a behemoth, weaponized against American citizens and conservative values, with freedom and liberty under siege as never before."[81] It is fairly jarring to realize that this language does not come from pamphlet being handed out on a street corner. It is a Heritage Foundation blueprint for the next Republican administration.

Even with that said, it would be easy to take *Project 2025* as empty rhetoric, but I think that we know better than that by now. It is a plan to "fix" the "long march of cultural Marxism through our institutions." But where? How? Against what? Where do we find these Marxists and their long march? I ask because I will be working as a precinct judge of election in November. I ran for that office as a Democrat. Does that qualify me as a Marxist if I use the Heritage Foundation's spongy logic? I ask because *Project 2025* puts a white collar, Beltway veneer on a political party that tolerates death threats against civil servants, volunteers or otherwise, especially when it comes to election conspiracies.[82]

In this environment, hope seems hard to come by. But there are reasons for hope.

The American court system offered us some answers. Multibillion-dollar lawsuits have a way of taking the starch out of conspiracists. Fox News found

that out with the Dominion Voting Systems lawsuit.[83] After years of litigation, a cohort of Sandy Hook families successfully sued *Infowars* host Alex
Jones and received approximately a $1.4 billion in judgments against him by
the end of 2022.[84]

Some citizens focused on the ballot box. Parents in Buck County, Pennsylvania, unhappy with school board policies, organized behind Democrats,
who reversed earlier Republican gains and took charge of all five school
districts.[85]

A few politicians have stepped up to the plate. A small group of Republicans defied their own party in 2021 when they voted in favor of Donald
Trump's second impeachment in the House and Senate. Wyoming Republican Liz Cheney ended her political career not only by supporting impeachment but also by joining the January 6th Committee as its vice chair in 2022.
Cheney's position eventually cost her a congressional seat. She was thrashed
in the August primary by Harriet Hageman, who gathered 66.3 percent of the
vote against Cheney's 28.9 percent.[86]

Cheney's political fate did not eliminate the spirit of bipartisanship. After
winning the Pennsylvania governor's race, Democrat Josh Shapiro appointed
a Republican, Al Schmidt, as his secretary of state.[87] During the 2020 election, Schmidt was the one Republican on a three-member Philadelphia
County board of elections. Despite Trump's relentless tweeting about the
dead voting in the city and the "mountain of corruption & dishonesty," he
refused block official certification of votes.[88] For keeping faith with the system, Schmidt and his staff received death threats. Almost a year later, before
the Senate Committee on Rules and Administration, he testified:

> After the president tweeted about me, my wife and I received threats that named
> our children, included my home address and images of my home, and threated to
> put their "heads on spikes." What was once a fairly obscure administrative job is
> now one where lunatics are threatening to murder your children.[89]

Schmidt also spoke to the January 6th Committee about some of Trump's
specific claims: "Not only was there not evidence of 8,000 dead voters voting
in Pennsylvania, there wasn't evidence of eight."[90]

When House Speaker Kevin McCarthy exclusively released thousands of
hours of Capitol riot footage to Tucker Carlson in February 2023, he likely
did not anticipate the response by his own party. On his popular Fox program,
Carlson summarized his own findings: "These were not insurrectionists. They
were sightseers."[91] A few lawmakers, like Representative Elise Stefanik
(R-NY), quickly jumped on board in a tweet: "Last night, @TuckerCarl-
son confirmed what I've been saying for well over a year. Nancy Pelosi's
sham, unconstitutional Jan 6th Committee was nothing more than a political

witch-hunt designed to punish the radical Far Left's political opponents."[92] Other prominent Republicans, however, disagreed. In comments to the press, Senate Majority Leader Mitch McConnell noted: "It was a mistake, in my view, for Fox News to depict this in a way that's completely at variance with what our chief law enforcement official here in the Capitol thinks." Senator Kevin Cramer, a North Dakota Republican, was less measured: "To somehow put [Jan. 6] in the same category as a permitted peaceful protest is just a lie."[93] Others were even more pointed. Mitt Romney described the Fox broadcast as "dangerous and disgusting." He went on to say: "You can't hide the truth by selectively picking a few minutes out of tapes and saying this is what went on. It's so absurd, it's nonsense."[94] Senator Thom Tillis (R-NC) fired his own broadside: "I think it's bullshit. I was here. I was down there and I saw maybe a few tourists, a few people who got caught up in things. But when you see police barricades breached, when you see police officers assaulted, all of that . . . if you were just a tourist you should've probably lined up at the visitors' center and came in on an orderly basis."[95]

* * *

One last reason for hope is personal. I have been teaching my conspiracy course for eight years now. It has grown from small twenty-five-seat sections to auditorium-style classes of seventy students each. Students run the gamut. Many are intrigued by the possibility of talking about their favorite conspiracies while meeting a general education requirement. Others are mildly curious about the topic and the possibility of waking up for a morning class.

But, as they do sometimes, students can restore an old teacher's faith. I had a class just like that during the spring 2024 semester. Almost seventy strong, most were not history majors. In fact, quite a few were from the sciences, and the cohort of seniors was higher than normal. Most of them did everything right. They were curious. They read. They attended class and participated in detailed discussions. They connected an array of complex ideas. On some days, individuals and groups took the class in original, unexpected directions.

They were outstanding, an absolute joy to teach, the kind of students we talk about for years.

Plato said educators are important less for imparting knowledge than pointing their students in the right direction to receive it. Where conspiracy theories are concerned, individual teachers and national organizations have ramped up their efforts against disinformation. Groups like the National Association for Media Literacy Education and Media Literacy Now gather thousands of teachers and develop strategies for evaluating conspiracy claims, the presence or absence of valid evidence, and tools for navigating the internet, whose platforms heavily influence young learners at every level, from grade school to college.[96] A joint study published in a 2022 edition of the *Journal of Educational Psychology* by faculty from Stanford University and the University of Maryland focused particularly on the "digital onslaught" presented by the World Wide Web.[97] The study is a good example of both the need for better educational strategies and some of their limits. The article examines the impact of online formats on student cognition and develops a more sophisticated understanding of "lateral" (leaving a familiar website for the unfamiliar web) and "vertical" (reading a whole website) learning processes.[98]

Our tools are getting better for the ongoing challenge of conspiracy theories. We have these and some of the other approaches mentioned in the first edition of the book—listening, patience, and persistence—as we navigate our task. At points, it might feel like a slog, but the results are important and still worth the effort. I have seen the results with my own eyes.

Notes

INTRODUCTION

1. Noam Chomsky, *The Prosperous Few and the Restless Many* (Berkeley, CA: Odonian Press, 1994), 7–8.

2. Speech, Dr. Neil deGrasse Tyson, "The Amazing Meeting" YouTube video, 12:14–12:32, from a talk given on June 6, 2008, posted by ChristopherHitchslap on January 4, 2012. https://www.youtube.com/watch?v=8vfOpZD4Sm8.

3. Stephanie Pappas, "How Big Is the Internet, Really?" *Live Science* (March 18, 2016). http://www.livescience.com/54094-how-big-is-the-internet.html.

4. Ibid.

5. Amy Mitchell, Jeffrey Gottfried, Michael Barthell, and Elisa Shearer, "Pathways to News," Pew Research Center website report (July 7, 2016). http://www.journalism.org/2016/07/07/pathways-to-news/.

6. Michael Crichton, *The Lost World* (New York: Ballantine Books, 1995), 339.

7. Rob Brotherton, *Suspicious Minds: Why We Believe in Conspiracy Theories* (New York: Bloomsbury Sigma, 2015), 112.

8. Ibid., 12–13.

9. Shahram Heshmat, "What Is Confirmation Bias?" *Psychology Today* (April 23, 2015). https://www.psychologytoday.com/us/blog/science-choice/201504/what-is-confirmation-bias.

CHAPTER ONE

1. G. Kitson Clark, *The Making of Victorian England* (New York: Routledge, 1962), 10.

2. *Oxford English Dictionary*, s.v. "conspiracy," https://en.oxforddictionaries.com/definition/conspiracy; as in Rob Brotherton, *Suspicious Minds: Why We Believe in Conspiracy Theories* (New York: Bloomsbury Sigma, 2015), 61.

3. *Merriam-Webster*, s.v. "conspiracy theory," https://www.merriam-webster.com/dictionary/conspiracy%20theory; as in Brotherton, *Suspicious Minds*, 61–62.

4. There are many examples online. One example is Paul Craig Roberts, "The Term 'Conspiracy Theory' Was Invented by the CIA in Order to Prevent Disbelief of Official Government Stories," LewRockwell.com (August 30, 2016). https://www.lewrockwell.com/2016/08/paul-craig-roberts/cia-invented-term-conspiracy-theory/.

5. See, for example, "Debunked: The CIA Invented the Term 'Conspiracy Theory' in 1967," Metabunk, November 29, 2012. https://www.metabunk.org/debunked-the-cia-invented-the-term-conspiracy-theory-in-1967-in-use-for-70-years-prior.t960/#post-68081.

6. The website can be found at https://www.ae911truth.org.

7. Kathryn S. Olmsted, *Real Enemies: Conspiracy Theories and American Democracy, World War I to 9/11* (New York: Oxford University Press, 2009), 3.

8. James and Flemming quoted in Brotherton, *Suspicious Minds*, 72; my emphasis.

9. "Offenses Known to Law Enforcement: Property Crime," *Crime in the United States*, 2015, Uniform Crime Reporting (UCR) Program, Federal Bureau of Investigation (website), https://ucr.fbi.gov/crime-in-the-u.s/2015/crime-in-the-u.s.-2015/offenses-known-to-law-enforcement/property-crime.

10. Brotherton, *Suspicious Minds*, 72.

11. Michael Barkun, *A Culture of Conspiracy: Apocalyptic Visions in Contemporary America*, second edition (Berkeley: University of California Press, 2013), 6.

12. Wikipedia, s.v. "David Icke," last modified October 30, 2021, 00:05 (UTC), https://en.wikipedia.org/wiki/David_Icke.

13. Helmuth C. Engelbrecht, and Frank C. Hanighen, *Merchants of Death: A Study of the International Armament Industry* (New York: Dodd, Mead & Company, 1934).

14. Richard Hofstadter, "The Paranoid Style of American Politics," *Harper's Magazine* (November 1964): 77–86.

15. Barkun, *A Culture of Conspiracy*, 11–14.

16. Public Policy Polling, *National Survey Results* (April 2, 2013), 27.

17. For example, see Dane Wigington, "Geoengineering Watch Global Alert News," Geoengineering Watch (July 1, 2017), https://www.geoengineeringwatch.org/geoengineering-watch-global-alert-news-july-1-2017/; and Wigington, "Fish Die-Off and Chemically Nucleated Ice Storms," Geoengineering Watch (March 26, 2015), https://www.geoengineeringwatch.org/?s=nucleated.

18. Glenn Kessler, "About the Fact Checker," *Washington Post* (September 11, 2013), https://www.washingtonpost.com/news/fact-checker/about-the-fact-checker/?utm_term=.6e838c988e1e.

19. Wikipedia, s.v. "Six Degrees of Kevin Bacon," last modified October 12, 2021, 02:02 (UTC), https://en.wikipedia.org/wiki/Six_Degrees_of_Kevin_Bacon.

20. These flowcharts can be found on Tyler Vigen's webpage *Spurious Correlations*: http://tylervigen.com/spurious-correlations.

21. *Merriam-Webster*, s.v. "causation," https://www.merriam-webster.com/dictionary/causation.

22. RationalWiki, s.v. "confirmation bias," last modified September 5, 2021, 16:37, https://rationalwiki.org/wiki/Confirmation_bias.

23. Boaventura de Sousa Santos, "Towards a Socio-Legal Theory of Indignation," in *Law's Ethical, Global, and Theoretical Contexts*, Upendra Baxi, Christopher McCrudden, Abdul Paliwala, eds. (New York: Cambridge University Press, 2015), 132–33.

24. Taken from the Quizlet.com "Fallacy Practice" flash cards, https://quizlet.com/53643438/fallacy-practice-flash-cards/.

25. Ibid., https://quizlet.com/167515650/fallacies-flash-cards/.

CHAPTER TWO

1. David Aaronvitch, *Voodoo Histories: The Role of Conspiracy Theory in Shaping Modern American History* (New York: Riverhead Books, 2010), 22.

2. *The Protocols of the Learned Elders of Zion*, available via biblebelievers.org, http://www.biblebelievers.org.au/przion2.htm#PROTOCOL%20No.%201.

3. Ibid.

4. Aaronvitch, *Voodoo Histories*, 44.

5. Howard Jones, *Crucible of Power: A History of American Foreign Relations from 1897*, second edition (New York: Rowman & Littlefield Publishers, Inc., 2008), 93–94.

6. Jackson J. Spielvogel, *Western Civilization*, 4th ed. (Belmont, CA: Wadsworth Thompson Learning, 2000), 782–83.

7. Gina Kolata, *Flu: The Story of the Great Influenza Pandemic of 1918 and the Search for the Virus That Caused It* (New York: Farrar, Straus, and Giroux, 1999), 7; The 675,000 figure is from http://www.history.com/topics/1918-flu-pandemic.

8. Kolata, *Flu*, 13–14.

9. Ibid., 19–20.

10. Theodore Ropp, *War in the Modern World* (New York: Collier Books, 1962), 243.

11. Ernest Hemingway, *The Collected Poems of Ernest Hemingway*. Pirated edition (San Francisco, 1960), xx.

12. Aaronvitch, *Voodoo Histories*, 18.

13. This quote is most likely a myth. The original source is a January 7, 1930, story about Ruth's contract negotiations with the Yankees; wikiquote, s.v. "Babe Ruth," https://en.wikiquote.org/wiki/Babe_Ruth.

14. Alexander Watson, *Enduring the Great War: Combat, Morale, and Collapse in the German and British Armies, 1914–1918* (New York: Cambridge University Press, 2008), 213.

15. Aaronovitch, *Voodoo History*, 19.

16. Ibid.

17. British Foreign Office report quoted in Aaronovitch, *Voodoo History*, 21.

18. Binjamin W. Segel, *A Lie and a Libel: A History of the Protocols of the Elders of Zion*, Richard S. Levy, trans. (Lincoln: University of Nebraska Press, 1995), 62.

19. Aaronovitch, *Voodoo History*, 20–21.

20. Robert K. Murray, *Red Scare: A Study of National Hysteria, 1919–1920* (New York: McGraw-Hill Book Company, 1964), 65.

21. Ibid., 70–71.

22. David M. Kennedy, *Over Here: The First World War and American Society* (New York: Oxford University Press, 1980), 288–90.

23. Aaronovitch, *Voodoo History*, 30.

24. Vincent Curcio, *Henry Ford* (New York: Oxford University Press, 2013), 138.

25. Ibid., 145.

26. Aaronovitch, *Voodoo History*, 31.

27. "The International Jew: The World's Problem," *The Dearborn Independent* (May 22, 1920): 1, Library of Congress, https://chroniclingamerica.loc.gov/lccn/2013218776/1920-05-22/ed-1/seq-1/.

28. Victoria Saker Woeste, *Henry Ford's War on Jews: And the Legal Battle Against Hate Speech* (Stanford, CA: Stanford University Press, 2012), 309. The second edition of *Mein Kampf* specifically said: "It is Jews who govern the stock exchange forces of the American Union. Every year makes them more and more the controlling masters of the producers in a nation of one hundred and twenty million; only a single great man, Ford, to their fury, still maintains full independence." See Adolph Hitler, *Mein Kampf*, Ralph Manheim, trans. (Boston: Houghton Mifflin Company, 1943), 639.

29. Michael Dobbs, "Ford and GM Scrutinized for Alleged Nazi Collaboration," *Washington Post* (November 30, 1998): A9.

30. Aaronovitch, *Voodoo History*, 38.

31. Ibid., 39.

32. Ibid., 40.

33. Adolph Hitler, *Mein Kampf* (Boston: Houghton Mifflin, 1971), 307–8.

34. Aaronovitch, *Voodoo History*, 46.

35. Ibid., 47.

36. *Hamas Covenant 1988: The Covenant of the Islamic Resistance Movement*, August 18, 1988, The Avalon Project digital documents website, Yale Law School, Lillian Goldman Law Library, http://avalon.law.yale.edu/20th_century/hamas.asp.

37. Aaronovitch, *Voodoo History*, 50.

38. Cynthia Dettelbach, "'Protocols of Zion' Are Alive and Well Post-9/11," *Cleveland Jewish News* (February 10, 2006). https://www.clevelandjewishnews.com/archives/protocols-of-zion-are-alive-and-well-post/article_a9e7dd3f-1737-5399-8eef-92feaf4650d9.html.

39. Rob Brotherton, *Suspicious Minds: Why We Believe Conspiracy Theories* (New York: Bloomsbury Sigma, 2015), 33–34.

40. Hannah Arendt, *The Origins of Totalitarianism* (New York: Harcourt Brace, 1951), 357.

CHAPTER THREE

1. Joseph McCarthy, *Major Speeches and Debates of Senator Joe McCarthy Delivered in the United States Senate, 1950–1951* (Washington: Government Printing Office, 1953), 215, 264, 307.

2. Wikiquote, s.v. "Joseph N. Welch," last modified April 12, 2017, 18:35, https://en.wikiquote.org/wiki/Joseph_N._Welch.

3. The Soviet Union officially ceased to exist on December 26, 1991.

4. An excellent study of the issue can be found in Robert Timberg, *The Nightingale's Song* (New York: Simon & Schuster, 1995).

5. Joseph McCarthy, Speech at Wheeling, West Virginia, February 9, 1950, http://historymatters.gmu.edu/d/6456/.

6. Harold B. Hinton, "M'Carthy Charges Spy for Russia Has a High State Department Post," *New York Times* (February 21, 1950): 13.

7. Nicholas V. Riasanovsky, *A History of Russia*, fourth edition (New York: Oxford University Press, 1984), 465–73.

8. Wikipedia, s.v. "Communist International," last modified October 31, 2021, 19:10, https://en.wikipedia.org/wiki/Communist_International#cite_ref-17.

9. Kathryn S. Olmsted, *Real Enemies: Conspiracy Theories and American Democracy, World War I to 9/11* (New York: Oxford University Press, 2009), 85.

10. Ibid., 86.

11. Katherine A. S. Sibley, *Red Spies in America: Stolen Secrets and the Dawn of the Cold War* (Lawrence, KS: University of Kansas Press, 2004), 133–74.

12. Olmsted, *Real Enemies*, 88–92.

13. Truman's Loyalty Program. Harry S. Truman Presidential Library and Museum. https://www.trumanlibrary.org/dbq/loyaltyprogram.php.

14. C. P. Trussell, "Woman Links Spies to US War Offices and White House," *New York Times* (July 31, 1948): 1.

15. David M. Oshinsky, *A Conspiracy So Immense: The World of Joe McCarthy* (New York: The Free Press, 1983), 104.

16. "US Reds Go Underground to Foil FBI, Hoover Says," *New York Times* (June 9, 1950): 1.

17. Oshinsky, *A Conspiracy So Immense*, 30–35; James Cross Giblin, *The Rise and Fall of Senator Joe McCarthy* (Boston, MA: Clarion Books, 2009), 34.

18. Oshinsky, *A Conspiracy So Immense*, 107.

19. James T. Patterson, *Grand Expectations: The United States, 1945–1974* (New York: Oxford University Press, 1996), 196.

20. Geoffrey R. Stone, *Perilous Times: Free Speech in Wartime from the Sedition Act of 1798 to the War on Terrorism* (New York: W.W. Norton & Company, 2004), 378.

21. David Aaronovitch, *Voodoo History: The Role of Conspiracy Theory in Shaping Modern History* (New York: Riverhead Books, 2010), 125.

22. Patterson, *Grand Expectation*, 190.

23. Oshinsky, *A Conspiracy So Immense*, 109–10.

24. Patterson, *Grand Expectation*, 267.

25. Wikipedia, s.v. "Joseph N. Welch," last modified September 15, 2021, 01:37, https://en.wikipedia.org/wiki/Joseph_N._Welch.

26. Richard M. Fried, *Nightmare in Red: The McCarthy Era in Perspective* (New York: Oxford University Press, 1990) 138.

27. Stephen E. Ambrose, *Eisenhower: The President*, vol. 2 (New York: Simon & Schuster, 1984), 162–63.

28. Andrea Friedman, "The Smearing of Joe McCarthy: The Lavender Scare, Gossip, and Cold War Politics," *American Quarterly* 57 (December 2005): 1107–8; Maryland State Department of Health, Certificate of Death, Joseph Raymond McCarthy, May 2, 1957.

29. David McCullough, *Truman* (New York: Simon & Schuster, 1992), 652 and 661.

30. McCarthy, Speech at Wheeling.

31. Olmsted, *Real Enemies*, 105.

32. Naoko Shibusawa, "The Lavender Scare and Empire: Rethinking Cold War Antigay Politics," *Diplomatic History* 36 (September 2012): 752.

33. Olmsted, *Real Enemies*, 105

34. K. A. Cuordileone, "'Politics in an Age of Anxiety': Cold War Political Culture and the Crisis in American Masculinity, 1949–1960," *Journal of American History* 87 (September 2000): 539.

35. Historian William Leuchtenberg argues that the postwar economic boom was the main goal of the American public. At the peak of McCarthy's public approval ratings in early 1954, polls indicated that less than 1 percent of the public was concerned about the Communist peril. William Leuchtenberg, *A Troubled Feast: American Society Since* 1945 (Boston: Little, Brown and Company, 1983), 34.

36. Scott W. Carmichael, *True Believer: Inside the Investigation and Capture of Ana Montes, Cuba's Master Spy* (Annapolis, MD: Naval Institute Press, 2007).

37. US Senate, Senate Select Committee to Study Governmental Operations, *Final Report of the Senate Select Committee to Study Governmental Operations with Respect to Intelligence Activities* (Washington, DC: Government Printing Office, 1976), 3.

38. Robert Pears, Foreign Agents Linked to Freeze, Reagan Says," *New York Times* (November 12, 1982): B7.

CHAPTER FOUR

1. Warren Commission Hearings, vol. I (Washington, DC: Government Printing Office, 1964), 19.

2. Central Intelligence Agency, Memorandum for J. Lee Rankin (General Counsel, President's Commission on the Assassination of President Kennedy, "Discussion Between Chairman Khrushchev and Mr. Drew Pearson re Lee Harvey Oswald," May 27, 1964, https://www.maryferrell.org/showDoc.html?docId=51190#relPageId=2.

3. Wikipedia, s.v. "Military-industrial complex," last modified October 5, 2021, 08:13 (UTC), https://en.wikipedia.org/wiki/Military–industrial_complex.

4. Probably the best example of a critic at the time is C. Wright Mills, *The Power Elite* (New York: Oxford University Press, 1956). For a more recent read on the same subject, there is Matt Taibbi, *The Divide: American Injustice in the Age of the Wealth Gap* (New York: Spiegel & Grau, 2014).

5. Lawrence R. Samuel, *Rich: The Rise and Fall of American Wealth Culture* (New York: American Management Association, 2009), 136–38. Martin P. Durkin, who served as Secretary of Labor, had been president of the United Association of Plumbers and Pipe Fitters Union.

6. Stephen E. Ambrose, *Eisenhower, vol. II: The President* (New York: Simon & Schuster, 1984), 40.

7. David Halberstam, *The Best and the Brightest* (Greenwich, CT: Fawcett Publications, Inc., 1973), 51.

8. Michael O'Brien, *John F. Kennedy: A Biography* (New York: Thomas Dunne Books, 2005), 333.

9. Quoted in Arthur M. Schlesinger, *A Thousand Days: John F. Kennedy in the White House* (New York: Houghton Mifflin, 1965), 14.

10. Address of Senator John F. Kennedy Accepting the Democratic Party Nomination for the Presidency of the United States—Memorial Coliseum, Los Angeles, July 15, 1960, http://www.presidency.ucsb.edu/ws/?pid=25966.

11. James T. Patterson, *Grand Expectations: The United States, 1945–1974* (New York: Oxford University Press, 1996), 459.

12. John F. Kennedy Presidential Approval, https://ropercenter.cornell.edu/presidential-approval.

13. Patterson, *Grand Expectations*, 465.

14. 1960 Presidential General Election Results—Texas, https://uselectionatlas.org/RESULTS/state.php?fips=48&year=1960.

15. Christopher Wynn, "Would a Bubble Top Have Saved Kennedy?" *Dallas Morning News* (May 5, 2013), https://www.dallasnews.com/news/jfk/2017/10/26/bubble-top-saved-kennedy-answers-strange-story-jfks-lincoln-limo.

16. Warren Commission Hearings, vol. I (Washington, DC: Government Printing Office, 1964), I, https://www.history-matters.com/archive/jfk/wc/wcvols/wh1/html/WC_Vol1_0001a.htm.

17. Kathryn S. Olmsted, *Real Enemies: Conspiracy Theories and American Democracy, World War I to 9/11* (New York: Oxford University Press, 2009), 113.

18. Ibid., 114 and 119.

19. Ibid., 126.

20. Warren Commission, *Report of the President's Commission on the Assassination of President Kennedy* (Washington: Government Printing Office, 1964), 23–24.

21. Ibid.

22. Office of the White House Press Secretary, Executive Order 11130: Appointing a Commission to Report Upon the Assassination of President John F. Kennedy, November 30, 1963, https://history-matters.com/archive/jfk/wc/wr/pdf/WR_A1_ExecOrder11130.pdf.

23. Gerald Posner, *Case Closed* (New York: Random House, 1993), 317, 407.

24. Ibid., 318.

25. Ibid., 300.

26. US House Select Committee on Assassinations, *Final Report* (Washington, DC: GPO, 1979), 41.

27. Olmsted, *Real Enemies*, 127.

28. Max Holland, *The Kennedy Assassination Tapes* (New York: Knopf, 2004), 250.

29. Art Swift, "Majority in US Still Believe JFK Killed in a Conspiracy," *Gallup* (November 15, 2013), http://www.gallup.com/poll/165893/majority-believe-jfk -killed-conspiracy.aspx.

30. Olmsted, *Real Enemies*, 132–33.

31. Richard Hofstadter, "The Paranoid Style of American Politics," *Harper's Magazine* (November 1964): 77–86.

32. Ibid., 80–81; my emphasis.

33. Mark Mazzetti, "Burglars Who Took on FBI Abandon Shadows," *New York Times* (January 7, 2014): A1.

34. "A Primer of Assassination Theories: The Whole Spectrum of Doubt, from the Warren Commissioners to Ousman Ba," *Esquire* (December 1966): 205–10.

35. Jay Epstein, *Inquest: The Warren Commission and the Establishment of Truth* (New York: Viking Press, 1966); Mark Lane, *Rush to Judgment: A Critique of the Warren Commission's Inquiry into the Murders of President John F. Kennedy, Officer J. D. Tippit, and Lee Harvey Oswald* (London: Bodley Head, 1966). See also Michael Wolff, "JFK and Fifty Years of Conspiracy," *USA Today* (October 13, 2013), https:// www.usatoday.com/story/money/columnist/wolff/2013/10/13/epstein-and-the-ken nedy-assassination/2960611/.

36. Lane, *Rush to Judgment*, 60–70.

37. Posner, *Case Closed*, 327.

38. Posner makes an interesting comment about the word "pristine" in *Case Closed*, 335–36. It implies no damage whatsoever.

39. Wikipedia, s.v. "Zapruder Film," last modified October 26, 2021, 17:10, https://en.wikipedia.org/wiki/Zapruder_film#cite_ref-3.

40. Posner, *Case Closed*, 454.

41. Ibid., 329–30.

42. Ibid., 336.

43. The United States House of Representatives Select Committee on Assassinations (HSCA) was established in 1976 to investigate the assassinations of John F. Kennedy and Martin Luther King Jr. The HSCA completed its investigation in 1978 and issued its final report the following year, concluding that Kennedy was probably assassinated as a result of a conspiracy.

44. Posner, *Case Closed*, 341–42. US House of Representatives, Select Committee on Assassinations, *Investigation of the Assassination of President John S. Kennedy*, vol. 1 (Washington, DC: Government Printing Office, 1978), 504. The complete report is available at http://www.maryferrell.org/showDoc.html?docId=95#relPageId=508.

45. *Findings of the House Select Committee on Assassinations in the Assassination of President John F. Kennedy* (Washington, DC: Government Printing Office, 1979), 3, https://www.archives.gov/research/jfk/select-committee-report.

46. Vincent Bugliosi, *Reclaiming History: The Assassination of President John F. Kennedy* (New York: W.W. Norton & Company, 2007), 177, 203.

47. National Academy of Sciences, *Report of the Committee on Ballistics Acoustics* (Washington, DC: National Academy Press, 1982), http://www.jfk-online.com/nas01.html#execsum.

48. Cliff Spiegelman, William A. Tobin, William D. James, et al., "Chemical and Forensic Analysis of JFK Assassination Bullet Lots: Is a Second Shooter Possible," *The Annals of Applied Statistics* 1 (2007): 1–16.

49. Olmsted, *Real Enemies*, 147.

50. One classic from that time is Francis Fukuyama, *The End of History and the Last Man* (New York: Avon Books, 1992).

CHAPTER FIVE

1. National Commission on Terrorist Attacks Upon the United States, *The 9/11 Commission Report* (Washington: Government Printing Office, 2004), xv.

2. David Ray Griffin, "The American Empire and 9/11," *Tikkun* 22 (March–April 2007): 23–32.

3. Tom Brokaw, "Tom Brokaw Adds His Perspective on the 2 Historic Events," *Chicago Tribune* (December 7, 2001), https://www.chicagotribune.com/news/ct-xpm-2001-12-07-0112070117-story.html.

4. Michael Barkun, *A Culture of Conspiracy: Apocalyptic Visions in Contemporary America* (Berkeley: University of California Press, 2013), 6.

5. A classic example is Gordon W. Prange, Donald M. Goldstein, and Katherine V. Dillon, *At Dawn We Slept: The Untold Story of Pearl Harbor* (New York: McGraw-Hill, 1981).

6. Stanley Karnow, *Vietnam: A History* (New York: The Viking Press, 1983), 601.

7. Bonnie Cordes, Bruce Hoffman, Brian M. Jenkins, et. al, *Trends in International Terrorism, 1982 and 1983* (Santa Monica, CA: RAND, 1984), 5.

8. Memorandum, Brian M. Jenkins to David Aaron (Special Assistant to the President for National Security Affairs), "An Independent Review of US Capabilities for Combating Terrorism," September 1979, The Jimmy Carter Presidential Library, Staff Office Files, National Security Advisor, Odom File, Box 52.

9. For an overview of terrorist incidents see US Department of State, Bureau of Intelligence and Research, *Thirteen Months of Anti-US Terrorism*, Report 1025-AR, March 13, 1985. Digital National Security Archive (DNSA). https://search-proquest-com.proxy-kutztown.klnpa.org/dnsa/advanced.

10. Walter Laqueur, "Postmodern Terrorism," *Foreign Affairs* 75 (September–October 1996): 25–27.

11. US Department of State, *Secretary of State's Advisory Panel Report on Overseas Security* (Washington, DC: Department of State, June 1985), 7–8. DNSA. Accessed May 11, 2009.

12. Federal Bureau of Investigation, "FBI 100: First Strike: Global Terror in America," https://archives.fbi.gov/archives/news/stories/2008/february/tradebom_022608.

13. Counterterrorist Center, Central Intelligence Agency, "International Terrorism in 1997: A Statistical View," 1. DNSA.

14. Susan B. Epstein, "Embassy Security: Background, Funding, and the Budget," *Congressional Research Service*, RL30662 (October 4, 2001): 7, 10. In 1998, it stood at $280.1 million. Total 1999 requests for appropriations were $1.7 billion.

15. Federal Bureau of Investigation "USS *Cole* Bombing," *History: Famous Cases & Criminals*, https://www.fbi.gov/history/famous-cases/uss-cole-bombing.

16. US Senate, Committee on Foreign Relations, *Countering the Changing Threat of International Terrorism: Report of the National Commission on Terrorism* (Washington, DC: Government Printing Office, 2001), 2.

17. See Raphael F. Perl, "National Commission on Terrorism Report: Background and Issues for Congress," *Congressional Research Service* RS20598 (February 6, 2001).

18. The title is an acronym. Public Law 107–56, Uniting and Strengthening America by Providing Appropriate Tools Required to Intercept and Obstruct Terrorism (USA Patriot) Act of 2001, October 26, 2001 https://www.gpo.gov/fdsys/pkg/PLAW-107publ56/pdf/PLAW-107publ56.pdf.

19. American Civil Liberties Union, "National Security Letters." https://www.aclu.org/other/national-security-letters.

20. American Civil Liberties Union, "Federal Court Strikes Down National Security Letter Provision of the Patriot Act," September 6, 2007, https://www.aclu.org/news/federal-court-strikes-down-national-security-letter-provision-patriot-act.

21. White House, Office of the Press Secretary, "President Establishes Office of Homeland Security: Summary of the President's Executive Order: The Office of Homeland Security & the Homeland Security Council," October 8, 2001, The Avalon Project digital documents archive, Yale Law School, Lillian Goldman Law Library, http://avalon.law.yale.edu/sept11/president_038.asp.

22. Department of Homeland Security, https://www.dhs.gov.

23. *The National Security Strategy of the United States of America*, September 17, 2002, https://2009-2017.state.gov/documents/organization/63562.pdf.

24. Richard B. Cheney, "Meeting the Challenge of the War on Terrorism," (Washington, DC: The Heritage Foundation, October 17, 2003), 2.

25. Melani McAlister, "A Cultural History of the War without End," *The Journal of American History* 89 (September 2002): 455.

26. Dana Priest and Glenn Kessler, "Iraq, 9/11 Still Linked Cheney," *Washington Post* (September 29, 2003), https://www.washingtonpost.com/archive/politics/2003/09/29/iraq-911-still-linked-cheney/5b56d29d-d5ba-43ec-8c57-3cec1dc713e6/.

27. "Transcript of the State of the Union: Part 8: Iraq," *CNN* (January 29, 2003), http://www.cnn.com/2003/ALLPOLITICS/01/28/sotu.transcript.8/index.html.

28. "The Case Against Iraq," *New York Times* (February 6, 2003): A38. See also Norman Solomon, "Ten Years After Colin Powell's UN Speech, Old Hands Are Ready for More Blood," *Common Dreams* (February 5, 2013), https://www.commondreams.org/views/2013/02/05/ten-years-after-colin-powells-un-speech-old-hands-are-ready-more-blood.

29. Kathryn S. Olmsted, *Real Enemies: Conspiracy Theories and American Democracy, World War I to 9/11* (New York: Oxford University Press, 2009), 209.

30. IAEA Directory General Dr. Mohamed El Baradei, "The Status of Nuclear Inspections in Iraq: An Update," International Atomic Energy Agency, March 7, 2003, https://www.iaea.org/newscenter/statements/status-nuclear-inspections-iraq-update.

31. Olmsted, *Real Enemies*, 211.

32. Republicans picked up two seats in the Senate and eight seats in the House of Representatives. See *Statistics of the Congressional Election of November 5, 2002* (Washington: Government Publication Office, 2003).

33. Joseph C. Wilson, "What I Didn't Find in Africa," *New York Times* (July 6, 2003): WK9.

34. Walter Pincus, "Richard Clarke Redux: Top Ex-CIA Official Says Bush Admin. 'Cherry Picked' Pre-war Intel . . . " *Huffington Post* (March 3, 2008), https://www.huffingtonpost.com/2006/02/10/richard-clarke-redux-top-_n_15405.html.

35. Dan Eggen, "No Evidence Connecting Iraq to Al-Qaeda, 9/11 Panel Says," *Washington Post* (June 16, 2004), http://www.washingtonpost.com/wp-dyn/articles/A46254-2004Jun16.html.

36. Fred Kaplan, "Let's Go to the Memo," *Slate* (June 15, 2005), http://www.slate.com/articles/news_and_politics/war_stories/2005/06/lets_go_to_the_memo.html.

37. Olmsted, *Real Enemies*, 220.

38. Thomas Hargrove, "Third of Americans Suspect 9-11 Government Conspiracy," *Scripps Howard News Service* (August 1, 2006), (https://web.archive.org/web/20060805052538/http://www.scrippsnews.com/911poll; Ben Smith, "More Than Half of Democrats Believed Bush Knew," *Politico* (22 March 2011), https://www.politico.com/blogs/ben-smith/2011/04/more-than-half-of-democrats-believed-bush-knew-035224.

39. Juliet Eilperin, "Democrat Implies Sept. 11 Administration Plot," *Washington Post* (April 12, 2002), https://www.washingtonpost.com/archive/politics/2002/04/12/democrat-implies-sept-11-administration-plot/258355b8-b645-43ab-b84c-d5bd500af172/?utm_term=.e4ad7d8d724a.

40. David Aaronovitch, *Voodoo Histories* (New York: Riverhead Books, 2010), 248.

41. 9/11 Myths . . . Reading between the lies, http://www.911myths.com/html/windfall.html.

42. Full text of Dick Cheney's speech to the Institute of Petroleum-Autumn Lunch, 1999, https://aleklett.wordpress.com/2013/03/25/full-text-dick-cheneys-speech-at-institute-of-petroleum-autumn-lunch-1999/; my emphasis.

43. David Ray Griffin, *The New Pearl Harbor: Disturbing Questions About the Bush Administration and 9/11* (Moreton-in-Marsh: Arris Publishing, 2004), 31.

44. "Major General Albert N. Stubblebine III," July 31, 2014, https://www.democraticunderground.com/11358419.

45. Architects & Engineers for 9/11 Truth, "World Trade Center-Twin Towers, Part 5: Evidence of Explosions," https://www.ae911truth.org/evidence/explosive-features.

46. Oxford English Dictionary, s.v. "conspiracy," https://en.oxforddictionaries.com/definition/conspiracy; as in Rob Brotherton, *Suspicious Minds: Why We Believe in Conspiracy Theories* (New York: Bloomsbury Sigma, 2015), 61.

47. Thomas W. Lippman, "In US, Calls Grow Louder for Saddam Hussein's Removal," *Washington Post* (February 5, 1998), https://www.washingtonpost.com/archive/politics/1998/02/05/in-us-calls-grow-louder-for-saddam-husseins-removal/55d294a8-4625-41bf-8ab8-fd6191463766/?utm_term=.358fe205582c.

48. Les Aspin, *The Bottom-Up Review: Forces for a New Era* (Washington, DC: Department of Defense, 1993), 1.

49. Ibid., 5.

50. "Full Text of Colin Powell's Speech," *The Guardian* (February 5, 2003), http://www.theguardian.com/world/2003/feb/05/iraq.usa.

51. Greg Miller, "CIA Study on Iraq Weapons is Off Course, Officials Say," *Los Angeles Times* (August 20, 2004), http://articles.latimes.com/2004/aug/20/nation/na-wmd20.

52. C. J. Chivers, "Abandoned Chemical Weapons and Secret Casualties in Iraq," *New York Times* (October 15, 2014): A1, A12–A15.

53. Statement of Judith S. Yaphe to the National Commission on Terrorist Attacks Upon the United States, July 9, 2003, http://www.911commission.gov/hearings/hearing3/witness_yaphe.htm.

54. US Senate Select Committee on Intelligence, *Report of the Senate Committee on Intelligence on the Postwar Findings About Iraq's WMD Programs and Links to Terrorism and How They Compare with Prewar Assessments Together with Additional Views* (Washington, DC, September 8, 2006), 83.

55. Ibid., 84.

56. Ibid., 85.

57. Jon Ronson, "Beset by Lizards," *The Guardian* (March 17, 2001), https://www.theguardian.com/books/2001/mar/17/features.weekend; Alex Abad-Santos, "Lizard People: The Greatest Political Conspiracy Ever Created," *Vox* (February 20, 2015), https://www.vox.com/2014/11/5/7158371/lizard-people-conspiracy-theory-explainer.

58. Aaronovitch, *Voodoo Histories*, 253.

59. Alfred Goldberg, Sarandis Papadopolous, Diane Putney, et al., *Pentagon 9/11* (Washington, DC: Office of the Secretary of Defense, 2007), https://www.history.navy.mil/research/library/online-reading-room/title-list-alphabetically/p/pentagon-9-11-footnotes.html.

60. Aaronovitch, *Voodoo Histories*, 254.

61. Riskus quoted in Aaronovitch, *Voodoo Histories*, 255.

62. "Evidence for the Explosive Demolition of World Trade Center Building 7 on 9/11," *Architects & Engineers for 9/11 Truth* (September 2009): 1.

63. Ibid., 4–5.

64. "9/11: Debunking the Myths," *Popular Mechanics* 182 (March 2005): 71–81.

65. Barkun, *A Culture of Conspiracy*, 174–75.

66. Aaronovitch, *Voodoo Histories*, 251.

67. Griffin, *The New Pearl Harbor*, xxiii.

68. Central Intelligence Agency, Freedom of Information Act Electronic Reading Room, https://www.cia.gov/library/readingroom/home.

69. National Security Archive, https://nsarchive.gwu.edu/digital-national-security -archive.

70. Olmsted, *Real Enemies*, 223.

71. Aaronovitch, *Voodoo Histories*, 242.

72. Jim Marrs, *The Terror Conspiracy: Deception, 9/11, and the Loss of Liberty* (New York: Disinformation, 2006), x.

73. Olmsted, *Real Enemies*, 225.

CHAPTER SIX

1. *Erica Lafferty et al. v. Alex Jones et al.*, Judicial District of Fairfield at Bridgeport, May 23, 2018, 13, https://cdn.theconversation.com/static_files/files/146/ JonesCTComplaint_.pdf?1527770307.

2. Nelba Marquez-Greene, "A Sandy Hook Parent's Letter to Teachers," *Education Week*, September 6, 2013, *Education Week*, https://www.edweek.org/leadership/ opinion-a-sandy-hook-parents-letter-to-teachers/2013/09.

3. Jerome P. Bjelopera, Kristine M. Finklea, Erin Bagalman, et al., *Public Mass Shootings in the United States: Selected Implications for Federal Public Health and Safety Policy*, R43004 (Washington, DC: Congressional Research Service, 2016), 2–3.

4. James Garbarino, Catherine P. Bradshaw, and Joseph A. Vorrasi, "Mitigating the Effects of Gun Violence on Children and Youth," *The Future of Children* 12 (Autumn 2002): 76.

5. Jon Rappoport, "Intelligent Questions Not Allowed on Sandy Hook," *Natural News*, January 23, 2013, https://www.naturalnews.com/038788_sandy_hook_ques tions_skepticism.html.

6. Jon Rappoport, "After Sandy Hook: How Psychiatrists Will Become Policemen," *Natural News*, January 7, 2013, https://www.naturalnews.com/038578_psy chiatrists_policemen_patient_prescriptions_database.html.

7. "Robby Parker Laughing a Day After His Daughter Was Murdered at S H," YouTube video, 3:07, posted by Conspiracy Mart July 5, 2020, accessed May 10, 2021, https://www.youtube.com/watch?v=7ir4sWOPEdM.

8. Mick West, "Debunked: FBI Says No One Killed at Sandy Hook [Included in CT State Total]," Metabunk, September 25, 2014, https://www.metabunk.org/threads/ debunked-fbi-says-no-one-killed-at-sandy-hook-included-in-ct-state-total.4570/.

9. Mick West, "Debunked: Sandy Hook Victims Not in Social Security Death Index (SSDI) Official Death Records," Metabunk, February 26, 2014, https://www .metabunk.org/threads/debunked-sandy-hook-victims-not-in-social-security-death -index-ssdi-official-death-records.3186/.

10. *Erica Lafferty et al,, v. Alex Jones et al.*, Judicial District of Fairfield at Bridgeport, May 23, 2018, 16.

11. James Fetzer and Mike Palecek, eds., *Nobody Died and Sandy Hook: It Was a FEMA Drill to Promote Gun Control* (Moon Rock Books, 2015), 183.

12. Reeves Wiedeman, "The Sandy Hook Hoax," *New York Magazine*, September 5, 2016, https://nymag.com/intelligencer/2016/09/the-sandy-hook-hoax.html.

13. Evelyn Schlatter, "Veterans Today Editor Blames Newtown Tragedy on Israel," *Southern Poverty Law Center*, January 10, 2013. https://www.splcenter.org/hatewatch/2013/01/10/veterans-today-editor-blames-newtown-tragedy-israel.

14. Ibid. Fetzer still maintains that Pozner is an imposter.

15. Amanda J. Crawford, "Professor of Denial," *Chronicle of Higher Education* February 20, 2020, https://www.chronicle.com/article/the-professor-of-denial/. See Jim Fetzer, "Why the Sandy Hook 'Pozner v. Fetzer' Lawsuit Matters: What's Really at Stake," *JamesFetzer.org*, January 18, 2020, accessed May 12, 2021, https://james fetzer.org/2020/01/jim-fetzer-why-the-sandy-hook-pozner-v-fetzer-lawsuit-matters -whats-really-at-stake/.

16. *Erica Lafferty et al. v. Alex Jones et al.*, Judicial District of Fairfield at Bridgeport, May 23, 2018, 2 and 12–14.

17. "Megyn Kelly Reports on Alex Jones and 'Infowars,'" *NBC News*, June 18, 2017, https://www.nbcnews.com/video/megyn-kelly-reports-on-alex-jones-and -infowars-970743875859.

18. Jack Nicas, "Alex Jones Said Bans Would Strengthen Him. He Was Wrong," *New York Times*, September 4, 2018, https://www.nytimes.com/2018/09/04/technol ogy/alex-jones-infowars-bans-traffic.html ; *Erica Lafferty et al. v. Alex Jones et al.*, Judicial District of Fairfield at Bridgeport, May 23, 2018, 5.

19. According to the *New York Times*, court documents recorded Jones's revenue at $20 million in 2014. See Elizabeth Williamson and Emily Steel, "Conspiracy Theories Made Alex Jones Very Rich. They May Bring Him Down," *New York Times*, September 7, 2018, https://www.nytimes.com/2018/09/07/us/politics/alex-jones -business-infowars-conspiracy.html.

20. Charlie Warzel, "Alex Jones Just Can't Help Himself," BuzzFeed News, May 3, 2017, https://www.buzzfeednews.com/article/charliewarzel/alex-jones-will-never -stop-being-alex-jones.

21. Ibid.

22. Wiedeman, "The Sandy Hook Hoax."

23. Ibid.

24. Connecticut Freedom of Information Commission, Final Decision FIC2014-461 in the Matter of a Complaint by Wolfgang Halbig against First Selectman, Town of Newton; Chief, Police Department, Town of Newton; Police Department, Town of Newton; Town of Newton; Chair, Board of Education, Newton Public Schools; and Board of Education, Newton Public Schools, Respondents, July 8, 2015, https://portal.ct.gov/FOI/Decisions/Final-Decisions-2015/FIC2014-461.

25. Nanci G. Hutson, "Newtown School Board Greets Sandy Hook Skeptics with Silence," *ctpost*, May 7, 2014, https://www.ctpost.com/local/article/Newtown-school -board-greets-Sandy-Hook-skeptics-5458643.php; *Erica Lafferty et al. v. Alex Jones et al.*, Judicial District of Fairfield at Bridgeport, May 23, 2018, 6.

26. *Erica Lafferty et al. v. Alex Jones et al.*, Judicial District of Fairfield at Bridgeport, May 23, 2018, 14–15

27. Ibid., 7–8, 15.

28. Crawford, "Professor of Denial."

29. Scott Jaschik, "Reprimand for a Blog," *Inside Higher Ed*, April 12, 2013, https://www.insidehighered.com/news/2013/04/12/florida-atlantic-reprimands-professor-over-his-blog.

30. Steven Novella, "Professor Fired over Sandy Hook Conspiracy Theory," *Neurologicablog*, December 18, 2015, https://theness.com/neurologicablog/index.php/professor-fired-over-sandy-hook-conspiracy-theory/.

31. Mark Follman, Gavin Aronsen, and Deanna Pan, "US Mass Shootings, 1982-2021: Data from Mother Jones Investigation," *Mother Jones*, April 16, 2021, https://www.motherjones.com/politics/2012/12/mass-shootings-mother-jones-full-data/.

32. Ibid.

33. For a complete inventory of the two dozen weapons recovered by police see "List: Guns and Evidence from Las Vegas Shooter Stephen Paddock," *KTNV Las Vegas*, January 19, 2018, https://www.ktnv.com/news/las-vegas-shooting/list-guns-and-evidence-from-las-vegas-shooter-stephen-paddock.

34. Las Vegas Metropolitan Police Department, *LVMPD Criminal Investigative Report of the 1 October Mass Casualty Shooting*, LVMPD Event Number 171001-3519, August 3, 2018, 19; Follman, Aronsen, and Pan, "US Mass Shootings, 1982–2021."

35. The official number for the Gulf War was 467. See Allan R. Millet, Peter Maslowski, and William B. Feis, *For the Common Defense: A Military History of the United States from 1607 to 2012* (New York: The Free Press, 2012), 681.

36. Christina Walker, "10 Years. 180 Shootings. 356 Victims," *CNN*, 2019, https://www.cnn.com/interactive/2019/07/us/ten-years-of-school-shootings-trnd/.

37. Follman, Aronsen, and Pan, "US Mass Shootings, 1982–2021."

38. White House, Office of the Press Secretary, "Remarks by the President on Reducing Gun Violence—Hartford, CT," April 8, 2013, https://obamawhitehouse.archives.gov/the-press-office/2013/04/08/remarks-president-reducing-gun-violence-hartford-ct.

39. Office of the White House, *Now Is the Time: The President's Plan to Protect Our Children and Our Communities by Reducing Gun Violence*, January 16, 2013, https://obamawhitehouse.archives.gov/sites/default/files/docs/wh_now_is_the_time_full.pdf; Lanza suffered from autism spectrum disorder and may have had obsessive compulsive disorder. See State of Connecticut, Office of the Child Advocate, *Shooting at Sandy Hook Elementary School: Report of the Office of the Child Advocate* (Hartford: Office of the Child Advocate, November 21, 2014), 3, 56.

40. Ed O'Keefe and Philip Rucker, "Gun-Control Overhaul Is Defeated in Senate," *Washington Post*, April 17, 2013, https://www.washingtonpost.com/politics/gun-control-overhaul-is-defeated-in-senate/2013/04/17/57eb028a-a77c-11e2-b029-8fb7e977ef71_story.html.

41. Reid Wilson, "Seven Years After Sandy Hill, The Politics of Guns Has Changed," *The Hill*, December 14, 2019, https://thehill.com/homenews/state

-watch/474479-seven-years-after-sandy-hook-the-politics-of-guns-has-changed; See, for example, Virginial General Assembly, 2020 Session, SB 240, Firearms; Removal from Persons Posing Substantial Risk of Injury to Himself, Etc., Penalties, April 8, 2020, https://lis.virginia.gov/cgi-bin/legp604.exe?201+sum+SB240.

42. Aaron Karp, *Estimating Global Civilian-Held Firearms Numbers* (Geneva: Small Arms Survey, June 2018), 4.

43. Martin Savidge and Maria Cartaya, "Americans Bought Guns in Record Numbers in 2020 During a Year of Unrest—and the Surge is Continuing," *CNN*, March 14, 2020, https://www.cnn.com/2021/03/14/us/us-gun-sales-record/index.html.

44. Hannah Denham and Andrew Ba Tran, "Fearing Violence and Political Uncertainty, Americans Are Buying Millions More Firearms," *Washington Post*, February 3, 2021, https://www.washingtonpost.com/business/2021/02/03/gun-sales-january-background-checks/.

45. See Connecticut State Police, Western District Major Crime Squad, Timeline [Redacted], n.d., https://wlad.com/assets/files/TimelineRedacted.pdf.

46. Abby Ohlheiser, "Why the Internet's Biggest Conspiracy Theories Don't Make Mathematical Sense," *Washington Post*, January 28, 2016, https://www.washingtonpost.com/news/the-intersect/wp/2016/01/28/the-internets-favorite-conspiracies-would-involve-too-many-people-to-stay-secret-says-science/.

47. See, for example, Newtown Public Schools Board of Education, *Requested Budget for the 2012–2013 School Year*, January 31, 2012, https://web.archive.org/web/20140926061038/http://www.newtown.k12.ct.us/Portals/Newtown/District/docs/BOARD%20OF%20EDUCATION/BOE%20Budgets/2012-2013%20Budgets/BOE%20Requested%20Budget%20Book.rev2.pdf.

48. Dan Zak, "Newtown School Shooting's First Responders Deal with Searing Memories," *Washington Post*, December 30, 2012, https://www.washingtonpost.com/national/newtown-school-shootings-first-responders-deal-with-searing-memories/2012/12/30/2ac5ba5e-5135-11e2-950a-7863a013264b_story.html.

49. Ken Dixon, "Sandy Hook Woes Included Too Many Ambulances," *EMSWorld*, March 3, 2014, https://www.emsworld.com/news/11321507/sandy-hook-woes-included-too-many-ambulances.

50. Deposition on H. Wayne Carver, State of Wisconsin, Circuit Court Dane County, Leonard Pozner v. James Fetzer, Mike Palecek, Wrongs Without Remedies, LLC, Case No. 18CV3122, May 21, 2019, https://www.poznervfetzer.com/videotaped-deposition-of-h-wayne-carver-md/.

51. Honr Network. https://www.honrnetwork.org.

52. "Sandy Hook Conspiracy Theorist Gets Prison Time for Threatening Victim's Family," *The Guardian*, June 9, 2017, https://www.theguardian.com/us-news/2017/jun/09/sandy-hook-conspiracy-theorist-death-threats-prison.

53. Lenny and Veronique Pozner, "Sandy Hook Massacre 3rd Anniversary: Two Parents Target FAU Conspiracy Theorist," *South Florida Sun Sentinel*, December 10, 2015, https://www.sun-sentinel.com/opinion/commentary/sfl-on-sandy-hook-anniversary-two-parents-target-fau-professor-who-taunts-family-victims-20151210-story.html.

54. Jaschik, "Reprimand for a Blog."

55. Letter, Diane Alperin (Vice Provost) to James Tracy, "Notice of Disciplinary Action—Termination," January 5, 2015. Susan Svrluga, "University Fires Professor Who Says Sandy Hook was a Hoax," *Washington Post*, January 6, 2016, https://www .washingtonpost.com/news/grade-point/wp/2016/01/06/university-fires-professor -who-says-sandy-hook-was-a-hoax/.

56. Daniel Trotta, "Infowars Founder Who Claimed Sandy Hook Was a Hoax Ordered to Pay $100,000," *Reuters*, December 31, 2019, https://www.reuters .com/article/us-texas-lawsuit-alex-jones/infowars-founder-who-claimed-sandy-hook -shooting-was-a-hoax-ordered-to-pay-100000-idUSKBN1YZ1BB.

57. "Alex Jones Ordered to Pay $100,000 in Sandy Hook Defamation Case," *BBC News*, December 31, 2019, https://www.bbc.com/news/world-us-canada-50960730.

58. Colin Kalmbacher, "Texas Supreme Court Silently Denies Alex Jones All Forms of Relief," *Law & Crime*, January 22, 2021, https://lawandcrime.com/high -profile/texas-supreme-court-silently-denies-alex-jones-all-forms-of-relief-sandy -hook-families-and-others-can-now-sue-conspiracy-theorist-and-infowars-into-the -ground/.

59. Emily S. Rueb, "Sandy Hook Father Awarded $450,000 in Defamation Case," *New York Times*, October 16, 2019, https://www.nytimes.com/2019/10/16/us/sandy -hook-defamation.html.

60. Ibid; Vanessa Romo, "Sandy Hook Father Wins Defamation Suit; Alex Jones Sanctioned," *NPR*, June 18, 2019, https://www.npr.org/2019/06/18/733880866/ sandy-hook-victims-father-wins-defamation-suit-alex-jones-sanctioned.

61. Elizabeth Williamson, "A Notorious Sandy Hook Tormentor Is Arrested in Florida," *New York Times*, January 20, 2020, https://www.nytimes.com/2020/01/27/ us/politics/sandy-hook-hoaxer-arrest.html.

62. See *James Fetzer: Exposing Falsehoods and Revealing Truths* at https://james fetzer.org/?s=posner. Accessed May 19, 2021.

63. Infowars. https://www.infowars.com. Accessed May 19, 2021.

64. Infowars Store. https://www.infowarsstore.com Accessed May 19, 2021.

65. Mike Adams, "Amazon Is the New Ministry of Truth: An Interview with Jim Fetzer, Editor of Sandy Hook Book BANNED By Amazon.com," *Natural News*, November 24, 2015, https://www.naturalnews.com/052096_sandy_hook_banned _book_amazon_ministry_of_truth.html.

CHAPTER SEVEN

1. Colonel Tamzy J. House, Lieutenant Colonel James B. Near, Jr., Lieutenant Colonel William B. Shields, et. al, *Weather as a Force Multiplier: Owning the Weather in 2025* (Air War College, August 1996), vi.

2. The respective websites may be found at: http://globalskywatch.com; https:// www.geoengineeringwatch.org.

3. For a description of the term see Moving the Goalposts, https://www.logical lyfallacious.com/logicalfallacies/Moving-the-Goalposts.

4. Murphy repeatedly made this claim in interviews. See "Chemtrails, Geoengineering and Climate Change from Cancun and Everywhere," *5 O'Clock Train* (December 9, 2010), http://trainradio.blogspot.com/2010/12/chemtrails-geoengineering-and-climate.html.

5. "Geoengineering Expert Dane Wigington: 'There Is No Natural Weather anymore!'" *The Event Chronicle* (October 23, 2017),http://www.theeventchronicle.com/geoengineering/geoengineering-expert-dane-wigington-no-natural-weather-anymore/.

6. "Chemtrail Syndrome: A Global Pandemic of Epic Proportions," *Cosmic Convergence* (May 3, 2014), http://cosmicconvergence.org/?p=6983.

7. Tanner has an entire section of his website dedicated to "Chemtrail Ailments." See http://globalskywatch.com/stories/my-chemtrail-story/story/16-Ailments.html#.W9sryC2ZNo4. For an examination of Morgellons Disease see https://www.mayoclinic.org/morgellons-disease/art-20044996.

8. David W. Keith, "Geoengineering the Climate: History and Prospect," *Annual Review of Energy and the Environment* vol. 25 (2000): 250.

9. Ibid., 254; Ty McCormick, "Geoengineering: A Short History," *Foreign Policy* (September 3, 2013), http://foreignpolicy.com/2013/09/03/geoengineering-a-short-history/.

10. Keith, "Geoengineering the Climate," 252.

11. Memorandum from the Deputy Under Secretary of State for Political Affairs (Kohler) to Secretary of State Rusk, January 13, 1967, https://history.state.gov/historicaldocuments/frus1964-68v28/d274.

12. H.H. Shugart, *Foundations of the Earth: Global Ecological Change and the Book of Job* (Columbia University Press: New York, 2014).

13. Memo from Kohler to Rusk, January 13, 1967.

14. Seymour Hersh, "Weather as a Weapon of War," *New York Times* (July 19, 1972): E3.

15. McCormack, "Geoengineering: A Short History."

16. IPCC, "Preface to the IPCC Overview," (n.d.),https://www.ipcc.ch/ipccreports/1992%20IPCC%20Supplement/IPCC_1990_and_1992_Assessments/English/ipcc_90_92_assessments_far_overview.pdf.

17. Craig R. Whitney, "Scientists Urge Rapid Action on Global Warming," *New York Times* (May 26, 1990): A6.

18. "Median Age of the Resident Population of the United States from 1960 to 2017." The media age increased from 28.1 in 1970 to 37.2 in 2010, https://www.statista.com/statistics/241494/median-age-of-the-us-population/.

19. Centers for Disease Control, Heart Disease Facts, https://www.cdc.gov/heartdisease/facts.htm; National Conference of State Legislators, Obesity Statistics in the United States, September 4, 2014, http://www.ncsl.org/research/health/obesity-statistics-in-the-united-states.aspx.

20. Frank Newport, "Top Issues for Voters: Healthcare, Economy, Immigration," *Gallup* (November 2, 2018), https://news.gallup.com/poll/244367/top-issues-voters-healthcare-economy-immigration.aspx?g_source=link_NEWSV9&g

_medium=TOPIC&g_campaign=item_&g_content=Top%2520Issues%2520for%25 20Voters%3a%2520Healthcare%2c%2520Economy%2c%2520Immigration.

21. Steve Conner, "Scientist Publishes 'Escape Route' from Global Warming," *Independent* (July 30, 2006), http://www.independent.co.uk/environment/scientist -publishes-escape-route-from-global-warming-409981.html.

22. Paul J. Crutzen, "Albedo Enhancement by Stratospheric Sulfur Injections: A Contribution to Resolve a Policy Dilemma?" *Climate Change* 77 (August 2006): 211–19.

23. James R. Fleming, "The Climate Engineers," *The Wilson Quarterly* 31 (Spring 2007): 46–60.

24. Heather Hansman, "Is This Plan to Combat Climate Change Insane or Insanely Genius?" *Smithsonian.com* (May 15, 2015), http://www.smithsonianmag.com/inno vation/is-this-plan-combat-climate-change-insane-insanely-genius-180955258/?no -ist.

25. "A Brief History of 'Chemtrails,'" *Contrail Science*, http://contrailscience com/a-brief-history-of-chemtrails/.

26. William Thomas, "Contrails Mystify, Sicken Americans," *Environment News Service* (January 8, 1999) http://web.archive.org/web/19990503013500/ens.lycos .com/ens/jan99/1999L-01-08-05.html.

27. Ibid.

28. Richard Corliss and Jeffrey Ressner, "The X Phones," *Time* (August 9, 1999): 64–65.

29. Ibid.

30. Ibid.

31. Global Skywatch, "About Us," http://globalskywatch.com/about-us.html# .VbYsdCSar-Y.

32. Global Skywatch, "Scientists & Specialists: Providing Information from Educated Sources," http://globalskywatch.com/scientists/francis-mangels/index .html#.W-RB3C2ZNo4.

33. Andrew Calbery, *The Fight against Geoengineering* (Victoria: Friesen Press, 2017), 83.

34. Carnicom Institute Board Members, https://carnicominstitute.org/wp/about/.

35. "Preliminary Meteorological Study: Unnatural Cloud Formations in Santa Fe NM." http://www.carnicominstitute.org/articles/study1.htm.

36. Clifford E. Carnicom, "Contrail Physics," September 17, 2000, http://www .carnicominstitute.org/articles/model1.htm.

37. Carnicom Institute, "We Do Scientific Research: Serving Humanity & Public Interest." https://carnicominstitute.org/html/mission.html.

38. "Geoengineering: A Dire Threat to the Planet," *Geoengineeringwatch* (December 5, 2012) http://www.geoengineeringwatch.org/tag/dane-wigington/.

39. Andrew Gumbel, "Drought Blamers: California Conspiracists See Government's Hand in Arid Climate," *The Guardian* (September 26, 2015), https://www .theguardian.com/us-news/2015/sep/26/california-drought-conspiracy-theories-geo engineering-climate.

40. Joseph Mercola, "Exclusive: Dr. Mercola Interviews Dane Wigington on Evidence of Geoengineering," *Project NSearch* (October 12, 2016), http://www.project.nsearch.com/profiles/blogs/exclusive-dr-mercola-interviews-dane-wigington-on-the-evidence-of.

41. Geoenginerring Watch, "Extensive List of Patents," http://www.geoengineeringwatch.org/links-to-geoengineering-patents/.

42. House, Near, Shields, et al., *Weather as a Force Multiplier*, vi.

43. Ibid., vii.

44. "Aluminum, What Is It Doing to Us?" *Geoengineering Watch* (September 24, 2014), http://www.geoengineeringwatch.org/aluminum-what-is-it-doing-to-us/; "Has the Primary Geoengineering Materials Supplier Been Identified?" *Geoengineering Watch* (October 3, 2017), http://www.geoengineeringwatch.org/has-the-primary-geoengineering-materials-supplier-been-identified/; "Geoengineering: Waging Weather Warfare on World Populations," *Geoengineering Watch* (January 2, 2018), http://www.geoengineeringwatch.org/geoengineering-waging-weather-warfare-on-world-populations/.

45. "How Persistent Aerosol Plumes are Being Changed to Short Non-Persistent Plumes to Fool the Public," *Global Sky Watch* (May 15, 2016), http://globalskywatch.com/stories/my-chemtrail-story/chemtrail-information/plumes-change.html#.VbpXMCSar-b.

46. Ibid; emphases in the original.

47. "I Am the Two Percent," *Global Sky Watch* (April 3, 2018), http://globalskywatch.com/stories/my-chemtrail-story/chemtrail-information/chemtrail-types.html#.WldopiOZO1s.

48. "Some Questions Regarding Chemtrails and Debunking," *Metabunk* (September 20, 2012), https://www.metabunk.org/some-questions-regarding-chemtrails-and-debunking.t790/#post-15498.

49. "Extensive List of Patents," *Geoengineering Watch* (n.d.), http://www.geoengineeringwatch.org/links-to-geoengineering-patents/.

50. "Debunked: Strontium as a Footprint of Geoengineering Proposals or Patents [There Is None]," *Metabunk* (July 7, 2015), https://www.metabunk.org/debunked-strontium-as-footprint-of-geoengineering-proposals-or-patents-there-is-none.t6502/#post-159266; my emphasis.

51. See, for example, Vojtech Mastny, Sven G. Holtsmark, and Andreas Wenger, eds., *War Plans and Alliances in the Cold War: Threat Perceptions in the East and West* (New York: Routledge, 2006).

52. House, Near, Shields, et al., *Weather as a Force Multiplier*, ii; my emphasis.

53. Homer E. Newell, *A Recommended National Program in Weather Modification: A Report to the Interdepartmental Committee for Atmospheric Sciences* (Washington, DC: Federal Council for Science and Technology, November 1966), 1.

54. Ibid., 12.

55. Aluminum Oxide, *Wikipedia*, https://en.wikipedia.org/wiki/Aluminium_oxide; My emphasis.

56. "Chemtrails, Geoengineering, and Climate Change from Cancun and Everywhere," *5'O'Clock Train—CHOU 89.1 FM* (December 9, 2010) http://trainradio.blogspot.com/2010/12/chemtrails-geoengineering-and-climate.html.

57. The term µg/l refers to parts per billion in water.

58. Shasta 12 Lake Shasta, Rain, May 22, 2008, Rainwater Tests, https://www.geoengineeringwatch.org/water-tests/.

59. Environmental Protection Agency, Drinking Water Contaminants—Standards and Regulations, http://water.epa.gov/drink/contaminants/.

60. "Chemtrails Debunked: Part 2 Metals," *Vaccine Papers* (December 22, 2016), http://vaccinepapers.org/chemtrails-debunked-part-2/.

61. "Chemtrails Additives in Jet Fuel: A Mathematical Analysis," *Metabunk* (September 8, 2014) https://www.metabunk.org/chemtrail-additives-in-jet-fuel-a-mathematical-analysis.t4426/#post-125241.

62. "14 Years of Chemtrails, Comments, and Suggestions," *Metabunk* (February 12, 2014) https://www.metabunk.org/14-years-of-chemtrails-comments-and-suggestions.t100/page-4#post-89102.

63. "Debunked: Monsanto's Aluminum Resistant GMO's and Chentrails," *Metabunk* (July 6, 2012) https://www.metabunk.org/debunked-monsantos-aluminum-resistant-gmos-and-chemtrails.t341/#post-10853.

64. Dane Wigington, "US Government Engineering the Climate to Control Populations," *Wake Up World* (July 12, 2015), https://wakeup-world.com/2015/07/12/u-s-government-engineering-the-climate-to-control-populations/.

65. "Non-Persistent and Non-Visible Chemtrails," *Metabunk* (August 1, 2015), (https://www.metabunk.org/non-persistant-and-non-visible-chemtrails.t6638/#post-161395.

66. See, for example, Alzheimer's Association, "Facts and Figures," https://www.alz.org/alzheimers-dementia/facts-figures.

CHAPTER EIGHT

1. Matt Taibbi, *Insane Clown President: Dispatches from the 2016 Circus* (New York: Spiegel & Grau, 2017), 5.

2. Steven Levitsky and Daniel Ziblatt "How a Democracy Dies," *New Republic* 249. (January/February 2018), 16–23.

3. The term is attributed to Trump advisor Kellyanne Conway. See Marilyn Wedge, "The Historical Origin of 'Alternative Facts'," *Psychology Today*, January 23, 2017, https://www.psychologytoday.com/us/blog/suffer-the-children/201701/the-historical-origin-alternative-facts.

4. Steven Levitsky and Daniel Ziblatt, "How Wobbly Is Our Democracy?" *New York Times*, January 27, 2018, https://www.nytimes.com/2018/01/27/opinion/sunday/democracy-polarization.html.

5. George B. Tindall and David E. Shi, *America: A Narrative History*, sixth edition (New York: W.W. Norton & Company, 2004), 331.

6. Ibid., 333.

7. John Quincy Adams, *Memoirs of John Quincy Adams: Comprising Portions of His Diaries from 1795 to 1848*, vol. 8 (Philadelphia: J. B. Lippincott, 1876), 546.

8. Emerson David Fite, *The Presidential Campaign of 1860* (New York: The Macmillan Company, 1911), 210.

9. Mark Bowden, "'Idiot,' 'Yahoo,' 'Original Gorilla': How Lincoln Was Dissed in His Day," *The Atlantic* 311 (June 2013); Doris Kearns Goodwin, *Team of Rivals: The Political Genius of Abraham Lincoln* (New York: Simon & Schuster, 2005), 383.

10. Maggie Haberman, "Donald Trump Accuses Ted Cruz's Father of Associating with Kennedy Assassin," *New York Times*, May 3, 2016, https://www.nytimes.com/politics/first-draft/2016/05/03/donald-trump-ted-cruz-father-jfk/.

11. Will Sommer, "Alt Right Conspiracy Theorists Obsess over Comet Ping Pong," *Washington City Paper*, November 6, 2016, https://www.washingtoncitypaper.com/food/blog/20840980/alt-right-conspiracy-theorists-obsess-over-comet-ping-pong.

12. Faiz Siddiqui and Susan Svrluga, "NC Man Told Police He Went to DC Pizzeria with Gun to Investigate Conspiracy Theory," *Washington Post*, December 5, 2016, https://www.washingtonpost.com/news/local/wp/2016/12/04/d-c-police-respond-to-report-of-a-man-with-a-gun-at-comet-ping-pong-restaurant/?utm_term=.43494d1a45d3.

13. Michael Schmidt, "Second Review Says Classified Information Was in Hillary Clinton's Email," *New York Times*, September 7, 2015, https://www.nytimes.com/2015/09/08/us/politics/second-review-says-classified-information-was-in-hillary-clintons-email.html.

14. Casey Hicks, "Timeline of Hillary Clinton's Email Scandal," *CNN Politics*, November 7, 2016, https://www.cnn.com/2016/10/28/politics/hillary-clinton-email-timeline/index.html.

15. US Department of Justice, Federal Bureau of Investigation, *Clinton E-Mail Investigation: Mishandling of Classified – Unknown Subject or Country (SIM)*, July 2016, 2, https://vault.fbi.gov/hillary-r.-clinton/Hillary%20R.%20Clinton%20Part%2002%20of%2020/view.

16. Ibid.

17. "CNN Exclusive: Hillary Clinton's First National Interview of 2016 Race," *CNN*, July 7, 2015, http://cnnpressroom.blogs.cnn.com/2015/07/07/cnn-exclusive-hillary-clintons-first-national-interview-of-2016-race/.

18. James B. Comey (Director, FBI) to Richard M. Burr (Chair, Senate Select Committee on Intelligence), Charles E. Grassley (Chair, Senate Committee on the Judiciary), Richard Shelby (Chair, Senate Committee on Appropriations), Ron Johnson (Chair, Senate Committee on Homeland Security and Governmental Affairs), Devin Johnson (Chair, House Permanent Select Committee on Intelligence), Robert Goodlatte (Chair, House Committee on the Judiciary), John Culberson (Chair, House Committee on Appropriations), Jason Chaffetz (Chair, House Committee on Oversight and Government Reform), October 28, 2016.

19. Full transcript: Donald Trump NYC Speech on Stakes of the Election, *Politico*, June 22, 2016, https://www.politico.com/story/2016/06/transcript-trump-speech-on-the-stakes-of-the-election-224654.

20. Frank Newport, "As Debate Looms, Voters Still Distrust Clinton and Trump," *Gallup* (23 September 2016), https://news.gallup.com/poll/195755/debate-looms-voters-distrust-clinton-trump.aspx.

21. "Report: Three Million Votes in Presidential Election Cast by Illegal Aliens," *Infowars*, November 14, 2016, Infowars https://www.infowars.com/report-three -million-votes-in-presidential-election-cast-by-illegal-aliens/.

22. Donald Trump, Twitter Post, January 27, 2017, 8:12 AM. This Twitter account has since been deactivated.

23. Melissa Chan, "Meet the Man Who May Have Convinced Trump Voter Fraud Exists," *Time*, January 17, 2017, http://time.com/4651634/gregg-phillips-voter-fraud -donald-trump/.

24. Brennan Center for Justice, "Background on the Trump 'Voter Fraud' Commission," (n.d.) https://www.brennancenter.org/everything-you-need-know-about -trumps-voter-fraud-commission.

25. Justin Levitt, "A Comprehensive Investigation of Voter Impersonation Finds 31 Credible Incidents Out of One Billion Votes Cast," *Washington Post*, August 6, 2014, https://www.washingtonpost.com/news/wonk/wp/2014/08/06/a-comprehen sive-investigation-of-voter-impersonation-finds-31-credible-incidents-out-of-one -billion-ballots-cast/?utm_term=.ef757f2e4c0b; Bryan Lowry, "Kobach: Kansas Won't Give Social Security Info to Kobach-Led Voter Commission at This Time," *The Kansas City Star*, June 30, 2017, http://www.kansascity.com/news/politics-govern ment/article159113369.html.

26. Aaron Klein, "Soros Army in Alabama to Register Convicted Felons to Vote Against Roy Moore *Breitbart*, December 3, 2017, https://www.breitbart.com/poli tics/2017/12/03/soros-army-alabama-register-convicted-felons-vote-roy-moore/.

27. David Ahle, "100,000 Illegal Aliens Registered to Vote in Pennsyalvania Spurs Lawsuit," *David Harris Jr: No Nonsense*, November 5, 2018, https://david harrisjr.com/politics/100000-illegal-aliens-registered-to-vote-in-pennsylvania-spurs -lawsuit/?fbclid=IwAR34mdOd5XKld-tLt14wioRtYYs5FZHjjZbheyxLYxjTDxD PUllLJs7XbZI.

28. Alec Tyson and Shiva Maniam, "Behind Trump's Victory: Divisions by Race, Gender, Education," *Pew Research Center*, November 9, 2016, http://www.pewre search.org/fact-tank/2016/11/09/behind-trumps-victory-divisions-by-race-gender -education/.

29. The term "low information" voter became common in 2016 discussions of the election. See Richard Fording and Sanford Schram, "'Low Information Voters' Are a Crucial Part of Trump's Support," *Washington Post*, November 7, 2016, https://www .washingtonpost.com/news/monkey-cage/wp/2016/11/07/low-information-voters -are-a-crucial-part-of-trumps-support/.

30. Peter Baker and Matthew Rosenberg, "Michael Flynn Was Paid to Represent Turkey's Interests During Trump Campaign," *New York Times*, March 10, 2017, https://www.nytimes.com/2017/03/10/us/politics/michael-flynn-turkey.html.

31. International Conference, "Information, Messages, Politics: The Shape-Shifting Powers of Today's World," December 10, 2015, https://conference.rt.com.

32. Eugene Kiely, "Michael Flynn's Russia Timeline," *Factcheck.org*, December 1, 2017, https://www.factcheck.org/2017/12/michael-flynns-russia-timeline/.

33. Craig Unger, "Trump's Russian Laundromat," *New Republic* 248 (August/ September 2017): 28.

34. Ibid., 30. Jonathan Stempel, "Trump Taj Mahal Casino Settles US Money Laundering Claims," *Reuters*, February 11, 2015, https://www.reuters.com/article/trump-ent-trumptajmahal-moneylaundering-idUSL1N0VL2L120150211.

35. "What to Ask about Russian Hacking," *New York Times*, March 17, 2017, https://www.nytimes.com/2017/03/17/opinion/what-to-ask-about-russian-hacking.html.

36. Office of National Intelligence, *Assessing Russian Activities and Intentions in Recent US Elections*, ICA 2017-01D, 6 January 2017), ii.

37. Heather A. Conley, James Mina, Ruslan Stefanov, and Martin Vladimirov, *The Kremlin Playbook* (New York: Rowman & Littlefield, 2016).

38. Office of the Deputy Attorney General, Order No. 3915-2017, "Appointment of Special Counsel to Investigate Russian Interference with the 2016 Presidential Election and Related Matters," May 17, 2017.

39. Andrew Prokop, "All of Robert Mueller's Indictments and Plea Deals in the Russia Investigation So Far," *Vox*, November 29, 2018, https://www.vox.com/policy-and-politics/2018/2/20/17031772/mueller-indictments-grand-jury.

40. Special Counsel Robert S. Mueller to US District Court for the Southern District of New York, "Government Sentencing Memorandum," December 7, 2018.

41. Robert Mueller, *Report on the Investigation into Russian Interference in the 2016 Election*, vol. 2 (Washington, DC: US Department of Justice, March 2019), 2.

42. Aaron Blake, "Pelosi's Impeachment Dam Has Been Breached," *Washington Post*, April 23, 2019, https://www.washingtonpost.com/politics/2019/04/23/democrats-dam-against-impeachment-fervor-has-been-breached/?utm_term=.b717122e6ad4.

43. Jordan Fabian, "Trump on Mueller Report: 'Complete and Total Exoneration'," *The Hill*, March 24, 2019, https://thehill.com/homenews/administration/435533-trump-on-mueller-report-complete-and-total-exoneration.

44. Colin Dickey, "The New Paranoia," *New Republic* 248 (July 2017): 27.

45. Matt Taibbi, "Why the Russia Story Is a Minefield for Democrats and the Media," *Rolling Stone*, March 8, 2017, http://www.rollingstone.com/politics/taibbi-russia-story-is-a-minefield-for-democrats-and-the-media-w471074.

46. Dickey, "The New Paranoia," 26.

47. Taibbi, *Insane Clown President*, 295–303.

48. Dickey, "The New Paranoia," 26.

49. Astead W. Herndon, "Elizabeth Warren, Speaking to Black Graduates, Warns 'the Rules Are Rigged,'" *New York Times*, 14 December 14, 2018.

50. Sophie Tatum, "Asked If DNC Was Rigged in Clinton's Favor, Warren Says 'Yes,'" *CNN*, November 3, 2017, https://www.cnn.com/2017/11/02/politics/elizabeth-warren-dnc-rigged/index.html; Garance Franke-Ruda, "Elizabeth Warren: 'The System Is Rigged,'" *The Atlantic*, September 6, 2012, https://www.theatlantic.com/politics/archive/2012/09/elizabeth-warren-the-system-is-rigged/262030/.

CHAPTER NINE

1. Dan Goldberg, "'It's Going to Disappear': Trump's Changing Tone on Coronavirus," *Politico*, March 17, 2020, https://www.politico.com/news/2020/03/17/how-trump-shifted-his-tone-on-coronavirus-134246.

2. Transcript, "Dr. Anthony Fauci Discusses Coronavirus on 'Face the Nation,'" March 15, 2020," *CBS News*, https://www.cbsnews.com/news/transcript-dr-anthony-fauci-discusses-coronavirus-on-face-the-nation-march-15-2020/.

3. Centers for Disease Control, 2009 H1N1 Pandemic (H1N1pdm2009 virus), https://www.cdc.gov/flu/pandemic-resources/2009-h1n1-pandemic.html.

4. Google News, *Cases*, May 25, 2021, https://news.google.com/covid19/map?hl=en-US&gl=US&ceid=US%3Aen.

5. Sui-Lee Wee and Donald G. McNeil, "China Identifies New Pneumonialike Illness," *New York Times,* January 8, 2020, https://www.nytimes.com/2020/01/08/health/china-pneumonia-outbreak-virus.html.

6. Derrick Bryson Taylor, "A Timeline of the Coronavirus Pandemic," *New York Times,* January 10, 2021, https://www.nytimes.com/article/coronavirus-timeline.html.

7. Ibid.

8. Governor's Press Office, "Amid COVID-19 Pandemic, Governor Cuomo, Governor Murphy, Governor Lamont, and Governor Wolf Direct Temporary Closure of Barber Shops, Nail and Hair Salons and Related Personal Care Services Effective by 8pm Saturday." March 20, 2020, https://www.governor.ny.gov/news/amid-covid-19-pandemic-governor-cuomo-governor-murphy-governor-lamont-and-governor-wolf-direct.

9. Mieszko Mazur, Man Dang, and Miguel Vega, "COVID-19 and the March 2020 Stock Market Crash: Evidence from S&P 1500," *Finance Research Letters* 38 (January 2021), https://www.ncbi.nlm.nih.gov/pmc/articles/PMC7343658/.

10. Justin Caruso, "Protest Showdowns: Anti-Lockdown Protestors Carry Guns in Pennsylvania, Kansas City; Counter-protestors Block Traffic," *Daily Caller,* April 20, 2020, https://dailycaller.com/2020/04/20/protest-showdowns-coronavirus-guns-block-traffic-pennsylvania-kansas-city/; Katelyn Burns, "Armed Protestors Entered Michigan's State Capital During Rally against Stay-at-Home Order," *Vox*, April 30, 2020, https://www.vox.com/policy-and-politics/2020/4/30/21243462/armed-protesters-michigan-capitol-rally-stay-at-home-order.

11. Manny Fernandez, "Conservatives Fuel Protests against Coronavirus Lockdowns," *New York Times,* April 18, 2020, https://www.nytimes.com/2020/04/18/us/texas-protests-stay-at-home.html.

12. Craig Mauger and Beth LeBlanc, "Trump Tweets 'Liberate' Michigan, Two Other States with Dem Governors," *The Detroit News,* April 17, 2020, https://www.detroitnews.com/story/news/politics/2020/04/17/trump-tweets-liberate-michigan-other-states-democratic-governors/5152037002/.

13. From Willis' LinkedIn profile, https://www.linkedin.com/in/mikki-willis-b3722311/.

14. Plandemic Movie, Part 1, https://www.bitchute.com/video/bZ2yliCyu373/.

15. Ibid.

16. Scott Neuman, "Seen 'Plandemic'? We Take a Close Look at the Viral Conspiracy Videos Claim," *NPR,* May 8, 2020, https://www.npr.org/2020/05/08/852451652/seen-plandemic-we-take-a-close-look-at-the-viral-conspiracy-video-s-claims.

17. Alex Kasprak, "Was a Scientist Jailed After Discovering a Deadly Virus Delivered Through Vaccines?" *Snopes.com,* December 8, 2018, https://www.snopes.com/fact-check/scientist-vaccine-jailed/.

18. Martin Enserink and Jon Cohen, "Fact-Checking Judy Mikovits, The Controversial Virologist Attacking Anthony Fauci in a Viral Conspiracy Video," *Science*, May 8, 2020. https://www.science.org/content/article/fact-checking-judy-mikovits-controversial-virologist-attacking-anthony-fauci-viral.

19. Plandemic Movie, Part 1, https://www.bitchute.com/video/bZ2yliCyu373/.

20. Enserink and Cohen, "Fact-Checking Judy Mikovits."

21. Plandemic Movie, Part 1, https://www.bitchute.com/video/bZ2yliCyu373/.

22. Matt Taibbi, *Hate Inc.: Why Today's Media Makes Us Despise One* Another (New York: OR Books, 2019), 18.

23. This story recently reappeared with respect to Robert F. Kennedy Jr. See Blake Montgomery, "Instagram Bans America's Worst Anti-Vaxxer," *Daily Beast*, February 10, 2021, https://www.thedailybeast.com/instagram-bans-americas-worst-anti-vaxxer-robert-f-kennedy-jr.

24. "The Online Anti-Vaccine Movement in the Age of COVID-19," *The Lancet* 2 (October 2020): 504, https://www.thelancet.com/action/showPdf?pii=S2589-7500%2820%2930227-2.

25. Nick Triggle, "MMR Scare Doctor 'Acted Unethically,' Panel Finds," *BBC News,* January 28, 2010, http://news.bbc.co.uk/2/hi/health/8483865.stm; Julia Belluz, "Research Fraud Catalyzed the Anti-Vaccination Movement. Let's Not Repeat History," *Vox*, March 5, 2019, https://www.vox.com/2018/2/27/17057990/andrew-wakefield-vaccines-autism-study.

26. Sara E. Gorman and Jack M. Gorman, *Denying to the Grave: Why We Ignore the Facts That Will Save Us* (New York: Oxford University Press, 2017), 79-81; Lindzi Wessel, "Four Vaccine Myths and Where They Came From," *Science,* April 27, 2017, https://www.sciencemag.org/news/2017/04/four-vaccine-myths-and-where-they.came.

27. *Vaxxed: From Cover-Up to Catastrophe*, https://vaxxedthemovie.com.

28. E. J. Dickson, "A Guide to 17 Anti-Vaccination Celebrities," *Rolling Stone*, June 14, 2019, https://www.rollingstone.com/culture/culture-features/celebrities-anti-vaxxers-jessica-biel-847779/.

29. Eric Boodman, "Robert DeNiro Defends Discredited Idea Linking Vaccines to Autism," *Stat*, April 13, 2016, https://www.statnews.com/2016/04/13/de-niro-vaccines-vaxxed-autism/.

30. Michael Hiltzik, "Trump Attacks Biden and Harris as Anti-Vaccine, but He's the One with the Anti-Vaxx Record," *Los Angeles Times*, September 8, 2020, https://www.latimes.com/business/story/2020-09-08/trump-anti-vaxx-record.

31. Ibid.

32. Gorman and Gorman, *Denying to the Grave*, 4.

33. Centers for Disease Control and Prevention, National Center for Health Statistics, Immunization, https://www.cdc.gov/nchs/fastats/immunize.htm.

34. Centers for Disease Control and Prevention, TB Incidence in the United States, 1953–2019, https://www.cdc.gov/tb/statistics/tbcases.htm.

35. Centers for Disease Control and Prevention, Measles Cases and Outbreaks, https://www.cdc.gov/measles/cases-outbreaks.html.

36. Department of Health and Human Services, Community-Based Testing Sites for COVID-19, https://www.hhs.gov/coronavirus/community-based-testing-sites/index.html#:~:text=COVID%2D19%20tests%20are,available%20in%20your%20area; Austin Williams and Stephanie Weaver, "The Cost of COVID-19: Amid Illness, Americans Face Heavy Financial Burden in Testing and Treatment," *Fox 10 Phoenix,* July 9, 2020, https://www.fox10phoenix.com/news/the-cost-of-covid-19-amid-illness-americans-face-heavy-financial-burden-in-testing-and-treatment.

37. "What Is the Cost of COVID-19 Treatment?" *NPR Weekend Edition Sunday,* March 29, 2020, https://www.npr.org/2020/03/29/823438983/what-is-the-cost-of-covid-19-treatment.

38. Bureau of Labor Statistics, TED: The Economics Daily, https://www.bls.gov/opub/ted/2020/unemployment-rate-falls-to-6-point-9-percent-in-october-2020.htm.

39. Dina Temple-Raston, "CDC Report: Officials Knew Coronavirus Test Was Flawed but Released It Anyway," *NPR Morning Edition,* November 6, 2020, https://www.npr.org/2020/11/06/929078678/cdc-report-officials-knew-coronavirus-test-was-flawed-but-released-it-anyway.

40. Becky Little, "Trump's 'Chinese' Virus Is Part of a Long History of Blaming Other Countries for Disease," *Time,* March 20, 2020, https://time.com/5807376/virus-name-foreign-history/.

41. See "Coronavirus COVID-19," Metabunk, https://www.metabunk.org/forums/coronavirus-covid-19.58/page-3. The debunking website features dozens of separate threads on COVID-19 conspiracies.

42. Amanda Seitz and Beatrice Dupuy, "Here Are 5 Debunked COVID-19 Myths That Just Won't Die," *Denver Post,* December 18, 2020, https://www.denverpost.com/2020/12/18/covid-19-myths-debunked/.

43. Coronavirus (COVID-19), https://news.google.com/covid19/map?hl=en-US&gl=US&ceid=US%3Aen.

44. Enserink and Cohen, "Fact-Checking Judy Mikovits."

45. Trine Tsouderos, "Covering the Stunning Fall of Judy Mikovits, Researcher of XMRV and Chronic Fatigue," *Chicago Tribune,* November 22, 2011, https://www.chicagotribune.com/news/chi-covering-the-stunning-fall-of-judy-mikovits-20111122-story.html.

46. Enserink and Cohen, "Fact-Checking Judy Mikovits."

47. Tina Hesman Saey, "No, The Coronavirus Wasn't Made in a Lab. A Genetic Analysis Shows It's from Nature," *ScienceNews,* March 26, 2020, https://www.sciencenews.org/article/coronavirus-covid-19-not-human-made-lab-genetic-analysis-nature.

48. CDC, *Key Facts about Seasonal Flu Vaccine,* https://www.cdc.gov/flu/prevent/keyfacts.htm.

49. See https://drjudyamikovits.com. Interestingly, the link for this topic was inactive in March 2021. By May, it had been removed from the website.

50. Daniel Funke, "Fact-Checking 'Plandemic': A Documentary Full of False Conspiracy Theories about the Coronavirus," *Politifact,* May 7, 2020, https://www.politifact.com/article/2020/may/08/fact-checking-plandemic-documentary-full-false-con/.

51. Trine Tsouderos, "Discredited Chronic Fatigue Researcher in California Jail," *Chicago Tribune*, November 22, 2011, https://www.chicagotribune.com/nation-world/ct-xpm-2011-11-22-ct-nw-chronic-fatigue-scientist-arrest-20111122-story.html.

52. "President Trump Calls Coronavirus 'Kung Flu," *BBC News*, June 24, 2020, https://www.bbc.com/news/av/world-us-canada-53173436.

53. Joe Walsh, "Trump Is Demanding China Pay 'Big Price' for COVID-19," *Forbes,* October 8, 2020, https://www.forbes.com/sites/joewalsh/2020/10/08/trump-is-demanding-china-pay-big-price-for-covid-19/#7b5cdf3b41c8.

54. John T. Bennett, "Trump Claims Border Wall 'Stopped Covid' in Arizona—Even as State Breaks Record for Coronavirus Cases," *Independent*, June 23, 2020, https://www.independent.co.uk/news/world/americas/us-politics/trump-arizona-coronavirus-cases-border-wall-covid-19-a9582141.html.

55. Susan Milligan, "Approval of Trump's Coronavirus Response Hits All-Time Low: Poll," *US News* July 10, 2020, https://www.usnews.com/news/elections/articles/2020-07-10/approval-of-trumps-coronavirus-response-hits-all-time-low-poll.

56. Peter Navarro, "Fauci Has Been Wrong About Everything I Have Interacted with Him On," *USA Today,* July 15, 2020, https://www.usatoday.com/story/opinion/todaysdebate/2020/07/14/anthony-fauci-wrong-with-me-peter-navarro-editorials-debates/5439374002/.

57. Mark Jurkowitz, "Majority of Americans Disapprove of Trump's COVID-19 Messaging, Though Large Partisan Gaps Persist," Pew Research Center, September 15, 2020, https://www.pewresearch.org/fact-tank/2020/09/15/majority-of-americans-disapprove-of-trumps-covid-19-messaging-though-large-partisan-gaps-persist/; See also Cary Funk, Brian Kennedy, and Courtney Jackson, "Trust in Medical Scientists Has Grown, but Mainly Among Democrats," Pew Research Center, May 21, 2020, https://www.pewresearch.org/science/2020/05/21/trust-in-medical-scientists-has-grown-in-u-s-but-mainly-among-democrats/.

58. Joel Achenbach and Laurie McGinley, "Another Casualty of the Coronavirus Panic: Trust in Government Science," *Washington Post*, October 11, 2020, https://www.washingtonpost.com/health/covid-trust-in-science/2020/10/11/b6048c14-03e1-11eb-a2db-417cddf4816a_story.html.

59. Nathalie Baptiste, "Scott Atlas Downplays Coronavirus and Rails Against Mask," *Mother Jones*, October 17, 2020, https://www.motherjones.com/politics/2020/10/scott-atlas-downplays-coronavirus-and-rails-against-masks/.

60. Ibid.

61. Kerry Breen, "Fauci Warns of 'Enormous' Death Toll If US Relies on Herd Immunity," *Today*, August 14, 2020, https://www.today.com/health/fauci-warns-enormous-death-toll-if-us-relies-herd-immunity-t189427.

62. Cary Funk, Meg Hefferon, Brian Kennedy, and Courtney Jackson, "Trust and Mistrust in Americans' Views of Scientific Experts," Pew Research Center, August 2, 2019, https://www.pewresearch.org/science/2019/08/02/trust-and-mistrust-in-ameri cans-views-of-scientific-experts/.

63. Margot Sanger-Katz, "On Coronavirus, Americans Still Trust the Experts," *New York Times*, June 27, 2020, https://www.nytimes.com/2020/06/27/upshot/coro navirus-americans-trust-experts.html.

64. Andrew Solender, "Amid White House Attacks, Polls Show Dr. Fauci Remains Nation's Most Trusted Voice on COVID-19," *Forbes*, July 15, 2020, https://www .forbes.com/sites/andrewsolender/2020/07/15/amid-white-house-attacks-polls-show -dr-fauci-remains-nations-most-trusted-voice-on-covid-19/#6f72ef181ee2.

65. Lauren Mascarenhaus and Kristen Holmes, "First Shipments of Pfizer Vaccine to Be Delivered December 15," *CNN Health*, December 2, 2020, https://www.cnn .com/2020/12/01/health/first-pfizer-vaccine-shipments/index.html.

66. Cary Funk and Alex Tyson, "Intent to Get a COVID-19 Vaccine Rises to 60% as Confidence in Research and Development Increases," Pew Research Center, December 3, 2020, https://www.pewresearch.org/science/2020/12/03/intent-to-get -a-covid-19-vaccine-rises-to-60-as-confidence-in-research-and-development-pro cess-increases/.

67. "1 in 4 Say 'No Thanks' to Vaccine," *Monmouth University Polling Institute*, February 3, 2021, https://www.monmouth.edu/polling-institute/reports/monmouth poll_us_020321/.

68. Gorman and Gorman, *Denying to the* Grave, 4.

69. (SARS) Severe Acute Respiratory Syndrome or SARS-CoV. Avian Flu is oth-erwise known as avian influenza. Swine flu is also known as influenza A (H1N1). The official term for Ebola is Ebola hemorrhagic fever.

70. Simon & Schuster, Mehmet Oz, "About the Author," https://www.simonand schuster.com/authors/Mehmet-Oz/50064466.

71. Paul Farhl and Elahe Isadi, "Dr. Phil and Dr. Oz Aren't Coronavirus Experts: So Why are They Talking About It on TV News?" *Washington Post*, April 18, 2020, https://www.washingtonpost.com/lifestyle/media/dr-phil-and-dr-oz-arent-coro navirus-experts-so-why-are-they-talking-about-it-on-tv-news/2020/04/17/09c2c410 -80bb-11ea-a3ee-13e1ae0a3571_story.html.

72. CDC, Measles Cases in 2020, https://www.cdc.gov/measles/cases-outbreaks .html.

73. CDC, Measles Data and Statistics, https://www.cdc.gov/measles/downloads/ measlesdataandstatsslideset.pdf.

CHAPTER TEN

1. There are multiple sources on the basic definition of QAnon. See Gregory Stan-ton, "QAnon is a Nazi Cult, Rebranded," *Just Security*, September 9, 2020, https:// www.justsecurity.org/72339/qanon-is-a-nazi-cult-rebranded/.

2. Kevin Roose, "Following Falsehoods: A Reporter's Approach on QAnon," *New York Times*, October 3, 2020, https://www.nytimes.com/2020/10/03/insider/qanon-reporter.html.

3. Todd Ruger, "FBI Director Describes Domestic Extremists in Homeland Threats Hearing," *Roll Call*, September 17, 2020, https://www.rollcall.com/2020/09/17/fbi-director-describes-domestic-extremists-in-homeland-threats-hearing/. See also Federal Bureau of Investigation, Phoenix Field Office, "Anti-Government, Identity Based, and Fringe Political Conspiracy Theories Very Likely Motivate Some Domestic Extremists to Commit Criminal, Sometimes Violent Activity," May 30, 2019.

4. "Report: Americans Pessimistic on Time Frame for Coronavirus Recovery," *Civiqs*, September 2, 2020, https://civiqs.com/reports/2020/9/2/report-americans-pessimistic-on-time-frame-for-coronavirus-recovery.

5. "More Than 1 in 3 Americans Believe a 'Deep State' Is Working to Undermine Trump," *Ipsos*, December 30, 2020, https://www.ipsos.com/en-us/news-polls/npr-misinformation-123020.

6. Mike Wendling, "QAnon: What Is It and Where Did It Come From?" *BBC.com* (August 20, 2020), https://www.bbc.com/news/53498434; Kevin Roose, "Following Falsehoods: A Reporter's Approach to QAnon," *New York Times,* 3 October 3, 2020, https://www.nytimes.com/2020/10/03/insider/qanon-reporter.html.

7. Ryan Grim, "Deconstructed: Is QAnon the Future of the Republican Party?" *The Intercept*, August 28, 2020, https://theintercept.com/2020/08/28/is-qanon-the-future-of-the-republican-party/.

8. Stanton, QAnon Is a Nazi Cult, Rebranded."

9. Katelyn Burns, "A QAnon Supporter Just Won a Republican Primary for US Senator," *Vox*, May 20, 2020, https://www.vox.com/policy-and-politics/2020/5/20/21264925/jo-rae-perkins-qanon-us-senate-oregon.

10. Kiera Butler, "The Mother of All Conspiracies," *Mother Jones* 46 (January/February 2021): 58.

11. Faiz Siddiqui and Susan Svrluga, "NC Man Told Police He Went to DC Pizzeria with Gun to Investigate Conspiracy Theory," *Washington Post*, December 5, 2016, https://www.washingtonpost.com/news/local/wp/2016/12/04/d-c-police-respond-to-report-of-a-man-with-a-gun-at-comet-ping-pong-restaurant/?utm_term=.43494d1a45d3.

12. William Mansell, "Man Pleads Guilty to Terrorism Charge After Blocking Hoover Dam Bridge with Armored Truck," *ABC News*, February 13, 2020, https://abcnews.go.com/US/man-pleads-guilty-terrorism-charge-blocking-bridge-armored/story?id=68955385.

13. Will Sommer, "QAnon Believer Teamed Up with Conspiracy Theorists to Plot Kidnapping, Police Say," *Daily Beast*, January 4, 2020, https://www.thedailybeast.com/cynthia-abcug-qanon-conspiracy-theorist-charged-in-kidnapping-plot.

14. Clive Thompson, "QAnon Is Like a Game—A Most Dangerous Game," *Wired*, September 22, 2020, https://www.wired.com/story/qanon-most-dangerous-multiplatform-game/.

15. Jarret Bencks-Brandeis, "Expert Decodes Trump Talk, Q Codes, and the Road to Insurrection," *Futurity*, January 14, 2021, https://www.futurity.org/trump-commu nication-supporters-2501462-2/.

16. "'Did You See That?' Donald Trump's Subtle Hand Gesture Triggers Bizarre Theory," Associated Press, February 7, 2020, https://au.news.yahoo.com/qanon -conspiracy-theorists-response-to-donald-trump-q-symbol-002645230.html.

17. Dan Barry and Sheera Frenkel, "'Be There, Will Be Wild': Trump All but Circled the Date," *New York Times*, January 6, 2021, https://www.nytimes .com/2021/01/06/us/politics/capitol-mob-trump-supporters.html.

18. Thompson, "QAnon Is Like a Game."

19. Matt Moore, "Stephen Colbert Checks in on the QAnon Shaman and More," *Fansided*, n.d., https://lastnighton.com/2021/03/05/stephen-colbert-qanon-shaman -seditionist-roundup/.

20. Ben Leonard, "'QAnon Shaman' Granted Organic Food in Jail After Report of Deteriorating Health," *Politico*, February 3, 2021, https://www.politico.com/ news/2021/02/03/qanon-shaman-organic-food-465563.

21. Eden Gillespie, "'Pastel QAnon': The Female Lifestyle Bloggers and Influ- encers Spreading Conspiracy Theories Through Instagram," *The Feed*, September 30, 2020, https://www.sbs.com.au/news/the-feed/pastel-qanon-the-female-lifestyle -bloggers-and-influencers-spreading-conspiracy-theories-through-instagram.

22. E. J. Dickson, "Pastel QAnon Is Infiltrating the Natural Parenting Com- munity," *Rolling Stone*, December 14, 2020, https://www.rollingstone.com/culture/ culture-news/qanon-pastel-antivax-natural-parenting-community-freebirth-1098518/.

23. Gillespie, "'Pastel QAnon'"

24. Ibid.

25. Lili Loofbourow, "It Makes Perfect Sense That QAnon Took Off with Women This Summer," *Slate*, September 18, 2020, https://slate.com/news-and -politics/2020/09/qanon-women-why.html.

26. Kiera Butler, "The Mother of All Conspiracies," *Mother Jones* 46 (January/ February 2021): 56.

27. Daniel Funke, "How the Wayfair Child Sex-Trafficking Conspiracy Theory Went Viral," *Politifact*, July 15, 2020, https://www.politifact.com/article/2020/jul/15/ how-wayfair-child-sex-trafficking-conspiracy-theor/; Neriah Swivel Bar & Counter Stool, https://www.wayfair.com/furniture/pdp/three-posts-neriah-swivel-bar-counter -stool-w004148314.html.

28. Butler, "The Mother of All Conspiracies," 56-57.

29. Daniel Dale and Jamie Gumbrecht, "Twitter Removes QAnon Supporter's False Claim about Coronavirus Death Statistics That Trump Retweeted," *CNN*, 31 August 31, 2020, https://www.cnn.com/2020/08/30/politics/twitter-coronavirus -deaths-false-claim-qanon-trump/index.html.

30. Kaitlyn Tiffany, "The Women Making Conspiracy Theories Beautiful," *The Atlantic*, August 18, 2020, https://www.theatlantic.com/technology/archive/2020/08/ how-instagram-aesthetics-repackage-qanon/615364/.

31. Loofbourow, "It Makes Perfect Sense That QAnon Took Off with Women This Summer."

32. Charlotte Ward and David Boas, "The Emergence of Conspirituality," *Journal of Contemporary Religion* 26 (2011) 103–21; Marisa Meltzer, "QAnon's Unexpected Roots in New Age Spirituality," *Washington Post*, March 29, 2021, https://www.washingtonpost.com/magazine/2021/03/29/qanon-new-age-spirituality/.

33. Meltzer, "QAnon's Unexpected Roots in New Age Spirituality."

34. Tiffany, "The Women Making Conspiracy Theories Beautiful."

35. Matthew Haag, "Florida SWAT Officer Is Demoted After Wearing QAnon Patch Next to Mike Pence, *New York Times*, December 4, 2018, https://www.nytimes.com/2018/12/04/us/swat-leader-qanon-patch.html.

36. Tina Nguyen, "Trump Isn't Secretly Winking at QAnon: He's Retweeting Its Followers," *Politico*, July 12, 2020, https://www.politico.com/news/2020/07/12/trump-tweeting-qanon-followers-357238.

37. Ewan Palmer, "Donald Trump Has Promoted QAnon-Linked Twitter Accounts More Than 250 Times," *Newsweek*, October 16, 2020, https://www.newsweek.com/qanon-trump-twitter-conspiracy-town-hall-pedophiles-1539698.

38. Patrick Svitek, "The Texas GOP's New Slogan Echoes a Conspiracy Group: Its Chair Says There Is No Connection," *Texas Tribune*, August 21, 2020, https://www.texastribune.org/2020/08/21/texas-gop-slogan-storm/.

39. Marshall Cohen, "Michael Flynn Posts Video Featuring QAnon Slogans," *CNN*, July 7, 2020, https://www.cnn.com/2020/07/07/politics/michael-flynn-qanon-video/index.html.

40. Katelyn Burns, "A QAnon Supports Just Won a Republican Primary for US Senator," *Vox*, May 20, 2020, https://www.vox.com/policy-and-politics/2020/5/20/21264925/jo-rae-perkins-qanon-us-senate-oregon.

41. Jacob Knutson, "11 GOP Candidates Who Support QAnon," *Axios*, July 12, 2020, https://www.axios.com/qanon-nominees-congress-gop-8086ed21-b7d3-46af-9016-d132e65ba801.html; See also *Right Wing Watch*, May 18, 2020, https://twitter.com/RightWingWatch/status/1262395371696816135?s=20, Accessed April 8, 2021.

42. Marjorie Taylor Greene—The Video She Wants You to Forget, November 26, 2017, https://www.youtube.com/watch?v=2rtYok4fdbQ, accessed April 8, 2021.

43. Ibid. See also Daniel Funke, "What Rep. Marjorie Taylor Green Has Said About Election Fraud, QAnon and Other Conspiracy Theories," *Politifact*, February 2, 2021, https://www.politifact.com/article/2021/feb/02/what-rep-marjorie-taylor-greene-has-said-about-ele/.

44. Jack Brewster, "'The Storm Is Here': GOP House Candidate Tweets QAnon Rallying Cry After Trump Retweets Her," *Forbes*, August 7, 2020, https://www.forbes.com/sites/jackbrewster/2020/08/07/the-storm-is-here-gop-house-candidate-tweets-qanon-rallying-cry-after-trump-retweets-her/#7f1224a84f59.

45. Alex Kaplan, "Here Are the QAnon Supporters Running for Congress in 2020," *Media Matters for America*, November 9, 2020, https://www.mediamatters.org/qanon-conspiracy-theory/here-are-qanon-supporters-running-congress-2020.

46. Ibid.

47. "2020 Oregon US Senate Election Results," *USA Today*, November 3, 2020, https://www.usatoday.com/elections/results/race/2020-11-03-senate-OR-38952/.

48. Rebecca Falconer, "GOP Sen. Ben Sasse: QAnon Is Destroying the Republican Party," *Axios*, January 17, 2021, https://www.axios.com/sen-ben-sasse-atlantic-op-ed -qanon-destroying-gop-c8f0b959-572d-447c-bfe5-d5bbbb80bf99.html.

49. Juliegrace Brufke, "Liz Cheney Condemns QAnon Conspiracy," *The Hill*, August 20, 2020, https://thehill.com/homenews/house/512959-liz-cheney-condemns -qanon-conspiracy.

50. Jeet Heer, "QAnon Is the Future of the Republican Party," *The Nation*, August 17, 2020, https://www.thenation.com/article/politics/qanon-future-republican-party/.

51. Khalida Volou, "Here's Everything You Need to Know About the 'March for Trump' Rally," *KVUE ABC*, January 5, 2021, https://www.kvue.com/article/news/ local/protests/march-for-trump-rally-dc-january-6-protest-pro-trump-demonstrators -event-details/65-2e019324-7861-48fa-8d78-d99b9617558b.

52. Katie Meyer, Miles Bryan, and Ryan Briggs, "Mastriano Campaign Spent Thousands on Buses Ahead of DC Insurrection," *WHYY PBS*, January 12, 2021, https://whyy.org/articles/mastriano-campaign-spent-thousands-on-buses-ahead-of-d -c-insurrection/.

53. Dave Wasserman@Redistrict, January 8, 2021, https://twitter.com/Redistrict/ status/1347614831071924227/photo/1.

54. Ryan Deto, "Former Congressional Candidate Rick Saccone Starts a Blog Called Veritas007 to Expose 'Hidden Agendas,'" *City Paper: Pittsburgh*, July 9, 2019, https://www.pghcitypaper.com/pittsburgh/former-congressional-can didate-rick-saccone-starts-a-blog-called-veritas007-to-expose-hidden-agendas/ Content?oid=15378781.

55. Ana Lucia Morillo, "57 GOP Officials Attended the Jan. 6 Rally That Preceded the Riot: Report," *Huffpost*, February 13, 2021, https://www.thedailybeast.com/57 -gop-officials-attended-jan-6-rally-that-preceded-capitol-riot-huffpost-reports.

56. Daniel A. Cox, "After the Ballots Are Counted: Conspiracies, Political Violence, and American Exceptionalism" *American Enterprise Institute*, February 11, 2021, https://www.americansurveycenter.org/research/after-the-ballots-are-counted -conspiracies-political-violence-and-american-exceptionalism/.

57. Will Sommer, "Cops Fear QAnon Violence: Diehards Call 'False Flag,'" *Daily Beast*, March 4, 2021, https://www.thedailybeast.com/cops-fear-qanon-violence-on -march-4-die-hards-call-false-flag.

58. Ali Breland, "Stranger Danger: Why Are the Conspiracy Theories of Pizzagate and QAnon So Obsessed with Pedophilia?" *Mother Jones* 44 (July/August 2019): 60.

59. Rob Brotherton, *Suspicious Minds: Why We Believe Conspiracy Theories* (New York: Bloomsbury Sigma, 2015), 34–35.

60. Breland, "Stranger Danger," 59.

61. Butler, "The Mother of Conspiracies," 58.

62. Meltzer, "QAnon's Unexpected Roots in New Age Spirituality."

63. Frida Ghitis, "QAnon is an American Invention, But It Has Become a Global Plague," *Washington Post*, March 10, 2021, https://www.washingtonpost.com/ opinions/2021/03/10/qanon-japan-germany-colombia-conspiracy-theories-disinfor mation/.

64. Craig Timberg and Elizabeth Dwoskin, "With Trump Gone, QAnon Groups Focus Fury on Attacking Coronavirus Vaccines," *Washington Post*, March 11, 2021, https://www.washingtonpost.com/technology/2021/03/11/with-trump-gone-qanon -groups-focus-fury-attacking-covid-vaccines/.

65. Butler, "The Mother of All Conspiracies," 57.

66. Cox, "After the Ballots Are Counted."

67. A good examination of this topic may be found in *A Contagion of Institutional Distrust: Viral Disinformation of the COVID Vaccine and the Road to Reconciliation*, National Contagious Research Institute, March 11, 2021, https://networkcontagion. us/reports/a-contagion-of-institutional-distrust/.

CHAPTER ELEVEN

1. "Watch ITV News' Eyewitness Report from Inside the US Capitol as Trump Supporters Storm Building," *ITV News*, January 6, 2021, https://www.itv.com/ news/2021-01-06/watch-itv-news-eyewitness-report-from-inside-the-us-capitol-as -protesters-storm-building.

2. Full Rashia Tlaib Fuck Trump Rant, January 4, 2019, https://www.youtube .com/watch?v=z8YW8lS4maY.

3. Terrance Smith, "Trump Has Longstanding History of Calling Election Re- sults 'Rigged' If He Doesn't Like the Results," *ABC News*, November 11, 2020, https://abcnews.go.com/Politics/trump-longstanding-history-calling-elections-rigged -doesnt-results/story?id=74126926.

4. Morgan Chalfant, "Trump: 'The Only Way We're Going to Lose This Election Is If the Election is Rigged'," *The Hill*, August 17, 2020, https://thehill.com/home news/administration/512424-trump-the-only-way-we-are-going-to-lose-this-election -is-if-the.

5. "2016 Presidential Election Results," *New York Times*, August 9, 2017, https:// www.nytimes.com/elections/2016/results/president; Election Results, 2020, https:// ballotpedia.org/Election_results,_2020. Ironically, as many commentators pointed out, Trump won by almost exactly the same Electoral College margin four years earlier (304 to 232).

6. 18 US Code § 2383 defines rebellion or insurrection as: "Whoever incites, sets on foot, assists, or engages in any rebellion or insurrection against the authority of the United States or the laws thereof, or gives aid or comfort thereto, shall be fined under this title or imprisoned not more than ten years, or both; and shall be incapable of holding any office under the United States." See Cornell Law School, Legal Informa- tion Institute, https://www.law.cornell.edu/uscode/text/18/2383.

7. Jake Kanter, "ITV News Journalist Goes Viral, Wins Praise After Extraordinary Report Following Trump Mob into Capitol," *Deadline*, January 7, 2021, https://dead line.com/2021/01/robert-moore-report-itv-news-capitol-donald-trump-1234666355/.

8. Boris Johnson, *@BorisJohnson*, January 6, 2021, https://twitter.com/borisjohn son/status/1346926138057220103?lang=en, accessed April 12, 2021.

9. Daniel Kreps, "'Deeply Disturbing and Alarming': World Leaders Condemn MAGA Uprising," *Rolling Stone*, January 6, 2021, https://www.rollingstone.com/politics/politics-news/world-leaders-react-trump-capitol-siege-assault-democracy-1110709/.

10. Shannon Tiezzi, "China Is Already Using the Storming of the US Capitol for Propaganda," *The Diplomat*, January 8, 2021, https://thediplomat.com/2021/01/china-is-already-using-the-storming-of-the-us-capitol-for-propaganda/.

11. For a good summary of events, see Federal Bureau of Investigation, Office of the Inspector General, Oversight and Review Divisions, *Review of Four FISA Applications and Other Aspects of the FBI's Crossfire Hurricane Investigation* (Washington, DC: Federal Bureau of Investigation, December 2019).

12. Jamie Ehrlich, "Jeff Session Says His Recusal from Russia Probe was an Attempt to Help Trump," *CNN Politics*, May 12, 2020, https://www.cnn.com/2020/05/12/politics/jeff-sessions-trump-alabama-tommy-tuberville/index.html.

13. Jessica Taylor, "Report: Trump told Russians He Fired 'Nut Job' Comey Because of Investigation," *NPR WHYY*, May 19, 2017, https://www.npr.org/2017/05/19/529171249/report-trump-told-russians-he-fired-nut-job-comey-because-of-investigation.

14. Department of Justice, Appointment of Special Counsel, May 17, 2017, https://www.justice.gov/opa/pr/appointment-special-counsel.

15. Carl Hulse, "'Moscow Mitch' Tag Enrages McConnell and Squeezes G.O.P. on Election Security," *New York Times*, July 30, 2019, https://www.nytimes.com/2019/07/30/us/politics/moscow-mitch-mcconnell.html.

16. Rich Lowry, "Rachel Maddow's Deep Delusion," *Politico*, March 27, 2019, https://www.politico.com/magazine/story/2019/03/27/rachel-maddows-deep-delusion-226266/.

17. Joe Otterson, "Rachel Maddow Tops Sean Hannity in March, Fox News Host Tops 2018 Q1," *Variety*, April 5, 2018, https://variety.com/2018/tv/news/rachel-maddow-ratings-sean-hannity-1202745403/.

18. Willa Paskin, "Rachel Maddow's Conspiracy Brain," *Slate*, March 29, 2019, https://slate.com/culture/2019/03/rachel-maddow-mueller-report-trump-barr.html.

19. "Mueller Indictments: Who's Who," *Wall Street Journal*, January 25, 2019, https://www.wsj.com/articles/mueller-indictments-whos-who-1531511838.

20. Dylan Matthews, "Why Paul Manafort Pleaded Guilty to 'Conspiracy Against the United States,'" *Vox*, March 13, 2019, https://www.vox.com/2018/9/14/17860410/conspiracy-against-the-united-states-paul-manafort-plea.

21. Matt Taibbi, "Master List of Official Russia Claims That Proved to Be Bogus," *TK News*, March 29, 2021, https://taibbi.substack.com/p/master-list-of-official-russia-claims.

22. Sharon LaFraniere, Mark Mazzetti, and Matt Apuzzo, "How the Russia Inquiry Began: A Campaign Aide, Drinks, and Talk of Political Dirt," *New York Times*, December 30, 2017, https://www.nytimes.com/2017/12/30/us/politics/how-fbi-russia-investigation-began-george-papadopoulos.html.

23. President Trump's Election Night Speech," *Reuters*, November 4, 2020, https://www.youtube.com/watch?v=K_ESXL7J6DY.

24. "President Trump's Remarks on Election Results," November 5, 2020, *C-SPAN*, https://www.c-span.org/video/?477858-1/president-trump-challenges-latest-election-results-claims-voter-fraud.

25. Alec Dent, "Fact Check: Explaining the False Allegations About Dominion Voting Systems," *The Dispatch*, November 10, 2020, https://factcheck.thedispatch.com/p/fact-check-explaining-the-false-allegations.

26. Mimi Dwyer and Sarah N. Lynch, "'Sharpiegate' Allegations Fuel Unproven Claims of Voter Fraud in Arizona," *Reuters*, November 4, 2020, https://www.reuters.com/article/uk-usa-election-arizona-sharpie-idUKKBN27K2QQ.

27. "AP Fact Check: Trump Wrong on Georgia Voter Signature Checks," *Associated Press*, November 15, 2020, https://apnews.com/article/ap-fact-check-donald-trump-georgia-elections-voter-registration-40bb602e6f0facf8eecc331e83ab36e0.

28. Kevin Roose, "No, the Army Didn't Seize a German Server Showing a Trump Landslide," *New York Times*, November 18, 2020, https://www.nytimes.com/2020/11/18/technology/scytl-trump.html; Jude Joffe-Block, "False Reports Claim Election Servers Were Seized in Germany," *Associated Press*, November 2020, https://apnews.com/article/fact-checking-9754011363.

29. George Papadopoulos @GeorgePapa19, November 13, 2021, https://twitter.com/georgepapa19/status/1327402113920602114?lang=en, accessed April 25, 2021.

30. Howard Altman and Davis Winkie, "This Retired Three-Star Falsely Claims US Soldiers Died Attacking a CIA Facility in Germany Tied to Election Fraud," *Military Times*, December 1, 2020, https://www.militarytimes.com/news/your-army/2020/12/01/this-retired-th...diers-died-attacking-a-cia-facility-in-germany-tied-to-election-fraud/.

31. Robert A. Caro, *Means of Ascent: The Years of Lyndon Johnson* (New York: Alfred A. Knopf, 1990), 360.

32. Josh Zeitz, "Worried About a Rigged Election? Here's One Way to Handle It," *Politico*, October 27, 2016, https://www.politico.com/magazine/story/2016/10/donald-trump-2016-rigged-nixon-kennedy-1960-214395/.

33. James T. Patterson, *Restless Giant: The United States from Watergate to Bush v. Gore* (New York: Oxford University Press, 2005), 412.

34. Michael E. Miller, "'It's Insanity!': How the 'Brooks Brothers Riot' Killed the 2000 Recount in Miami," *Washington Post*, November 15, 2018, https://www.washingtonpost.com/history/2018/11/15/its-insanity-how-brooks-brothers-riot-killed-recount-miami/.

35. Patterson, *Restless Giant*, 419.

36. Ibid., 418.

37. John Maines, Sean Cavanagh, and Megan O'Matz, "Florida 2000: The Lost Vote," *South Florida Sun Sentinel*, January 28, 2001, https://www.sun-sentinel.com/news/fl-xpm-2001-01-28-0101280213-story.html.

38. CDC, Epidemic Intelligence Service, Community Congregate Settings, https://www.cdc.gov/eis/field-epi-manual/chapters/community-settings.html.

39. "Wisconsin Primary Recap: Voters Forced to Choose Between Their Health and Their Civic Duty," *New York Times*, April 7, 2020, https://www.nytimes.com/2020/04/07/us/politics/wisconsin-primary-election.html.

40. Richard H. Pildes and Charles Stewart, "The Wisconsin Primary Had Extraordinarily High Voter Turnout," *Washington Post*, April 15, 2020, https://www.washingtonpost.com/politics/2020/04/15/wisconsin-primary-had-extraordinarily-high-voter-turnout/.

41. Florida Department of State, Division of Elections, Early Voting, https://dos.myflorida.com/elections/for-voters/voting/early-voting/.

42. Compromise Settlement and Release, Case 1:19-cv-05028-WMR, Document 56-1, March 6, 2020, https://demdoc2.perkinscoieblogs.com/wp-content/uploads/sites/45/2020/07/GA-Settlement-1.pdf.

43. The author was an election judge for both the 2020 primary and general election in Pennsylvania.

44. Roose, "No, the Army Didn't Seize a German Server Showing a Trump Landslide."; Joffe-Block, "False Reports Claim Election Servers Were Seized in Germany."

45. Jeremy W. Peters and Alan Feuer, "How is Trump's Lawyer Jenna Ellis 'Elite Strike Force' Material?" *New York Times*, December 3, 2020, https://www.nytimes.com/2020/12/03/us/politics/jenna-ellis-trump.html.

46. Elizabeth Thompson, "5 Things to Know About Sydney Powell, the Dallas Lawyer Formerly on Trump's Legal Team," *Dallas Morning News*, November 20, 2020, https://www.dallasnews.com/news/politics/2020/11/20/5-things-to-know-about-sidney-powell-the-dallas-lawyer-on-trumps-legal-team-alleging-election-fraud/.

47. Cybersecurity and Infrastructure Security Agency, Joint Statement from Elections Infrastructure Government Coordinating Council and the Election Infrastructure Sector Coordinating Executive Committees, November 12, 2020, https://www.cisa.gov/news/2020/11/12/joint-statement-elections-infrastructure-government-coordinating-council-election.

48. Pam Fessler, Miles Parks, Barbara Sprunt, "As Trump Pushes Election Falsehoods, His Cybersecurity Agency Pushes Back," *WHYY PBS*, November 14, 2020, https://www.npr.org/sections/live-updates-2020-election-results/2020/11/14/934220380/as-trump-pushes-election-falsehoods-his-cybersecurity-agency-pushes-back.

49. "US Attorney General Finds 'No Voter Fraud That Could Overturn Election,'" *BBC News*, December 2, 2020, https://www.bbc.com/news/world-us-canada-55153366.

50. Matt Zapotosky, "Undercutting Trump, Barr Says There's No Basis for Seizing Voting Machines, Using Special Counsels for Election Fraud, Hunter Biden," *Washington Post*, December 21, 2020, https://www.washingtonpost.com/national-security/barr-trump-special-counsel-voter-fraud-hunter-biden/2020/12/21/4d85f060-439c-11eb-b0e4-0f182923a025_story.html.

51. Jacob Sullum, "An Autopsy of Sidney Powell's 'Kraken' Reveals Suspiciously Similar Affidavits," *Reason.com*, December 25, 2020, https://reason.com/2020/12/25/an-autopsy-of-sidney-powells-kraken-reveals-suspiciously-similar-affidavits/.

52. Ibid.

53. *Tyler Bower et al. v. Doug Ducey et al.*, US District Court for the District of Arizona, Order No. CV-20-02321-PHX-DJH, December 9, 2020, 23, https://www .courtlistener.com/recap/gov.uscourts.azd.1255923/gov.uscourts.azd.12559 23.84.0_2.pdf.

54. *Timothy King, Marian Ellen Sheridan, John Earl Haggard, et al. v. Gretchen Witmer, Jocelyn Benson, and Michigan Board of Canvassers*, US District Court, Eastern District of Michigan, Southern Division, Civil Case No. 20-13134, December 7, 2020, 34, https://reason.com/wp-content/uploads/2020/12/King-v-Whitmer -ruling-12-7-20.pdf.

55. William Cummings, Joey Garrison, and Jim Sergent, "By the Numbers: President Trump's Failed Efforts to Overturn the Election," *USA Today*, January 6, 2021, https://www.usatoday.com/in-depth/news/politics/elections/2021/01/06/ trumps-failed-efforts-overturn-election-numbers/4130307001/.

56. Zeke Miller and Jill Colvin, "'I Hope Mike Pence Comes Through for Us': Pence Caught Between Trump, Constitution," *Associated Press*, January 5, 2021, https://www.dailyherald.com/news/20210105/i-hope-mike-pence-comes-through -for-us-pence-caught-between-trump-constitution.

57. Nick Niedzwiadek and Kyle Cheney," Trump Pressures Pence to Throw Out Election Results—Even Though He Can't," *Politico*, January 5, 2021, https://www .politico.com/news/2021/01/05/trump-pressures-pence-election-results-455069.

58. Cameron Peters, "Louie Gohmert's Failed Election Lawsuit, Briefly Explained," *Vox*, January 2, 2021, https://www.vox.com/2021/1/2/22210169/louie -gohmert-mike-pence-trump-hawley-election-lawsuit.

59. Tina Nguyen, "MAGA Marchers Plot Final DC Stand on Jan. 6," *Politico*, January 4, 2021, https://www.politico.com/news/2021/01/04/maga-marchers-trump -last-stand-454382.

60. Ibid.

61. Joseph Tanfani, Michael Berens, and Ned Parker, "How Trump's Pied Pipers Rallied a Faithful Mob to the Capitol," *Reuters*, January 11, 2021, https://www .reuters.com/article/uk-usa-trump-protest-organizers-insight/how-trumps-pied-pip ers-rallied-a-faithful-mob-to-the-capitol-idINKBN29H00H; Matthew Choi, "Trump is on Trial for Inciting an Insurrection: What About the 12 People Who Spoke Before Him?" *Politico*, February 10, 2021, https://www.politico.com/news/2021/02/10/ trump-impeachment-stop-the-steal-speakers-467554

62. Dan Barry and Sheera Frenkel, "'Be There. Will Be Wild': Trump All but Circled the Date," *New York Times*, January 8, 2021, https://www.nytimes .com/2021/01/06/us/politics/capitol-mob-trump-supporters.html.

63. Ibid.

64. For example, Red-State Secession is at https://redstatesecession.org.

65. Tanfani, Berens, and Parker, "How Trump's Pied Pipers Rallied a Faithful Mob to the Capitol."

66. Shayna Jacobs, "Giuliani Hit with Disbarment Complaint, Faces Possible Expulsion from New York Lawyers Association," *Washington Post*, January 11, 2021, https://www.washingtonpost.com/national-security/rudy-giuliani-new-york -bar-association/2021/01/11/5cfaf084-544c-11eb-a931-5b162d0d033d_story.html.

67. "Cawthorn—Constitution Was Violated by 2020 Election," *Fox Carolina News*, January 6, 2021, https://www.youtube.com/watch?v=w9FDABDlx_k.

68. "Mo Brooks Gives Fiery Speech Against Anti-Trump Republicans, Socialists," *The Hill*, January 6, 2021, https://www.youtube.com/watch?v=ZKHwV6sdrMk.

69. Choi, "Trump is on Trial for Inciting an Insurrection."

70. Tanfani, Berens, and Parker, "How Trump's Pied Pipers Rallied a Faithful Mob to the Capitol."

71. Calvin Woodward, "AP Fact Check: Trump Team Glosses over His Jan. 6 Tirade," *Associated Press*, February 12, 2021, https://apnews.com/article/ap-fact-check-donald-trump-capitol-siege-violence-elections-507f4febbadecb84e1637e55999ac0ea; See also, "Transcript of Trump's Speech at Rally Before US Capitol Riot," January 6, 2021, https://www.usnews.com/news/politics/articles/2021-01-13/transcript-of-trumps-speech-at-rally-before-us-capitol-riot.

72. Tanfani, Berens, and Parker, "How Trump's Pied Pipers Rallied a Faithful Mob to the Capitol."; Tom Jackman, "Police Union Says 140 Officers Injured in Capitol Riot," *Washington Post* 27 January 2021, https://www.washingtonpost.com/local/public-safety/police-union-says-140-officers-injured-in-capitol-riot/2021/01/27/60743642-60e2-11eb-9430-e7c77b5b0297_story.html.

73. Bart Jansen, "Cause of Death Release for 4 of 5 People at Capitol Riot-But Not Officer Brian Sicknick," *USA Today*, April 7, 2021, https://www.usatoday.com/story/news/politics/2021/04/07/capitol-riot-deaths-cause-death-released-4-5-not-sicknick/7128040002/.

74. Aruna Viswanatha, "Officer Brian Sicknick: What We Know about His Death," *Wall Street Journal*, April 21, 2021, https://www.wsj.com/articles/officer-brian-sicknick-what-we-know-about-his-death-11619010119; Peter Hermann, "Two Officers Who Helped Fight the Capitol Mob Died by Suicide. Many More Are Hurting," *Washington Post*, February 12, 2021, https://www.washingtonpost.com/local/public-safety/police-officer-suicides-capitol-riot/2021/02/11/94804ee2-665c-11eb-886d-5264d4ceb46d_story.html.

75. Tal Axelrod, "RNC Launches 'Committee on Election Integrity'," *The Hill*, February 17, 2021, https://thehill.com/homenews/campaign/539271-rnc-launches-committee-on-election-integrity; Amber Phillips, "How Republicans Are Spinning Their Election Fraud Falsehoods Now That Many Are Acknowledging Biden's Win," *Washington Post*, December 16, 2020, https://www.washingtonpost.com/politics/2020/12/16/how-republicans-are-spinning-their-unproven-election-fraud-claims-now-that-many-are-acknowledging-bidens-win/.

76. Will Steakin and Libby Cathey, "Trump's CPAC Speech Repeats False Claims Election Fraud Claims, Teases 2024 Presidential Run," *ABC News*, February 28, 2021, https://abcnews.go.com/Politics/trumps-cpac-speech-repeats-false-election-fraud-claims/story?id=76173257.

77. "Voting Laws Roundup: March 2021," Brennan Center for Justice, April 1, 2021, https://www.brennancenter.org/our-work/research-reports/voting-laws-roundup-march-2021.

78. Katanga Johnson and Heather Timmons, "How Stacy Abrams Paved the Way for a Democrat Victory in 'New Georgia,'" *Reuters*, November 11, 2020, https://

www.reuters.com/article/usa-election-georgia/how-stacey-abr...paved-the-way-for-a
-democratic-victory-in-new-georgia-idUSKBN27P197.

79. Amy Gardner and Amy B. Wang, "Georgia Governor Signs into Law
Sweeping Voting Bill That Curtails the Use of Drop Boxes and Imposes New ID
Requirements for Mail Voting," *Washington Post*, March 25, 2021, https://www
.washingtonpost.com/politics/georgia-voting-restrictions/2021/03/25/91009e72
-8da1-11eb-9423-04079921c915_story.html.

80. Nick Corasaniti and Reid J. Epstein, "What Georgia's Voting Law Really
Does," *New York Times*, April 7, 2021, https://www.nytimes.com/2021/04/02/us/
politics/georgia-voting-law-annotated.html.

81. Gabriel Sterling, "Opinion: Mr. President, Your Misinformation on Georgia's
Voting Law Is Dangerous," *Washington Post*, April 14, 2021, https://www.washing
tonpost.com/opinions/mr-president-your-misinformation-on-georgias-voting-law-is
-dangerous/2021/04/14/59b8a53c-9d4f-11eb-9d05-ae06f4529ece_story.html.

82. Ibid.

83. Jane C. Timm, "In Supreme Court, GOP Attorney Defends Voting Restrictions
by Saying They Help Republicans Win," *NBC News*, March 2, 2021, https://www
.nbcnews.com/politics/elections/supreme-court-gop-attorney-defends-voting-restric
tions-saying-they-help-n1259305.

84. Daniel A. Cox, "After the Ballots Are Counted: Conspiracies, Violence, and
American Exceptionalism," *Survey Center on American Life*, February 11, 2021,
https://www.americansurveycenter.org/research/after-the-ballots-are-counted-con
spiracies-political-violence-and-american-exceptionalism/.

85. Jan Wolfe, "Trump Advisor Giuliani Asks Judge to Throw Out $1.3 Billion
Lawsuit over His 'Big Lie' Election Claims," *Reuters*, April 7, 2021, https://www.re
uters.com/article/us-usa-election-dominion/trump-advise...t-1-3-billion-lawsuit-over
-his-big-lie-election-claims-idUSKBN2BU2NS.

86. Matt Lewis, "Sidney Powell's 'Just Kidding' Defense Is Seriously, Literally
Nuts," *Daily Beast*, March 28, 2021, https://news.yahoo.com/sidney-powell-just
-kidding-defense-085824126.html.

87. *US Dominion Inc. v. Sydney Powell and Defending the Republic Inc.*, Defen-
dants' Motion to Dismiss, March 22, 2021, 21.

CONCLUSIONS

1. Metabunk, "Posting Guidelines," https://www.metabunk.org/threads/posting
-guidelines.2064/.

2. See Conspirituality at https://conspirituality.net/about/.

3. Tom Wolfe, "The Me Decade and the Third Great Awakening," in Tom Wolfe,
The Purple Decades: A Reader (New York: Farrar, Straus, Giroux, 1982), 265–93.

4. Gerald Posner, *Case Closed* (New York: Random House, 1993), 469.

5. Centers for Disease Control and Prevention, Zombie Preparedness, https://
www.cdc.gov/cpr/campaigns/index.htm.

6. Geoengineering Watch, Extensive List of Patents, http://www.geoengineer ingwatch.org/links-to-geoengineering-patents/. It is interesting that this part of the website has more than fifteen thousand shares.

7. Jeffrey Gottfried, Katerina Eva Matsa, and Michael Barthel, "As Jon Stewart Steps Down, 5 Facts about the Daily Show," Pew Research Center, August 6, 2015, http://www.pewresearch.org/fact-tank/2015/08/06/5-facts-daily-show/.

8. Brian Steinberg, "And Now This: John Oliver Just Might Be a Journalist," *Variety*, February 16, 2018, https://variety.com/2018/tv/news/john-oliver-journalist -hbo-last-week-tonight-1202702144/.

9. Elizabeth Williamson, "Alex Jones Podcasting Hecklers Face Their Foils Downward Slide," *New York Times*, April 18, 2021, https://www.nytimes.com/2021/04/18/ us/politics/alex-jones.html.

10. Matt Taibbi, "Why the Russia Story Is a Minefield for Democrats and the Media," *Rolling Stone*, March 8, 2017, http://www.rollingstone.com/politics/taibbi -russia-story-is-a-minefield-for-democrats-and-the-media-w471074.

11. Sara E. Gorman and Jack M. Gorman, *Denying to the Grave: Why We Ignore the Facts That Will Save Us* (New York: Oxford University Press, 2017), 47–50.

12. Ibid., 65–106. The Gormans cite Jenny McCarthy's anti-vaccination activities as one particular example.

13. Marisa Meltzer, "QAnon's Unexpected Roots in New Age Spirituality," *Washington Post*, March 29, 2021, https://www.washingtonpost.com/magazine/2021/03/29/ qanon-new-age-spirituality/.

AFTERWORD

1. Plato, *The Republic*, Book VII. See also Roosevelt Montás, *Rescuing Socrates: How the Great Books Changed My Life and Why They Matter for a New Generation* (Princeton: Princeton University Press, 2021), 64.

2. See, for example, Michael Kunzelman, Lindsay Whitehurst, and Allana Durkin Richer, "Proud Boys' Enrique Tarrio Gets Record 22 Years in Prison for Seditious Conspiracy," *Associated Press*, September 6, 2023. https://apnews.com/article /enrique-tarrio-capitol-riot-seditious-conspiracy-sentencing-da60222b3e1e54902db 2bbbb219dc3fb

3. Chicago Project on Security and Threats, Findings from the fall 2021 CPOST (NORC) American Political Violence Survey January 2, 2022. https://d3qi0qp-55mx5f5.cloudfront.net/cpost/i/docs/Pape_AmericanInsurrectionistMovement_2022 -01-02.pdf?mtime=1641247264

4. Katherine Schaeffer, "A Look at the Americans Who Believe There is Some Truth to the Conspiracy Theory That COVID 19 was Planned," *Pew Research Center*, July 24, 2020. https://www.pewresearch.org/fact-tank/2020/07/24/a-look-at-the -americans-who-believe-there-is-some-truth-to-the-conspiracy-theory-that-covid-19 -was-planned/ ; Susan Milligan, "A Quarter of Republicans Believe Central Views of QAnon Conspiracy Movement," *U.S. News*, February 24, 2022. https://www

.usnews.com/news/politics/articles/2022-02-24/a-quarter-of-republicans-believe-central-views-of-qanon-conspiracy-movement

5. Arthur Goldwag, *The Politics of Fear: The Peculiar Persistence of American Paranoia* (New York: Vintage Books, 2024), 46.

6. Ibid., 41.

7. The term is old and usually referred to corporations, policy makers, and the U.S. military during the Cold War or, to use Eisenhower's term, "the military-industrial complex." For a recent example, see Michael McNerny, "Military Partisanship," *Journal of Political & Military Sociology*, vol. 34 (Winter 2006): 281-288.

8. See Doug McAdam, *Freedom Summer* (New York: Oxford University Press, 1988).

9. For an excellent study of this relationship, see Adam J. Berinsky, *In Time of War: Understanding American Public Opinion from World War II to Iraq* (Chicago: The University of Chicago Press, 2009).

10. Steve Benen, "Former Intel Director Reportedly Feared Putin 'Had Something on Trump'," *MaddowBlog,* September 10, 2020. https://www.msnbc.com/rachel-maddow-show/maddowblog/former-intel-director-reportedly-feared-putin-had-something-trump-n1239781; Veronica Stracqualursi, "Clapper Suggestions 'Parallelism' in Actions of Russia, Trump Campaign," *CNN Politics*, May 24, 2018. Coats served as the Director of National Intelligence (DNI) from 2017 to 2019. Clapper served as DNI from 2010 to 2017.

11. Bryan Bender, "'Disturbing and Reckless': Retired Brass Spread Election Lie in Attack on Biden, Democrats," *Politico*, May 11, 2021. https://www.politico.com/news/2021/05/11/retired-brass-biden-election-487374. There is a link to the open letter in the article.

12. Matt Brown and James Pollard, "Conspiracy Theories Swirl Around Taylor Swift. These Republican Voters Say They Don't Care," *Associated Press*, February 8, 2024. https://apnews.com/article/taylor-swift-conspiracies-biden-republican-voters-reaction-b5192ca92541f1f04485e3d8c7c24e53

13. Public Religion Research Institute, *The Persistence of QAnon in the Post-Trump Era: An Analysis of Who Believes in Conspiracy Theories*, February 24, 2022. https://www.prri.org/research/the-persistence-of-qanon-in-the-post-trump-era-an-analysis-of-who-believes-the-conspiracies/

14. Partially quoted from Goldwag, *The Politics of Fear*, 38-39. The complete quote is in Brian Stelter, "The Infamous Steve Bannon Quote is Key to Understanding America's Crazy Politics," *CNN Business*, November 16, 2012. https://www.cnn.com/2021/11/16/media/steve-bannon-reliable-sources/index.html

15. Michael N. Grynbaum, "Elon Musk, Matt Taibbi, and a Very Modern Media Maelstrom," *New York Times*, December 4, 2022. https://www.nytimes.com/2022/12/04/business/media/elon-musk-twitter-matt-taibbi.html

16. "Note to Readers," December 2, 2022. https://taibbi.substack.com/p/note-to-readers-8d4

17. Grynbaum, "Elon Musk, Matt Taibbi, and a Very Modern Media Maelstrom."

18. Ibid.

19. David Folkenflik, "The 'Wackadoodle' Foundation of Fox News' Election-Fraud Claims," *NPR*, February 20, 2023. https://www.npr.org/2023/02/20/1158223099/fox-news-dominion-wackadoodle-election-fraud-claim

20. Google News, *Cases*, May 25, 2021. https://news.google.com/covid19/map?hl=en-US&gl=US&ceid=US%3Aen

21. Kaiser Family Foundation, Global COVID Tracker, May 22, 2024. https://www.kff.org/coronavirus-covid-19/issue-brief/global-covid-19-tracker/

22. Adam Taylor, "China is Finally Divulging COVID Data. The WHO Says There is More to the Story," *Washington Post*, January 17, 2023. https://www.washingtonpost.com/world/2023/01/16/china-who-covid-data/

23. Joby Warrick, Ellen Nakashima, and Shane Harris, "Little-Known Scientific Team Behind New Assessment on COVID-19 Origins," *Washington Post*, February 27, 2023. https://www.washingtonpost.com/national-security/2023/02/27/little-known-scientific-team-behind-new-assessment-covid-19-origins/

24. E&C GOP Leaders Statement on COVID-19 Lab Leak Theory, February 26, 2023. https://energycommerce.house.gov/posts/e-and-c-gop-leaders-statement-on-covid-19-lab-leak-theory-report. Rogers chairs the House Energy and Commerce Committee. Griffith chairs the House Subcommittee on Oversight and Investigations. Guthrie chairs the House Subcommittee on Health.

25. Ashley Capoot, "The U.S. is 'Certainly' Still in a COVID-19 Pandemic, Dr. Fauci Says," *CNBC*, 27 November 2022. https://www.cnbc.com/2022/11/27/the-us-is-certainly-still-in-a-covid-19-pandemic-dr-fauci-says.html

26. Zeke Miller, "Trump Threatens to Fire Fauci in Rift with Disease Expert," *Associated Press*, November 2, 2020. https://apnews.com/article/trump-threatens-fire-fauci-rift-disease-57c804db048aa7f1c99f227b495f52e6

27. Josephine Harvey, "Ron DeSantis Unleashes Disturbing Attack on 'Little Elf' Fauci," *Huffpost*, August 25, 2022. https://news.yahoo.com/ron-desantis-unleashes-disturbing-attack-042501046.html

28. Sam Tabahriti, "Elon Musk Teases Release of the 'Fauci Files,' Following His Previous Scathing Criticism of the Medical Expert," *Business Insider*, January 2, 2023. https://www.businessinsider.com/elon-musk-twitter-teases-release-fauci-files-amid-spat-2023-1

29. For the entire hearing, see C-SPAN, Dr. Fauci Testifies on U.S. Response to COVID-19 Pandemic, June 3, 2024. https://www.c-span.org/video/?536025-1/dr-fauci-testifies-us-response-covid-19-pandemic&live&vod

30. Dana Milbank, "Opinion: Another Committee to Confirm Our Conspiracy Theories comes up short," *Washington Post*, June 3, 2024. https://www.washingtonpost.com/opinions/2024/06/03/fauci-testimony-congress-covid-conspiracy/

31. C-SPAN, "Rep. Marjorie Taylor Greene: 'You belong in prison, Dr. Fauci," June 3, 2024. https://www.c-span.org/video/?c5119599/rep-marjorie-taylor-greene-belong-prison-dr-fauci

32. Bradley Jones, "The Changing Political Geography of COVID-19 Over the Last Two Year," *Pew Research Center*, March 3, 2022. https://www.pewresearch.org/politics/2022/03/03/the-changing-political-geography-of-covid-19-over-the-last-two-years/. For a detailed study, see Nancy Krieger, Christian Testa, Jarvis T. Chen,

William P. Hanage, and Alecia J. McGregor, "Relationship of Political Ideology of U.S. Federal and State Elected Officials and Key COVID Pandemic Outcomes Following Vaccine Rollout to Adults: April 2021-March 2022," *The Lancet*, vol. 16 (December 1, 2022).
　　https://www.thelancet.com/journals/lanam/article/PIIS2667-193X(22)00201-0/fulltext

33. CDC, COVID-19 Vaccinations in the United States, Percent of the Population 5 Years of Age or Older with at Least One Dose Reported to the CDC by Jurisdiction of Select Federal Entities, January 6, 2023. https://covid.cdc.gov/covid-data-tracker/#vaccinations_vacc-people-onedose-pop-5yr

34. CDC, Trends in Number of COVID Vaccinations in the US, March 2, 2023. https://covid.cdc.gov/covid-data-tracker/#vaccination-trends

35. CDC, COVID Data Tracker, Summary of Variant Surveillance, January 6, 2023. https://covid.cdc.gov/covid-data-tracker/#variant-summary

36. McKenzie Beard, "Covid is No Longer Mainly a Pandemic of the Unvaccinated: Here's Why," *Washington Post*, November 23, 2022. https://www.washingtonpost.com/politics/2022/11/23/vaccinated-people-now-make-up-majority-covid-deaths/

37. CDC, COVID-19 Integrated County View, March 2, 2023; CDC, Percent Positivity of COVID-19 Nucleic Acid Amplification Tests (NAATs) in the Past Week by HHS Region – United States, May 30, 2024. https://covid.cdc.gov/covid-data-tracker/#county-view?list_select_state=all_states&list_select_county=all_counties&data-type=CommunityLevels

38. The White House, *National Biodefense Strategy and Implementation Plan: For Countering Biological Threats, Enhancing Pandemic Preparedness, and Achieving Global Health Security,* October 2022, 5.

39. Erin Banco, "Biden Admin Unveils New Pandemic Preparedness and Biodefense Strategy," *Politico*, October 18, 2022. https://www.politico.com/news/2022/10/18/biden-pandemic-biodefense-strategy-00062207

40. American Hospital Association, "White House Creates Pandemic Preparedness Office," July 2023. https://www.aha.org/news/headline/2023-07-21-white-house-creates-pandemic-preparedness-office

41. Katelyn Jetelina, "State of Affairs: Jan 9," *Your Local Epidemiologist*, January 9, 2024. https://yourlocalepidemiologist.substack.com/p/state-of-affairs-jan-9

42. Jim Banks, "Fighting the Woke Agenda in Congress," *The American Mind*, January 13, 2023. https://americanmind.org/memo/fighting-the-woke-agenda-in-congress/

43. Richard Hofstadter, "The Paranoid Style of American Politics," *Harper's Magazine* (November 1964): 77-86.

44. "Trump: 'I'm a Very Innocent Man'," *Politico*, May 30, 2024. https://www.politico.com/live-updates/2024/05/30/trump-hush-money-criminal-trial/while-he-waits-trump-is-working-00160686

45. Ryan J. Reilly, "Trump supporters try to dox jurors and post violent threats after his conviction," *NBC News*, May 31, 2024. https://www.nbcnews.com/politics/donald-trump/trump-supporters-try-doxx-jurors-violent-threats-conviction-rcna154882#

46. Cyril Mychalejko, "Project Veritas Wants Parents to Send Their Kids to School Armed with Secret Cameras," *Bucks County Beacon*, December 12, 2022. https://buckscountybeacon.com/2022/12/project-veritas-wants-parents-to-send-their-kids-to-school-armed-with-secret-cameras/

47. Pennsylvania Family Institute, School Incident Report for Parents/Students/Educators, March 31, 2022. Note: the actual form no longer appears on the website. https://pafamily.org/2022/03/31/school-incident-report-for-parents-students-educators/

48. Cyril Mychalejko, "Mastriano Accuses Elementary School Teachers of Showing Students Porn, Pushing Them to be Transgender," *Bucks County Beacon*, August 30, 2022. https://buckscountybeacon.com/2022/08/mastriano-accuses-elementary-school-teachers-of-showing-students-porn-pushing-them-to-be-transgender/

49. The actual News Talk 103.7 interview on August 24, 2022 is at: https://soundcloud.com/newstalk1037fm/24-august-state-senator-mastriano-on-news-talk-1037fmmp3?utm_source=clipboard&utm_medium=text&utm_campaign=social_sharing

50. Campbell Robertson, "While Politics Consume School Board Meetings, A Very Different Crisis Festers," *New York Times*, December 1, 2021. https://www.nytimes.com/2021/12/01/us/central-bucks-school-board-politics-pennsylvania.html

51. Chris Ullery, "Group Calls Off Plan to Gather Before Central Buck District Meeting After Militia Fears Spread Online," *Bucks County Courier Times*, August 23, 2021. https://www.buckscountycouriertimes.com/story/news/2021/08/24/group-calls-off-plans-gather-before-central-bucks-district-meeting-after-militia-fears-spread-online/8239862002/

52. Peter Blanchard, "2021 Candidate Profile: Jim Pepper, Central Bucks School Board," *Patch*, May 4. 2021. https://patch.com/pennsylvania/doylestown/2021-candidate-profile-jim-pepper-central-bucks-school-board

53. David Murrell, "Inside the Ridiculously Vicious and Increasingly Nasty Elections in Bucks County," *Philadelphia Magazine*, December 18, 2021. https://www.phillymag.com/news/2021/12/18/bucks-county-school-board-elections/. See also Cyril Mychalejko, "Three Percent Militia-Endorsed School Board Candidate Debra Cannon & Her Crusade Against 'Evil' and 'Demonic' Adults," *Bucks County Progressive*, October 6, 2021. https://cyrilmychalejko.substack.com/p/three-percent-militia-endorsed-school

54. Central Bucks School District. https://www.cbsd.org/schoolboard

55. Eric Garcia, "We Asked Conservatives at CPAC What 'Woke' Means. Their Replies were Revealing," *Independent*, March 5, 2023. https://www.independent.co.uk/news/world/americas/us-politics/cpac-woke-capitalism-meaning-trump-b2294257.html See also Kevin M. Kruse and Julian E. Zelizer, eds., *Myth America: Historians Take on the Biggest Legends and Lies About Our Past* (New York: Basic Books, 2022).

56. Trip Gabriel, "Driven by Election Deniers, This County Recounted 2020 Votes Last Week," *New York Times*, January 15, 2023. https://www.nytimes.com/2023/01/15/us/politics/2020-recount-lycoming-county.html

57. Patrick Svitek, "Donald Trump Energizes South Texas Voters Ahead of Early Voting as Republicans Predict Red 'Tsunami,'" *The Texas Tribune*, October 22, 2022. https://www.texastribune.org/2022/10/22/donald-trump-election-republicans/

58. Louis Jacobson and Amy Sherman, "Trump's Baseless Claim About 2020 Election Fraud and Suspending the Constitution," *Politifact*, December 6, 2022. https://www.politifact.com/factchecks/2022/dec/06/donald-trump/trump-said-2020 -fraud-calls-for-termination-of-rul/

59. "Our View: Doug Mastriano's Dangerous History of Election Denial and Contemptuous Disdain for the System," *USA Today*, October 19, 2022. https://www.buc kscountycouriertimes.com/story/opinion/editorials/2022/10/20/doug-mastrianos-dan gerous-history-of-election-denial-our-view-opinion-pennsylvania-governor-election /69568785007/

60. The link appears in the October 19th editorial cited above. For the specific document, go to: https://www.justice.gov/oip/foia-library/foia-processed/general_topics/ comms_doj_and_reps_djt_campaign_09_13_22/download

61. Rachel Alexander, "Kari Lake Challenges Fox News Host Bret Baier for Not Covering Election Fraud: 'Mama Bear Takes Down a Fake News Baier'," *The Tennessee Star*, June 30, 2022. https://tennesseestar.com/the-west/arizona/kari-lake-chal lenges-fox-news-host-bret-baier-for-not-covering-election-fraud-mama-bear-takes -down-a-fake-news-baier/rachel-alexander/2022/06/30/

62. For the complete report, see U.S. House of Representatives, *Final Report of the Select Committee to Investigate the January 6th Attack on the United States Capitol*, House Report 117-663 (Washington: Government Printing Office, December 22, 2022).

63. John Koblin, "At Least 20 Million Watched Jan. 6 Hearing," *New York Times*, June 10, 2022. https://www.nytimes.com/2022/06/10/business/media/jan-6-hearing -ratings.html

64. Ryan Nobles, Annie Grayer, Zachary Cohen, and Jamie Gangel, "First on CNN: January 6 Committee Has Text Messages Between Ginni Thomas and Mark Meadows," *CNN Politics*, March 25, 2022. https://www.cnn.com/2022/03/24/politics /ginni-thomas-mark-meadows-text-messages/index.html

65. Ibid.

66. Mary Clare Jalonick and Lisa Mascaro, "Ginni Thomas Says She Regrets Post-Election Texts to Mark Meadows," *Associated Press*, December 30, 2022. https:// whyy.org/articles/ginni-thomas-says-she-regrets-post-election-texts-to-meadows/

67. Nicole Narea, "Sean Hannity's Damning Deposition in the Fox News Defamation Lawsuit, Explained," *Vox*, December 22, 2022. https://www.vox.com/policy-and -politics/2022/12/22/23523385/sean-hannity-fox-news-defamation-dominion-lawsuit

68. Department of Justice, United States Attorney's Office, District of Columbia, *Three Years Since the Jan. 6 Attack on the Capitol*, https://www.justice.gov/usao-dc /36-months-jan-6-attack-capitol-0#:~:text=Approximately%20718%20individuals %20have%20pleaded,have%20pleaded%20guilty%20to%20misdemeanors.

69. Ibid.

70. Patrick Marley, "Here are the States Where Trump Electors Have Been Charged," *Washington Post*, April 24, 2024. https://www.washingtonpost.com/

politics/2024/04/24/trump-electors-state-investigations-indictments/; Yvonne Wing-ett Sanchez, "Rudy Giuliani and Other Trump Allies Plead Not Guilty in Arizona," *Washington Post*, May 21, 2024. https://www.washingtonpost.com/politics/2024/05/21/rudy-giuliani-christina-bobb-arizona-not-guilty/

71. "Read the Full Georgia Indictment Against Trump and 18 Allies," *PBS*, August 15, 2023. https://www.pbs.org/newshour/politics/read-the-full-georgia-indictment-against-trump-and-18-allies. The actual indictment is linked through the article.

72. Adam Edelman, "Election Deniers Overwhelmingly Lost in Battleground States," *NBC News*, November 16, 2022. https://www.nbcnews.com/politics/2022-election/election-deniers-overwhelmingly-lost-battleground-states-rcna57058

73. Sarah Ewall-Wice, "2022 Pennsylvania Governor's Race: Josh Shapiro Projected as Winner Over Doug Mastriano," *CBS News*, November 2022. https://www.cbsnews.com/live-updates/election-2022-pennsylvania-governor-results-josh-shapiro-doug-mastriano-2022-11-08/

74. Caitlin Sievers, "Kari Lake Election Suit Shot Down, Says She'll Appeal," *Arizona Mirror*, December 22, 2022. https://www.azmirror.com/2022/12/24/kari-lake-election-suit-shot-down-says-shell-appeal/

75. Monmouth University, "January 6 Hearings Have No Impact on Opinion," August 9, 2022.
https://www.monmouth.edu/polling-institute/reports/monmouthpoll_us_080922/

76. Monmouth University, "National: Faith in American System Drops," July 7, 2022. https://www.monmouth.edu/polling-institute/documents/monmouthpoll_us_070722.pdf/

77. Quinnipiac University, "Lowest Opinion of Trump Among Voters in Seven Years, Quinnipiac University National Poll Finds, Biden Approval Rating Climbs," December 14, 2022. https://poll.qu.edu/poll-release?releaseid=3863

78. "Do Americans Have a Favorable or Unfavorable Opinion of Donald Trump," *FiveThirtyEight*, June 5, 2024. https://projects.fivethirtyeight.com/polls/favorability/donald-trump/

79. "Do Americans Approve or Disapprove of Joe Biden?" *FiveThirtyEight*, June 6, 2024. https://projects.fivethirtyeight.com/polls/approval/joe-biden/?ex_cid=abcpromo

80. Michelle Goldberg, "Leopards Eat Kevin McCarthy's Face," *New York Times*, January 5, 2023. https://www.nytimes.com/2023/01/04/opinion/kevin-mccarthy-speaker-race.html

81. Paul Dans, "A Note on "Project 2025," in *Mandate for Leadership: The Conservative Promise: Project 2025: Presidential Transition Project*, Paul Dans and Steven Groves, eds. (Washington: Heritage Foundation, 2023), xiv. https://static.project2025.org/2025_MandateForLeadership_P2025-NOTE.pdf

82. "Election Workers are Being Bombarded with Death Threats, the U.S. Government Says," *PBS News Hour*, August 31, 2023. https://www.pbs.org/newshour/politics/election-workers-are-being-bombarded-with-death-threats-the-u-s-government-says#:~:text=Election%20workers%20are%20being%20bombarded%20with%20death%20threats%2C%20the%20U.S.%20government%20says,

-Politics%20Aug%2031&text=WASHINGTON%20(AP)%20—%20More%20 than,count%20and%20secure%20the%20vote; Eileen Sullivan, "Election Workers Face Flood of Threats, but Charges Are Few," *New York Times*, April 13, 2024. https://www.nytimes.com/2024/04/13/us/politics/election-workers-threats.html

83. David Bauder, Randall Chase, and Geoff Mulvihill, "Fox, Dominion reach $787M settlement over election claims," *Associated Press*, April 18, 2023. https:// apnews.com/article/fox-news-dominion-lawsuit-trial-trump-2020-0ac71f75acfacc5 2ea80b3e747fb0afe

84. Elizabeth Williamson, "With New Ruling, Sandy Hook Families Win Over $1.4 Billion from Alex Jones," *New York Times*, November 10, 2022. https://www .nytimes.com/2022/11/10/us/politics/alex-jones-sandy-hook-damages.html; Roxanna Asgarian, "Texas Judge Rules Alex Jones Must Pay Sandy Hook Parents Full $48 Million in Defamation Case," *The Texas Tribune*, November 23, 2022. https:// www.texastribune.org/2022/11/23/alex-jones-texas-lawsuit-damages/; Dave Collins, Michael Hill, and Jake Bleiberg," "$1B Judgement Against Alex Jones Not the Final Word," *Associated Press*, October 13, 2022. https://apnews.com/article/business -shootings-connecticut-conspiracy-theories-alex-jones-fbb3ae82129f39e71989839 f6074c356

85. Kenny Cooper, "How Democrats Flipped a Central Bucks School Board Embroiled in Controversy," WHYY, November 8, 2023. https://whyy.org/articles/ central-bucks-school-board-elections-democrats-sweep/

86. "Wyoming At-Large Congressional District Primary Election Results," *New York Times*, August 18, 2022. https://www.nytimes.com/interactive/2022/08/16/us/ elections/results-wyoming-us-house-district-1.html

87. Gillian McGoldrick and Jonathan Lai, "Al Schmidt, A Republican Former Philly Election Official, Named as Secretary of State," *Philadelphia Inquirer*, January 5, 2023. https://www.inquirer.com/politics/election/al-schmidt-pennsylvania-secre-tary-of-state-20230105.html

88. Chris Cameron, "Al Schmidt: A Philadelphia Republican Who Continued Counting Votes as Trump's Pressure Mounted," *New York Times*, June 13, 2022. https://www.nytimes.com/2022/06/13/us/al-schmidt-jan-6-hearing-witness.html

89. Senate Committee on Rules and Administration, "Emerging Threats to Elec-tion Administration," Testimony of Al Schmidt, City Commissioner of Philadelphia, Tuesday, October 26, 2021. https://www.rules.senate.gov/imo/media/doc/Testimony _Schmidt.pdf

90. "Who is Al Schmidt and Why Did He Testify in the Jan. 6 Hearings?," *PBS News Hour*, June 13, 2022. https://www.pbs.org/newshour/politics/who-is-al-schmidt -and-why-did-he-testify-in-the-jan-6-hearings

91. Lisa Mascaro, Mary Clarke Jalonick, and Faroush Amiri, "Tucker Carlson Amplifies Jan. 6 Lies with GOP-Provided Video, *Associated Press*, March 7, 2023. https://apnews.com/article/jan-6-tucker-carlson-capitol-riot-mccarthy-adc245e22f5 0b076925eb72948062808

92. https://twitter.com/EliseStefanik/status/1633227562737364993

93. Paul Kane, "'Just a Lie': Senate Republicans Blast Tucker Carlson's Jan. 6 Narrative," *Washington Post*, March 7, 2023. https://www.washingtonpost.com/politics/2023/03/07/tucker-carlson-jan-6-senate-republicans/

94. Luke Broadwater and Stephanie Lai, "Republican Lawmakers Split Over Carlson's False Jan. 6 Claims," *New York Times*, March 7,2023. https://www.nytimes.com/2023/03/07/us/republicans-tucker-carlson-jan-6.html

95. Ryan Bort, "Even Republicans are Bashing Tucker Carlson for Lying About Jan. 6 Violence," *Rolling Stone*, March 7, 2023. https://www.rollingstone.com/politics/politics-news/republicans-bash-tucker-carlson-lying-jan-6-violence-1234692024/

96. Tiffany Hsu, "When Teens Find Misinformation, These Teachers are Ready," *New York Times*, September 8, 2022. https://www.nytimes.com/2022/09/08/technology/misinformation-students-media-literacy.html?searchResultPosition=7; See also Alina Tugend, "These Students are Learning About Fake News and How to Spot It," *New York Times*, February 20, 2020. https://www.nytimes.com/2020/02/20/education/learning/news-literacy-2016-election.html

97. Sam Wineburg, Joel Breakstone, Sarah McGrew, Mark D. Smith, and Teresa Ortega, "Lateral Reading on the Open Internet: A District-Wide Field Study in High School Classes," *Journal of Educational Psychology*, vol. 114 (July 2022): 893.

98. Ibid., 895, 897, 900.

Glossary of Terms

ACADEMIC TERMS

analogy. A similarity between like features of two things, on which a comparison may be based.

causation. The act or process of causing something to happen or exist.

claim. An assertion of the truth of something, typically one that is disputed or in doubt.

confirmation bias. A tendency for people to prefer information that confirms their preconceptions or hypotheses, independently of whether they are true.

correlation. A mutual relation or connection between two or more things.

false analogy. An informal fallacy that applies to inductive arguments. It is an informal fallacy because the error is about what the argument is about, not the argument itself. An analogy proposes that two concepts that are similar (A and B) have a common relationship to some property.

normalcy bias. A mental state people enter when facing a disaster. It causes people to underestimate both the possibility of a disaster and its possible effects.

proof. Evidence or argument establishing or helping to establish a fact or the truth of a statement.

primary source. A source with direct access to an event.

secondary source. A source that has indirect access to an event.

syllogism. A kind of logical argument that applies deductive reasoning to arrive at a conclusion based on two or more propositions that are asserted or assumed to be true.

INTERNET TERMS

connecting the dots. Pulling together different forms of evidence to make a point. *See* correlation

disinformation. Intentionally false or inaccurate information that is deliberately spread.

disinformation agent. An individual who distributes disinformation.

false flag. An attack deliberately and falsely attributed to an enemy.

Gish gallop. A debating technique used by creationist Duane Gish in which the speaker drowns the other side in a torrent of arguments or assertions that cannot be answered.

global power structure. A group that dominates the entire world.

going down the rabbit hole. A metaphor for an entry into the unknown, the disorientating or the mentally deranging, from its use in Alice's Adventures in Wonderland.

mainstream media (MSM). Media comprising the major networks, print, and electronic news outlets.

moving the goalposts. Changing the conditions of either the argument or the evidence during a debate.

new world order. A generic term to describe a global conspiracy to dominate the world.

official story. Official document addressing or investigating an event. Sometimes interpreted as propaganda.

PSYOPS. Military acronym for "psychological operations."

sheeple. A term describing the general public as people compared to sheep in being docile, foolish, or easily led.

shill. An accomplice of a hawker, gambler, or swindler who acts as an enthusiastic customer to entice or encourage others. *See* disinformation agent.

truther. A label created by the 9/11 Truth movement to reframe their activities away from media descriptions of conspiracy theories.

Selected Bibliography

PODCASTS

Conspirituality: https://conspirituality.net/about/
Generation Why: http://thegenerationwhypodcast.com
Knowledge Fight: https://knowledgefight.com
The Skeptics' Guide to the Universe: http://www.theskepticsguide.org/podcast/5x5
Skeptoid: http://skeptoid.com
Stuff They Don't Want You to Know: http://www.stufftheydontwantyoutoknow.com/podcasts/
The Unbelievable Podcast: http://www.unbelievablepodcast.com

WEBSITES

General

Metabunk.org: https://www.metabunk.org
Politifact: https://www.politifact.com
Snopes: http://www.snopes.com

9/11

9/11 Conspiracy Theories—Debunking the Myths: http://www.popularmechanics.com/military/a6384/debunking-911-myths-world-trade-center/
Architects and Engineers for 9/11 Truth: http://www.ae911truth.org
Debunking 9/11 Conspiracy Theories and Controlled Demolition Myths: http://debunking911.com Physics911: http://physics911.net/thermite/

Chemtrails and Contrails

Carnicom Institute: https://carnicominstitute.org/wp/
Geoengineering Watch: http://www.geoengineeringwatch.org
Global Skywatch: http://globalskywatch.com
Contrail Science: http://contrailscience.com

VIDEOS

"Plandemic Movie" (Part 1): https://www.bitchute.com/video/bZ2yliCyu373/
Loose Change (third edition): https://www.youtube.com/watch?v=7GwFs7mPh0Q
What in the World Are They Spraying?: https://www.youtube.com/watch?v=
  jf0khstYDLA

DOCUMENTS

Comey, James B. (Director, FBI) to Richard M. Burr (Chair, Senate Select Committee
  on Intelligence), Charles E. Grassley (Chair, Senate Committee on the Judiciary),
  Richard Shelby (Chair, Senate Committee on Appropriations), Ron Johnson (Chair,
  Senate Committee on Homeland Security and Governmental Affairs), Devin John-
  son (Chair, House Permanent Select Committee on Intelligence), Robert Goodlatte
  (Chair, House Committee on the Judiciary), John Culberson (Chair, House Com-
  mittee on Appropriations), Jason Chaffetz (Chair, House Committee on Oversight
  and Government Reform), October 28, 2016.
"Evidence for the Explosive Demolition of World Trade Center Building 7 on 9/11,"
  Architects & Engineers for 9/11 Truth (September 2009).
National Commission on Terrorist Attacks Upon the United States, *The 9/11 Commis-
  sion Report*. New York: W.W. Norton & Company, 2004.
The National Security Strategy of the United States of America, September 17, 2002.
Newell, Homer E. *A Recommended National Program in Weather Modification: A
  Report to the Interdepartmental Committee for Atmospheric Sciences*. Washington,
  DC: Federal Council for Science and Technology, November 1966.
Office of the Director of National Intelligence. *Intelligence Community Assessment:
  Assessing Russian Activities and Intentions in Recent US Elections*. ICA-2017-
  01D, January 6, 2017.
Office of the White House Press Secretary, Executive Order 11130: Appointing a
  Commission to Report Upon the Assassination of President John F. Kennedy, No-
  vember 30, 1963.
US Department of Justice. Federal Bureau of Investigation. *Clinton E-Mail Investiga-
  tion: Mishandling of Classified – Unknown Subject or Country (SIM)*. July 2016.
US House of Representatives. Select Committee on Assassinations, *Final Report*.
  Washington, DC: GPO, 1979.

Warren Commission. *Hearings before the President's Commission on the Assassination of John F. Kennedy*. 26 vols. Washington, DC: Government Printing Office, 1964.

Warren Commission, *Report of the President's Commission on the Assassination of President Kennedy*. Washington, DC: Government Printing Office, 1964.

BOOKS AND ARTICLES

"9/11: Debunking the Myths," *Popular Mechanics* 182 (March 2005): 71–81.

Aaronovitch, David. *Voodoo History: The Role of Conspiracy Theory in Shaping Modern History*. New York: Riverhead Books, 2010.

"A Brief History of Chemtrails," *Contrail Science*, May 11, 2007. http://con trailscience.com/a-brief-history-of-chemtrails/.

Barkun, Michael. *A Culture of Conspiracy: Apocalyptic Visions in Contemporary America*. Second edition. Berkeley: University of California Press, 2013.

Brotherton, Rob. *Suspicious Minds: Why We Believe in Conspiracy Theories*. New York: Bloomsbury Sigma, 2015.

Bugliosi, Vincent. *Reclaiming History: The Assassination of President John F. Kennedy*. New York: W.W. Norton & Company, 2007.

Carmichael, Scott W. *True Believer: Inside the Investigation and Capture of Ana Montes, Cuba's Master Spy*. Annapolis, MD: Naval Institute Press, 2007.

Chomsky, Noam. *How the World Works*. New York: Penguin, 2015.

———. *The Prosperous Few and the Restless Many*. Tuscon, AR: Odonian Press, 1993.

Conley, Heather A., James Mina, Ruslan Stefanov, and Martin Vladimirov. *The Kremlin Playbook*. Lanham, MD: Rowman & Littlefield, 2016.

Crutzen, Paul J. "Albedo Enhancement by Stratospheric Sulfur Injections: A Contribution to Resolve a Policy Dilemma?" *Climate Change* 77 (August 2006): 211–19.

Curcio, Vincent. *Henry Ford*. New York: Oxford University Press, 2013.

Dickey, Colin. "The New Paranoia." *New Republic* 248 (July 2017): 22–31.

Eisner, Will. *The Plot: The Secret Story of the Protocols of the Elders of Zion*. New York: W.W. Norton & Company, 2005.

Engelbrecht, Helmuth C. and Frank C. Hanighen. *Merchants of Death: A Study of the International Armament Industry*. New York: Dodd, Mead & Company, 1934.

Epstein, Jay. *Inquest: The Warren Commission and the Establishment of Truth*. New York: Viking Press, 1966.

Freeland, Elana. *Chemtrails, HAARP, and the Full Spectrum Dominance of Planet Earth*. Port Townsend: Feral House, 2014.

Giblin, James Cross. The Rise and Fall of Senator Joe McCarthy. Boston, MA: Clarion Books, 2009.

Gorman, Sara E., and Jack M. Gorman. *Denying to the Grave: Why We Ignore the Facts That Will Save Us*. New York: Oxford University Press, 2017.

Greenstein, Fred I. *The Hidden Hand Presidency: Eisenhower as Leader*. Baltimore, MD: Johns Hopkins University Press, 1994.

Halberstam, David. *The Best and the Brightest*. Greenwich, CT: Fawcett Publications, Inc., 1973.

Herman, Arthur. *Joseph McCarthy: Re-examining the Life and Legacy of America's Most Hated Senator*. New York: The Free Press, 2000.

Hitler, Adolph. *Mein Kampf*. Berlin: Verlag, 1925.

Hofstadter, Richard. "The Paranoid Style of American Politics," *Harper's Magazine* (November 1964): 77–86.

Holland, Max. *The Kennedy Assassination Tapes*. New York: Knopf, 2004.

House, J., Lieutenant Colonel James B. Near Jr., Lietenant Colonel William B. Shields, et al. *Weather as a Force Multiplier: Owning the Weather in 2025*. Air War College, August 1996.

Keith, David W. "Geoengineering and Climate: History and Prospect," *Annual Review of Energy and the Environment* 25 (2000): 245–84.

Kennedy, David M. *Freedom from Fear: The American People in Depression and War, 1929–1945*. New York: Oxford University Press, 1999.

———. *Over Here: The First World War and American Society*. New York: Oxford University Press, 1980.

Kimball, Jeffrey. "The Enduring Paradigm of the 'Lost Cause': Defeat in Vietnam, the Stab-in-the-Back Legend, and the Construction of a Myth," in *Defeat and Memory: Cultural Histories of Military Defeat in the Modern Era*, edited by Jenny Macleod, 233–50. New York: Palgrave Macmillan, 2008.

Kolata, Gina. *Flu: The Story of the Great Influenza Pandemic of 1918 and the Search for the Virus That Caused It*. New York: Farrar, Straus and Giroux, 1999.

Lane, Mark. *Rush to Judgment: A Critique of the Warren Commission's Inquiry into the Murders of President John F. Kennedy, Officer J. D. Tippit and Lee Harvey Oswald*. Harmondsworth: Penguin, 1967.

Levitsky, Steven, and Daniel Ziblatt. "How a Democracy Dies." *New Republic* 249 (January/February 2018): 16–23.

McCormick, Ty. "Geoengineering: A Short History." *Foreign Policy*, September 3, 2013. http://foreignpolicy.com/2013/09/03/geoengineering-a-short-history/.

McCullough, David. *Truman*. New York: Simon & Schuster, 1992.

Mensch, Louise. "What to Ask About Russian Hacking," *New York Times*, March 17, 2017.

Mills, C. Wright. *The Power Elite*. New York: Oxford University Press, 1956.

Murray, Robert K. *Red Scare: A Study of National Hysteria, 1919–1920*. New York: McGraw-Hill Book Company, 1964.

Neyman, Jerzy. "Experimentation with Weather Control." *Journal of the Royal Statistical Society* 130 (1967): 285–326.

Olmsted, Kathryn S. *Real Enemies: Conspiracy Theories and American Democracy, World War I to 9/11*. New York: Oxford University Press, 2009.

Oshinsky, David M. *A Conspiracy So Immense: The World of Joe McCarthy*. New York: The Free Press, 1983.

Patterson, James T. *Grand Expectations: The United States, 1945–1974*. New York: Oxford University Press, 1996.

Posner, Gerald. *Case Closed: Lee Harvey Oswald and the Assassination of JFK.* New York: Random House, 1993.

Report of the Warren Commission on the Assassination of President Kennedy. New York: McGraw-Hill Book Company, 1964.

Riasanovsky, Nicholas V. *A History of Russia.* Fourth edition. New York: Oxford University Press, 1984.

Ropp, Theodore. *War in the Modern World.* New York: Collier Books, 1962.

Saker Woeste, Victoria. *Henry Ford's War on Jews: And the Legal Battle Against Hate Speech.* Stanford, CA: Stanford University Press, 2012.

Schlesinger, Arthur M. *A Thousand Days: John F. Kennedy in the White House.* New York: Houghton Mifflin, 1965.

Sibley, Katherine A. S. *Red Spies in America: Stolen Secrets and the Dawn of the Cold War.* Lawrence, KS: University of Kansas Press, 2004.

Stone, Geoffrey R. *Perilous Times: Free Speech in Wartime from the Sedition Act of 1798 to the War on Terrorism.* New York: W.W. Norton & Company, 2004.

Summers, Harry. *On Strategy: A Critical Analysis of the Vietnam War.* Novato, CA: Presidio Press, 1982.

Taibbi, Matt. *Insane Clown President: Dispatches from the 2016 Circus.* New York: Spiegel & Grau, 2017.

———. *The Divide: American Injustice in the Age of the Wealth Gap.* New York: Spiegel & Grau, 2014.

Taylor, Adam. "Debunking the Real 9/11 Myths: Why Popular Mechanics Can't Face up to Reality–Part 2" Architects & Engineers for 9/11 Truth (March 2, 2012).

Unger, Craig. "Trump's Russian Laundromat." *New Republic* (August/September 2017): 26–35.

Watson, Alexander. *Enduring the Great War: Combat, Morale, and Collapse in the German and British Armies, 1914–1918.* New York: Cambridge University Press, 2008.

Index